THE
GNOSTIC HERESIES
OF THE
FIRST AND SECOND CENTURIES

THE GNOSTIC HERESIES
OF THE
FIRST AND SECOND CENTURIES

BY

HENRY LONGUEVILLE MANSEL D.D.

Athens ‡ Manchester

The Gnostic Heresies of the First and Second Centuries

Published by: Old Book Publishing Ltd

Book Cover Design: Old Book Publishing Ltd

Copyright © 2012 Old Book Publishing Ltd
All rights reserved.

Originally published in 1875

Title of original: The Gnostic Heresies of the First and Second Centuries

Cover image: These Abrasax-stones often bear Hebraic names of God: Iao, Sabaoth, Adonai, Eloai. The name ΙΑΩ, to which ΣΑΒΑΩΘ is sometimes added, is found with this figure even more frequently than ΑΒΡΑΣΑΞ, and they are often combined. Beside an Abrasax figure the following, for instance, is found: ΙΑΩ ΑΒΡΑΣΑΞ ΑΔΩΝ ΑΤΑ, "Iao Abrasax, thou art the Lord". With the Abrasax-shield are also found the divine names Sabaoth Iao, Iao Abrasax, Adonai Abrasax, etc.

ISBN–10: 1-78107-164-0
ISBN–13: 978-1-78107-164-9

EDITOR'S NOTE

Old Book Publishing Ltd takes care in preserving the wording and images of the original books. For this reason we have invested in technology that enables us to enhance the quality of such reproduction. This investment helps overcome problems encountered when reproducing old books, such as stains, coloured paper, discolouration of ink, yellowed pages, see-through and onion skin type paper.

This reproduction book, produced from digital images of the original, may contain occasional defects such as missing pages or blemishes due to the original source content or were introduced by the scanning process.

These are scanned pages and the quality of print represents accurately the print quality of the original book, though we may have been able to enhance it.

As this book has been scanned and/or reformatted from the original we cannot guarantee that it is error-free or contains the full content of the original.

However, we believe that this work is culturally important, and despite its imperfections, have elected to bring it back into print as part of our commitment to the preservation of printed works.

Old Book Publishing

THE
GNOSTIC HERESIES

OF THE

FIRST AND SECOND CENTURIES

BY THE LATE

HENRY LONGUEVILLE MANSEL, D.D.

DEAN OF ST. PAUL'S

SOMETIME PROFESSOR OF ECCLESIASTICAL HISTORY AT OXFORD

WITH A SKETCH OF HIS WORK, LIFE, AND CHARACTER

BY THE EARL OF CARNARVON

EDITED

BY J. B. LIGHTFOOT, D.D

CANON OF ST. PAUL'S

LONDON
JOHN MURRAY, ALBEMARLE STREET
1875

LONDON : PRINTED BY
SPOTTISWOODE AND CO., NEW-STREET SQUARE
AND PARLIAMENT STREET

INTRODUCTION

At the request of some common friends, I have endeavoured to put upon paper some few recollections of the late Dean Mansel. I do not pretend to write a memoir of his life; my principal, and indeed my only, object in this letter is to retrace the impressions which many years of close friendship and unrestrained intercourse have left on my mind; and if, indeed, I have occasionally diverged into the public side of his character, it has been because I knew him so well in every aspect and relation of life, that I have found it difficult to confine myself to that with which I feel I am and ought to be here mainly concerned.

My first acquaintance with Dean Mansel was made twenty years ago at the University, when he had everything to give, and I had everything to receive. As I think of him, his likeness seems to rise before me. In one of those picturesque and old-world colleges, in rooms which, if I remember rightly, on one side looked upon the collegiate quadrangle with its sober and meditative architecture, and on the other caught the play of light and shade cast by trees almost as venerable on the garden grass—in one of those rooms, whose walls were built up to the ceiling with books, which, nevertheless, overflowed on the floor, and were piled in masses of disorderly order upon chairs and tables, might have been seen sitting day after day the late Dean, then my private tutor, and the most successful teacher of his time in the University. Young men are no bad judges of the capabilities of a teacher; and those who sought the highest honours of the University in the Class schools thought themselves fortunate to secure instruction such as he gave, transparently lucid, accurate, and without stint, flowing on through the whole morning continuously, making the most complicated questions clear.

But if, as chanced sometimes with me, they returned later as guests in the winter evening to the cheery and old-fashioned hospitality of the Common Room, they might have seen the same man, the centre of conversation, full of anecdote and humour and wit, applying the resources of a prodigious memory and keen intellect to the genial intercourse of society.

The life of old Oxford has nearly passed away. New ideas are now accepted, old traditions almost cease to have a part in the existence of the place, the very studies have greatly changed, and—whether for good or evil—except for the grey walls which seem to upbraid the altered conditions of thought around them, Oxford bids fair to represent modern Liberalism, rather than the Church and State doctrines of the early part of the century. But of that earlier creed, which was one characteristic of the University, Dean Mansel was an eminent type. Looked up to and trusted by his friends, he was viewed by his opponents as worthy of their highest antagonism, and whilst he reflected the qualities which the lovers of an older system have delighted to honour, he freely expressed opinions which modern reformers select for their strongest condemnation. The lines of that character were not traced in sand. They were graven in the very nature of the man, part of himself, and often influencing the mind of those with whom he came in contact.

Such he was when I first knew him twenty years ago—in the zenith of his teaching reputation, though on the point of withdrawing himself from it to a career even more worthy of his great abilities. It was then that I formed an acquaintance which ripened into deep and sincere friendship, which grew closer and more valued as life went on, over which no shadow of variation ever passed, and which was abruptly snapped at the very time when it had become most highly prized.

Dean Mansel's mind was one of the highest order. Its greatness perhaps, as was truly said by Canon Liddon, was not such as best commands immediate popular recognition or sympathy, but it was not on that account the less powerful. The intellect was of such a kind that some may have failed to appreciate it, and to understand that they 'were close to a mind—almost the only mind in England—to which all the heights and all the depths of the most recent speculation respecting the highest truth that can be grasped by the human understanding were perfectly familiar;' but now that death has intervened, a truer estimate, as so often happens, is possible; and both by those who knew him personally, and by those who can only know him in his writings, his very great power will perhaps be more fully acknowledged. I do not mean that his remarkable capacity was or could be ignored. The honours that he had gained, and the position that he had achieved, would alone have rendered this impossible; and at Oxford there was no misapprehension, on this point, as to the man. There the wide range of his mind and attainments was correctly appreciated; but the outer world knew him chiefly as a great metaphysical thinker, and perhaps only a minority even of those few who have an acquaintance with metaphysical studies rated him at his true standard. Of his consummate gifts in the province of metaphysics none, indeed, but a professed metaphysician can with propriety speak; yet this an outsider and an old pupil may say —that for clear thought, full knowledge, and an unsurpassed gift of expression—qualities which give especial value to this branch of study—he was second to none. So singularly lucid was the language in which difficult and involved subjects were presented by him to the reader or hearer, that none had the excuse that Bishop Butler modestly suggests to those who may be perplexed with the hardness of style which is to be found in his own masterly works. If, indeed, from a different point of view, Dean Mansel's writings were open to criticism, it was that this extreme lucidity and force of expression were such that in literary controversy he sometimes dealt out to his opponents heavier blows than he possibly intended. One of his antagonists, worthy of all respect—and all the more that, like Dean Mansel, he has passed away from the arena of earthly controversy to a scene where those higher questions of a future life on which he sometimes dwelt are now all solved—has left a proof of his candour and truthfulness in the admission that, although still adhering to his own view of a particular subject under dispute, he was overmatched by the Dean in the actual dialectics of debate. It often occurred to me that his possession of this singularly transparent style, when dealing with the most abstract and complicated questions, was in a great measure due to a perfect familiarity with classical literature. He sought and mastered it in early life, and, unlike many who are inclined to disparage, for more modern studies, the learning which for so many generations gave to the world its greatest minds and its most humanising gifts, he followed and delighted in it to the last. And, like a grateful mistress, classical learning rewarded his devotion with that style and skill of fence which lent him so formidable a superiority in the literary warfare of theological discussion.

Nowhere was this more conspicuous than in the now famous Bampton Lectures on the 'Limits of Religious Thought,' which he preached in 1858. But for him those lectures had a yet greater importance. They were a new point of departure, and, in a somewhat wider sense, the beginning of his public life. From the pulpit of St. Mary's he stepped at once into the foremost rank of modern theological writers; and the classical tutor, the professor of moral philosophy, however eminent locally, became at once a power in, and even beyond, the walls of the University. From this time he wielded an influence which he never lost, and which, had he lived, he would, I believe, have largely increased. But those lectures were its origin. They passed through several editions, they were repeatedly reviewed and canvassed, and they became almost a text-book in the schools of the University. They had as readers alike those who could appreciate, and those who were incapable of apprehending, the reasoning; they became the subject both of an understanding and of an unintelligent discussion ; until at last some one was found who from impatience of argument, or from love of paradox, or from jealousy of the logical limits assigned to the liberty of human thought, declared that he had discovered a latent heresy in a chain of reasoning which to the great majority of men seemed orthodox and plain enough. But the ingenuity of a somewhat perverse reasoning was attractive, and so others—often but little qualified to form a judgment on such a subject—not only accepted on trust the statement, but repeated it in every exaggerated form of expression.

It would be entirely beyond my meaning were I

to enter in any way upon such a controversy. Yet I will venture to assert that, when these criticisms have passed away and are almost forgotten, the lectures will remain amongst those monuments of theological argument which it is the boast of the University to have raised up for the guidance of her children in defence of the truth. Certainly those who knew the sincere piety and devoted orthodoxy of the lecturer were aware how little there was in the personal character of the man to lend confirmation to the charge.

I do not think that Dean Mansel would have desired to be spared the free comments of those who differed from him. His character was in this respect so robust and fearless, and he had such well-founded confidence in his mental powers of self-defence, that he was the last man to shrink from the challenge of a fair fight. But it is remarkable to observe how before his death—through the gradual recognition of his great powers—he had almost lived down the adverse, if not unfriendly, criticisms of an earlier period, and to compare the public estimate of his fitness for the Chair of Ecclesiastical History and for the Deanery of St. Paul's. When, indeed, the honours and responsibilities of this first office came to him, some cavils and questions were suggested; and, though no one could venture to allege in such a man unfitness for the office, it was hinted that political and undiscriminating favour had placed him in a sphere which was less than congenial to his ordinary habits of study. There was so far doubtless the semblance of fact in this allegation that Dean Mansel's literary work had followed the line of abstract rather than historical study. But his earlier if not his earliest predilections, as those who knew him best were aware, inclined to a theological rather than a philosophical course of study. Philosophy was, I think, in his eyes the companion of theology; and, though the accidents of his literary life gave a predominance to the philosophical side, the theological inclination remained undisturbed. Thus, if any there were who hoped or thought to trace a flaw or an inequality of power in this to him comparatively new field of labour, they were disappointed. No really weak point in the harness could be detected; and I believe that it will be generally as it was then locally admitted, that his vigour, knowledge, and logical capacity were as eminent here as they were elsewhere. It is perhaps an evidence of his singular ability that whilst few men in such circumstances as his have more frequently or fearlessly laid themselves open to criticism, none came off more unscathed by the attacks which those who descend into the arena of polemical controversy must expect to meet. But perhaps the secret of his almost unvaried success lay in this, that he never undertook what he could not do, and thus never failed to do what he undertook.

Dean Mansel did not long hold the Chair of Ecclesiastical History. He held it, indeed, barely long enough to justify the choice made of him ; but his lectures on the Gnostic heresies of the early centuries, of which, fortunately, the MS. notes remain and form the volume, in which it is desired to include this short notice of him, furnish some illustration of the power which he brought to bear in the discharge of his task. The events of his later life are crowded into a narrow compass. He had been appointed by the Crown to the Professorship of Ecclesiastical History on the advice of Lord Derby; he was transferred from it on the nomination of Mr. Disraeli, Lord Derby's successor, to the Deanery of St. Paul's. By this time his powers were so fully recognised that criticism itself was silent, and from all parties and individuals there was an acknowledgment that no better man could have been selected.

He addressed himself with all the vigour of his character to the work which lay before him. The commutation of the estates belonging to St. Paul's Cathedral had to be carried through, and it was, I believe, by the laborious and minute calculations into which he entered that the bases of the present arrangements were laid. But whilst the best part of his day was devoted to these public duties, all available leisure was still given, as formerly, to the work of the student and the scholar, in which his real nature was centered. Time was not, indeed, allowed to enable him to give to the world one of those great philosophical works in defence of the principles of religious faith which his friends expected, which perhaps he meditated, and to which none could have done more justice than himself; but, during the short interval that remained, he nearly performed the part which he had undertaken in 'the Speaker's Bible,' and he completed within the last two chapters his commentary on the Gospel of St. Matthew.

But there were other public duties which his new position entailed upon him ; and they were not altogether easy; for in the Deanery of St. Paul's he succeeded one who was as eminent in letters as he was deservedly popular in general society. And his time was very short. Little more than one year of life remained ; yet in that year he made a probably lasting mark, and he gave a great impulse to a work which others must carry to completion.

Of all the many architectural restorations which taste and devotional feeling have dictated to this generation, none can be the subject of a heartier and more undivided agreement than the revival of the Metropolitan Cathedral for its religious uses. The most sensitive of critics will not easily discover an objection to such a work ; the coldest cannot see unmoved the crowd of men and women gathered on some Sunday evening under that airy dome—the forest of upturned faces directed to the preacher, who sways at will an audience of thousands drawn together from the busiest, wealthiest, most cultivated, and varied capital of the world. But the spectacle, grand as it is, is full of inequalities and contrasts. The great Cathedral, indeed—rebuilt by Wren after the Fire of London, and the masterpiece of his genius—bears comparison with the stateliest churches of other countries, but bears comparison only in its outlines and general proportions. Without, it is a pile of most noble parts and lofty conceptions : within, the bare walls, naked of the enrichment and ornament which the architect designed, chill the rising enthusiasm, while the fantastic cenotaphs and tasteless monuments that are grouped along the aisles mock the glorious span and the ascending lines of the dome. Since Wren's death little or nothing had been done towards the completion of his great work; but the desire had not been wanting. Dean Mansel's able and cultivated predecessor had expressed himself ten or twelve years previously in a letter, which has been incorporated in his 'Annals of St. Paul's,' as follows :—

' I should wish to see such decorations introduced into St. Paul's as may give some splendour, while they would not disturb the solemnity or the exquisitely harmonious simplicity of the edifice ; some colour to enliven and gladden the eye, from foreign or native marbles, the most permanent and safe modes of embellishing a building exposed to the atmosphere of London. I would see the dome, instead of brooding like a dead weight over the area below, expanding and elevating the soul towards heaven. I would see the sullen white of the roof, the arches, the cornices, the capitals, and the walls broken and relieved by gilding, as we find it by experience the most lasting as well as the most appropriate decoration. I would see the adornment carried out in a rich but harmonious (and as far as possible from gaudy) style in unison with our simpler form of worship.'

These words, which deserve to be rescued from

the oblivion of an appendix, and which are worthy of the learned and accomplished man who wrote them, seem equally to represent the feelings of Dean Mansel, and recall to me not only the anxiety with which his mind was set upon the task of embellishment and completion, but almost the words in which he often spoke to me of it. The great meeting which through his means was convened at the Mansion House, and the large contributions that at once flowed in, were an earnest of the probable success of the undertaking, which, large as it undoubtedly was, had yet been fully measured beforehand in his mind. But, unhappily, hostilities between France and Germany broke out, money was needed for other purposes, and the designs and arts of peace were swept away into the bottomless pit of an all-absorbing war. Still, in spite of the difficulties which a vast Continental struggle created, the work advanced, though slowly. A committee, consisting of men of very various attainments, pursuits, and views, had been brought together, and under the Dean's guidance and good sense they had entered upon large improvements.

Differences were being smoothed, difficulties were being overcome, when, in the midst of scheme and purpose, in the full vigour of ripe intellect, in the midst also of the domestic repose which a singularly happy marriage had conferred upon him, death came suddenly like a thief in the night, and in one moment of time arrested for ever the active brain, and closed the career of administrative power and promise.

Others have succeeded to him. They have taken

up the work as it fell from his hands : it is to be hoped that they may continue it in a manner and spirit worthy of its commencement.

These were the public duties to which the last few years of Dean Mansel's life were devoted with a singleness and completeness of purpose that those only who knew him can fairly estimate ; but there was also a private side of his character which the outside world perhaps hardly suspected.

His range both of reading and of observation was very large, and it was perpetually widening under the desire to know more. To him the words which were once spoken of a great writer might perhaps not unfairly be applied—

> His learning such, no author old or new
> Escaped his reading that deserved his view,
> And such his judgment, so exact his test
> Of what was best in books, as what books best—

so readily did his mind embrace each new subject of interest, foreign though it might be supposed to be to his ordinary habits of life and study. As fast as he came in contact with new information or ideas he took them in and assimilated them in such a manner as to have them at command. Every fact, every illustration, was available for its purpose, every argument was duly marshalled under its respective principle. I cannot recall an intellect more solid, compact, and balanced, or where everything was, so to speak, more in its place, and more susceptible of immediate employment. This was doubtless due to a large combination of qualities; to abilities of a very high order, to learning, accuracy, careful cultivation and self-discipline, with no inconsiderable play of the imaginative faculties, which lent a freshness to every subject that he touched; and, lastly, to a prodigious memory, which had the rare gift of being as discriminating as it was powerful. If he retained with absolute exactitude things great and small, and seemed never to forget what he had read or heard, it was that all those facts or statements were, in his opinion, worth remembering. He seemed, moreover—which is very rare with such memories—to be able to reject the useless matter which forms so large a portion of every subject, whilst he made absolutely his own everything that he might hereafter need. Lord Macaulay once told me that with a little effort he could recall all the Latin themes and verses which he had written since the age of twelve or thirteen, and he implied, if he did not actually say, that there was a burden as well as a delight in such a marvellous power. Dean Mansel's mind, though singularly retentive, was not, as I have said, of this kind ; nor was it one of those very rapid memories which are instinctive and instantaneous in their operation : his mind seemed rather to go through a sort of mechanical process until the missing fragment for which he sought was recovered, and—like the pattern of a mosaic pavement—was recovered perfect in all its details.

But, though this complete precision of memory was a counterpart of the exactness of his logical faculty, it never dried up in him, as in so many persons, the sense of humour or the springs of imagination. He had a genuine love of poetry, to which he constantly recurred; and, though he treated it only as a pastime, he could on occasion show himself a graceful writer of verse. In the 'Phrontisterion,' a squib written at the time of the issue of the University Commission—but one which few will hesitate to acknowledge as of the highest literary merit which this generation has produced, and worthy to be read by the side of Frere's Aristophanic translations—there are lines not only remarkable for their wit, but of very noble thought and expression. And this sense of humour was a genuine characteristic of the man. His conversation was full of it; his private letters overflowed with it; he had an inexhaustible reserve at command for every occasion, and, it may be added, for every society. And yet it was always lit up by the light of kindness; it ceased with an instinctive and immediate sympathy in the presence of a friend's anxiety or sorrow; and if ever the edge of his wit was for the moment unduly sharpened, as in controversy may have happened, it arose rather from a strong sense of the wrong which he thought he was opposing, than from any personal antagonism to his opponent. He was, in fact, one of the truest, steadiest, and most warm-hearted of friends, never varying with change of circumstance or lapse of time; sometimes even with an amiable inconsistency, reconciling the mistakes or shortcomings of those in whom he was warmly interested, to a standard which his affection or regard had set up.

To this must be added—perhaps from this in a

certain measure proceeded—that which constituted one of the great charms of his character, a perfect simplicity of feeling and taste. No amusement was too simple, no occupation was unworthy of him, just as he considered no person below the level of his mind. He would come down to the dullest; and would either learn whatever there was to be acquired, or would pour out the abundant stores of his own knowledge, without a thought that he was intellectually condescending to one less competent than himself. I remember, during part of a summer that I spent with him by the seaside, his characteristic determination to understand the method of sailing a boat, and the acuteness with which he resolved the practical details, as he got them from an old fisherman, into the more scientific principles by which they were really governed. I remember, on another occasion, the keen interest with which he learnt from a gamekeeper some of the mysteries of his craft in the rearing of birds; and though Dean Mansel would never have become a good pilot or gamekeeper, yet this keen interest in the occupations of others kept his own mind singularly fresh and active. Nor was this simplicity confined to the intellectual side of his character. He was morally most just and single of purpose. It would be to such a man a poor compliment to say that he was as entirely above the temptations of profit and personal interest, and as incapable of an unworthy act, as any whom I have ever known. I would rather say that he was one whose scrupulous conscientiousness was hard to satisfy, and in whose mind the conflicting pretensions of duty and interest never held debate.

In politics he, like many others, lived too late for his generation. He saw the decay and change of ideas and institutions which were precious in his eyes; and, though he resisted it to the utmost of his power, he watched with pain the revolution of thought that has carried so far from her old moorings the University which had been long his home, and with which his earlier life, and fortunes, and affections were all so closely intertwined. It can be no offence to any one to say that, during the last few years of his residence at Oxford, he was the pillar and centre of the Conservative cause. By wisdom of counsel, ability of speech, fertility of resource, he vindicated it in the eyes of the outer world, and gave it at once strength and ornament; for of him, in letters at least, it might be truly said that he touched no subject that he did not in some way embellish it. His Liberal opponents knew it, and have left it on record that, when he was transferred from the Chair of Ecclesiastical History to St. Paul's, the ablest head had been taken away from the Conservative party. I have, indeed, heard some who knew Dean Mansel very slightly, say or imply that in the affairs of public life, where conciliation and the spirit of 'give and take' are necessary, he was of a somewhat impracticable disposition; but such an opinion was incorrect. His contemporaries were perhaps sometimes misled by the force with which his opinions were expressed. Nor was his intellect one naturally favourable to compromise. It was of too logical and incisive a kind. But his strong common sense and his keen appreciation of the course of events led him to apply the strength of his mind to any reasonable compromise which had a chance of lasting; and thus, though practically averse from change, he was, as I have often had reason to observe in my intercourse with him, always moderate in counsel, and anxious for expedients to reconcile his love of the Church and University with those alterations of public or Parliamentary opinion, to which he was not blind, however he might seem to shrink from the open recognition of them. His Conservatism, in short, was not the Conservatism of prejudice, but of individual conviction, founded on severe thought, adorned by no common learning, and bound up through the entire course of his life with the principles of his religious belief. In these days—when fundamental principles are raised and burning questions are too often discussed with moderate knowledge, excessive asperity, and sometimes hysterical passion—that fine intellect, ripe learning, and even judgment can be ill spared from the service of the Church. And if I often have cause to lament the loss of a private friend, there is still greater reason to regret from the wide sphere of public usefulness, and especially from the world of letters, the withdrawal of one whose qualities peculiarly fitted him for the work of his time.

CARNARVON.

September 25, 1874.

PREFACE.

THE course of Lectures on the Gnostic Heresies which is published in this volume was delivered before the University of Oxford by Dr. Mansel, as Regius Professor of Ecclesiastical History, in the Lent Term 1868. He had been appointed to this chair by the Crown in the preceding year, having previously held the Waynflete Professorship of Moral and Metaphysical Philosophy. Some regret was felt at the time that one who had shown himself eminently competent as a teacher of philosophy should be transferred to another branch of study, which did not seem to be so peculiarly his own. These lectures are a complete answer to any such misgivings. There were extensive provinces of Ecclesiastical History — more especially of early Ecclesiastical History—which could only be successfully occupied by one who had a familiar acquaintance with ancient and modern philosophy. To these provinces more especially Professor Mansel directed his attention ; and the present volume is one of the fruits of a very brief but energetic professoriate.

I do not think that I need offer any apology for having recommended the publication of these lectures. The student will be grateful for the guidance of a singularly clear and well-trained thinker through the mazes of this intricate subject. Since the discovery of the work of Hippolytus, which has added largely to the materials for a history of Gnosticism, English literature has furnished no connected account of this important chapter in the progress of religious thought. Indeed, with the single exception of Lipsius' elaborate article in Ersch and Gruber, which was written subsequently to this discovery, all the French and German works (so far as I am aware), which treat of the subject as a whole, labour under the same defect. Nor again, will the subject itself stand in need of any apology. The time is gone by when the Gnostic theories could be regarded as the mere ravings of religious lunatics. The problems which taxed the powers of a Basilides and a Valentinus are felt to be among the most profound and most difficult which can occupy the human mind. Even the Gnostic solutions of these problems are not altogether out of date in the second half of this nineteenth century, as the dualistic tendencies of Mr. John Stuart Mill's posthumous Three Essays will show. At such a time an exposition of the subject from a distinctly Christian point of view, written by one who apprehended with singular clearness the gravity of the issues involved, cannot be regarded as otherwise than opportune. It is only by the study of Gnostic aberrations that the true import of the teaching of Catholic Christianity, in its moral as well as its theological bearings, can be fully appreciated.

There is some reason for believing that Dean Mansel at one time contemplated the publication of these lectures; but, if so, he was prevented by pressure of other work from fulfilling his intention. Had he lived to carry out this design, the work would doubtless have received considerable additions from his hands. But it is not probable that in any essential points he would have found it necessary to modify his opinions. I am informed by those who knew him best, that he never set pen to paper until he had thoroughly worked out his subject, in all its main points, to his own satisfaction; and this representation is fully borne out by the appearance of his manuscripts, which are singularly free from corrections. It would therefore have been in the more finished execution, and in the fuller illustration, that the latest hand of the author would have been discerned. But this want did not seem to be a sufficient reason for withholding the lectures from the public.

For the reason indicated, the amount of labour which has fallen to my share has been much less than usually devolves on the editor of a posthumous work. With the exception of the alteration or addition of a word here and there, or the occasional transposition of a clause for the sake of clearness, the lectures are printed exactly as they appear in the manuscript. Any attempt to supplement them with matter of my own would have destroyed the unity of the work, without any countervailing advantage. In the verification of the references I have had the assistance of the Rev. Dr. Baker, Head Master of Merchant Taylors' School, to whom my sincere thanks are due for relieving me in great measure of this laborious task; and for the preparation of the index I am indebted to the Rev. J. J. Scott, M.A., of Trinity College, Cambridge. Such labour as I myself have bestowed on the publication of these lectures has been cheerfully tendered as a tribute of respect to the memory of one from whom, during the very short period of my connection with him as a member of the Chapter of St. Paul's, I received nothing but kindness.

J. B. LIGHTFOOT.

TRINITY COLLEGE, CAMBRIDGE:
Christmas 1874.

CONTENTS.

LECTURE I.

INTRODUCTION.

                                                                                                                                                                   PAGE

Meaning of term *Gnosis*—Gnosticism applied in actual use only to perversions of Christianity—Idea of Redemption foreign to Greek philosophy—This idea the distinctive feature of Gnosticism—Indicates its partly Christian source—Language adopted from Christianity—Title *Gnostic*—Distinction between true and false knowledge by St. Paul; by Clement of Alexandria—Gnostic estimate of the relation of Christianity to Gnosticism—Gnostic doctrines of Absolute Existence and Origin of Evil—Destroy personality and free-will—Hostile to Christianity—Lead to the same conclusions as modern Materialism 1–15

LECTURE II.

SOURCES OF GNOSTICISM.

Absolute Existence and Origin of Evil merged into one problem by the Gnostics—Absolute Existence handed down to them from Plato—Philo—The *Logos*—The *Powers*—Gnostics differ from Philo in substituting Christianity for Judaism—Judaizing and Anti-Jewish Gnostics—Origin of Evil, in Greek Philosophy little more than glanced at—Reason of this—In the East, two principal theories—Dualistic or Persian—Zoroaster—His system—Resemblance to Mosaic narrative—Influenced by intercourse with the Hebrews—The Persian theory compared with the Indian or Emanation theory—Brahmanism and Buddhism—Their doctrines—Persian influence on Gnosticism in Syria—Indian influence in Egypt—Therapeutæ—Conclusion, three principal sources of Gnosticism 16–32

LECTURE III.

SOURCES OF GNOSTICISM—CLASSIFICATION OF GNOSTIC SECTS.

PAGE

Sources of Gnosticism—The Kabbala—Jewish Metaphysics—Resembles the philosophy of Spinoza—Its teaching—'Sepher Yetzirah,' or 'Book of Creation'—'Zohar,' or 'Light'—Theory of the latter—Emanations—Adam Kadmon—Three worlds, two spiritual, one material—Final destiny of all—Resemblance to Gnosticism—Chronological difficulties—Date and authorship of the books of the Kabbala—Influenced by Persian philosophy—Relation to Gnosticism—Simon Magus—The Marcosians—Basilides and Valentinus—Classifications of Gnostic sects—Mosheim—Giescler—Neander—Baur—Matter—Order adopted in these Lectures 33–47

LECTURE IV.

NOTICES OF GNOSTICISM IN THE NEW TESTAMENT.

Simon Magus mentioned in the Acts of the Apostles—Earliest notices of Gnostic teaching found in the Epistles of St. Paul to the Asiatic Churches and to Corinth—Epistles to the Corinthians—Ephesians—Colossians—Gnostic term *Pleroma*—Pastoral Epistles—The Resurrection spiritually understood—Epistle to the Hebrews—*Æon* occurs in these Epistles—Not used in the Gnostic sense till later 48–63

LECTURE V.

NOTICES OF GNOSTICISM IN THE NEW TESTAMENT.

Prophecies of Gnosticism by St. Paul and St. Peter—Epistle of St. Jude—References to the Nicalaitans—St. John, Apocalypse—Date—Nicolaitans mentioned by name—Nicolas, one of the seven deacons—Reference to Ophites—The Gospel written to refute Gnosticism—Cerinthus and others who denied the Deity of our Lord—The Epistles directed against the Docetæ—In the First Epistle references also to Cerinthus—Apostolic treatment of heresies   64–78

LECTURE VI.

PRECURSORS OF GNOSTICISM—SIMON MAGUS AND MENANDER.

PAGE

Simon Magus mentioned in the New Testament—His pretensions—Hostile both to Christianity and Judaism—Adopts the titles *Logos* and *Power*—His *Ennoia*—His teaching—The Great 'Announcement'—The first principle, *Fire* or *Silence*—Has two natures—The world generated by six emanations or 'Roots'—The Perfect man the complete manifestation of the whole—Relation to Persian theosophy and Jewish Kabbala—This theory figurative—Fragment of 'the Announcement' preserved by Hippolytus—Simon a false Christ, not merely a false prophet—Personal history—Statue at Rome—Accounts of his death—Menander 79–94

LECTURE VII.

THE OPHITE SECTS.

Simon Magus and Gnosticism — Ophite sects—Naassenes — Ophite Trinity — The Serpent— Cainites —Sethites — Peratæ — Ophite heresies recognise Jesus as a Redeemer—Ophite doctrine of Redemption—Sources and date of the first Ophite sects—Relation to Pantheism—Ophite doctrine of the Fall identical with that of Hegel—Conclusion 95–109

LECTURE VIII.

CERINTHUS—CARPOCRATES—THE NAZARENES AND EBIONITES.

Gnostic errors in relation to the Person of Christ—Result of regarding matter as evil and the source of evil—Docetic heresy in the Apostolic age—Ebionite heresy—Cerinthus—Early mention of him—Teaching borrowed from Philo—Regarded Judaism as imperfect, but not evil—His Christology—Opposed by St. John—Baptism for the dead—Carpocrates—Date—Teaching—Differs from Cerinthus —Licentiousness of his teaching—His son Epiphanes—This teaching, how reconciled with the Gospel—Prodicus and the Adamites—Nazarenes and Ebionites—Their doctrine—Origin of the names—Gospel of the Ebionites—Testimony borne by heretics to the Catholic Faith 110–128

LECTURE IX.

SYRIAN GNOSTICISM—SATURNINUS—TATIAN—BARDESANES.

Menander the parent of Syrian and Egyptian Gnosticism—Saturninus—His relation to Simon and Menander—His teaching—A combination of Persian and Alexandrian doctrine—The moral alternative, asceticism or licentiousness—Tatian—Life and tenets—Hydroparastatæ—Bardesanes—A pervert from Catholic Christianity—His Gnostic teaching—Does not separate the Supreme God from the Creator—The Book of the Laws of Countries—His son Harmonius—Their hymns—Syrian Gnosis—Its peculiar tenet . 129-143

LECTURE X.

EGYPTIAN GNOSTICISM—BASILIDES.

Basilides—His teaching—Non-existent Deity—Non-existent world—The Word the seed of the world—Rejects common Gnostic accounts of the Origin of Evil—Influenced by Greek philosophy and Alexandrian Judaism—Introduces a Christian element from the Gospel of St. John—The seed of the world a threefold sonship—Relation of this allegory to the Mosaic account of Creation—The Great Ruler—The Ogdoad—The Hebdomad—The first Archon, the Ruler of the Ogdoad—Abrasax—The Ruler of the Hebdomad—His idea of Redemption—The Gospel the means of deliverance—Three periods of the world—Period of the Revelation of the Sons of God—The Illumination—The Great Ignorance—Basilideans accepted the reality of the life and passion of Jesus—Basilides does not adopt the Docetic heresy—Nor Persian Dualism—Nor Emanations—The account given by Irenæus probably later—His relation to Plato—Caulacau—His teaching not immoral—His relation to Judaism—Position of his teaching as a system of philosophy 144-165

LECTURE XI.

EGYPTIAN GNOSTICISM—VALENTINUS AND THE VALENTINIANS.

Valentinus—His heresy refuted by Irenæus—Sources of his system—Differs from that of Basilides—Primary Being, Depth, Unspeakable—Three series of Æons—Principle of his system—Deals with ideal archetypes—Claims support from the Gospel of St. John—Use of terms Æon, Pleroma—Valentinian theory of the Fall a desire after knowledge—The Redemption a communication of knowledge effected by Christ—A second Christ, Jesus or Logos—Emanates from the thank-offerings of the Æons—The Divine Nature represented by a plurality of distinct attributes—Relation to the philosophical theology of St. Augustine . . . 166–183

LECTURE XII.

VALENTINUS AND THE VALENTINIANS.

Romance of Valentinus in three parts—The second part—*Achamoth*—Her sorrows and sufferings—Her offspring, material, animal, spiritual—The theory an attempt to explain how the Spiritual gives existence to Matter—The third part of the romance—Formation of the visible world—The Demiurge—His work—This theory recognises three classes of men, material, animal, spiritual—Valentinian theory of Redemption—Two kinds of Redemption for the two higher classes of men—No Redemption for the material part—Valentinian views of the nature of Christ—Tendency of this teaching about Redemption—Followers of Valentinus—Ptolemæus—His letter to Flora—Marcus—Heracleon—His commentary on St. John's Gospel—The Coptic Pistis Sophia not written by Valentinus—System of Valentinus in principle Pantheistic—Its relation to the Kabbala 184–202

LECTURE XIII.

ASIATIC GNOSTICISM—MARCION.

Marcion—His position—His life—His teaching, a combination of Rationalism and 'higher criticism'—His system critical, not metaphysical—He began by criticising the Old Testament—His Antitheseis—Meaning of the term 'just'—Tertullian's answers to Marcion—Marcion distinguishes between two Gods and two Christs—His Christ of the Old Testament—His Christ of the New Testament has neither a human soul nor a seeming birth, only a seeming death—The contest between Christ and the Demiurge—The relation of Christ to the Supreme God unexplained—He denies the resurrection of the body—Condemns marriage—Marcionite baptism—Asceticism—Assumes only three principles, but none essentially evil—His teaching the transition of Christian speculation from philosophy to pure theology . 203–219

LECTURE XIV.

JUDAIZING REACTION—THE CLEMENTINES—THE ELKESAITES.

Comparison of earlier and later Gnosticism—Judaizing reaction—The Clementines—Writings included under this title—Introduction to the Homilies—Their contents—Their teaching—Leading feature, hostility to Marcionism—External history—Most nearly akin to the doctrines of the Elkesaites—Account of Elxai and the Elkesaites as given by Epiphanius—Relation of the teaching of the Clementines to the tenets of the Elkesaites . . . 220–238

LECTURE XV.

CHRISTIAN OPPONENTS OF GNOSTICISM, IRENÆUS, TERTULLIAN.

Antagonists of Gnosticism—Irenæus—'Five Books of the Refutation and Overthrow of Knowledge falsely so called'—Date—Account of Contents—Tertullian—His 'Præscriptio adversus Hæreticos'—His treatise against the Valentinians—Against Marcion—Comparison of these writers 239–260

LECTURE XVI.

CLEMENT OF ALEXANDRIA—HIPPOLYTUS.

The Christian School at Alexandria—Clement succeeds Pantænus—His estimate of Philosophy—His principal works—His doctrine of the Logos—Account of the 'Stromateis'—In opposition to Gnosticism he asserts the free will of man—The true value of the material creation—He defends marriage—He answers the Gnostic theories by a counter-sketch of the true Gnostic—Difference between his true knowledge and the knowledge claimed by the Gnostic heretics—Comparison of Clement with Irenæus—Hippolytus 261–275

THE
GNOSTIC HERESIES

OF THE

FIRST AND SECOND CENTURIES.

LECTURE I.

INTRODUCTION.

THE meaning of the term *Gnosis* or *Knowledge*, as applied to a system of philosophy, may be illustrated by the language of Plato towards the end of the fifth book of the Republic, in which he distinguishes between knowledge (γνῶσις) and opinion (δόξα) as being concerned respectively with the real (τὸ ὄν) and the apparent (τὸ φαινόμενον). When to this distinction is added the further explanation that the objects of sense, the visible things of the world, belong to the class of phenomena and are objects of opinion, while the invisible essence of things, the one as distinguished from the many, is the true reality, discerned not by sense but by intellect, we shall be justified in identifying 'knowledge' with that apprehension of things which penetrates beyond their sensible appearances to their essence and cause, and which differs in name only from that 'wisdom' (σοφία) which Aristotle tells us is by common consent admitted to consist in a knowledge of

First Causes or Principles.[1] In this general sense however, the term γνῶσις has nothing to distinguish it from the ordinary Greek conception of 'philosophy,' and so long as it remains solely within the region of philosophical inquiry and terminology, we do not find it generally employed to designate either philosophy as a whole or any special philosophical system.[2] It is not till after the Christian era that the term comes into use as the distinct designation of a certain form of religious philosophy, emanating in some degree from Christian sources, and influenced by Christian ideas and Christian language. Even in the earlier association of Greek philosophy with a revealed religion, which is manifested in the Græco-Jewish philosophy of Alexandria, though the teaching of Philo may be regarded as embodying the essential constituents of Gnosticism in an entire if an undeveloped form, we do not find the distinctive name of Gnosis or Gnostic applied to designate the system or its teachers. It is not indeed difficult to detect in Philo the germs of the later Gnosticism, but they are present under other names. The wise man, the perfect man, the philosopher, the contemplative man,[3] are names applied by Philo to those favoured persons who are permitted to attain to a knowledge of divine things, so far as it is attainable by man; the peculiar designations of Gnosis and Gnostic do not appear.[4] In their actual use, if not in their etymological meaning, the terms Gnostic, Gnosis, Gnosticism, as names of a sect of philosophers or the doctrines professed by them, have been employed exclusively with reference to philosophical systems which have distinguished themselves,

[1] *Metaph.* i. 1: τὴν ὀνομαζομένην σοφίαν περὶ τὰ πρῶτα αἴτια καὶ ἀρχὰς ὑπολαμβάνουσι πάντες.

[2] Cf. Burton, *Bampton Lectures*, p. 358.

[3] *Legis Alleg.* iii. 73, p. 128;
Fragm. p. 637; *De Conf. Ling.* 20, p. 419; *De Præm. et Pæn.* 7, p. 415.

[4] Cf. Harvey's *Irenæus*, vol. I. p. cxl; Matter, *Histoire du Gnosticisme*, vol. I. p. 62 (2nd edit.)

not merely as ontological speculations, but also as heretical perversions of Christianity. It is necessary therefore to a full explanation of the historical import of the terms that we should pay attention, not merely to the general distinctions between knowledge and opinion, between the real and the apparent, between ontology and phenomenology, but also to the especially Christian feature, the perversion of which distinguishes Gnosticism as a heresy from other forms of speculation, which, however extravagant in their pretensions, however erroneous in their results, however alien from or opposed to the doctrines of the Christian revelation, have never been classified as *heresies*, but only as *philosophies*, heathenish it may be or anti-Christian, but not properly heretical. The feature in question will be found in the idea, common alike to Gnosticism and Christianity, but not shared by that philosophy from which the name and many of the leading ideas of Gnosticism are borrowed—the idea of a Redemption—of a Divine interposition to deliver the world from the dominion of evil and its consequences.[1]

Among the Greek philosophical systems, as the idea of evil holds a very subordinate and insignificant place, so the idea of redemption seems not to be recognised at all. The world and its phenomena are regarded from the most various points of view. It may be as the spontaneous development of some primitive vital force, as in the hylozoism of the early Ionians; it may be as the momentary collision of opposite forces and the perpetual passing from one state of being to another, as in the system of Heraclitus; it may be as a motionless uniformity, without plurality and without change, as in the theory of the Eleatics; it may be as a continuous development under the influence of an external power, as in the philosophy

[1] Cf. Baur, *Die Christliche Gnosis* p. 27.

of Anaxagoras; it may be as the subject of successive cycles, of opposite states alternating with each other, as in the doctrine of Empedocles, and again in that of Plato, and more distinctly still in that of the Stoics; it may be as an organised system in eternal revolution, as in the Peripatetic philosophy; but in all these systems alike, the world, through all its changes or appearances of change, does but exhibit the working of one law or one nature essentially belonging to it, and continuing to act upon it or in it throughout its whole existence: there is no trace of any such conception as that of a new power introduced into the world to deliver it from the law to which it is subject, to exalt it permanently and progressively to a higher and better existence and destiny. This one pervading deficiency, which characterizes the whole current of Greek thought, is strikingly and painfully brought into light in the lines of a great poet of our own country, one who, unhappily an unbeliever in the truths of Christianity, endeavoured to replace what he had rejected by elevating the speculations of Pagan philosophy to the Christian level. The Great Year of the Stoics, the destruction of the old world, the commencement of the new cycle, takes the place of the Christian expectation of the delivery of the creature from the bondage of corruption; but after the triumphant opening of the poem with its exulting description of the regenerated world in its new cycle, the melancholy conclusion tells us too plainly, by the unwilling confession of an advocate, that the vaunted regeneration of philosophy is but an endless repetition of the old evil:

> The world's great age begins anew,
>   The golden years return;
> The earth doth like a snake renew
>   Her winter weeds outworn;

Heaven smiles; and faiths and empires gleam
Like wrecks of a dissolving dream.

A brighter Hellas rears its mountains
   From waves serener far,
A new Peneus rolls its fountains
   Against the morning star,
Where fairer Tempes bloom, there sleep
Young Cyclads on a sunnier deep.

A loftier Argo cleaves the main,
   Fraught with a later prize;
Another Orpheus sings again,
   And loves, and weeps, and dies;
A new Ulysses leaves once more
Calypso for his native shore.

Another Athens shall arise,
   And to remoter time
Bequeath, like sunset to the skies,
   The splendour of its prime;
And leave, if nought so bright may live,
All earth can take or heaven can give.

*   *   *   *   *

O cease! must hate and death return?
   Cease! must men kill and die?
Cease! drain not to its dregs the urn
   Of bitter prophecy.
The world is weary of the past;
O might it die, or rest at last![1]

The distinctive feature which marks Gnosticism in all its schools as a religious heresy, and not as a mere philosophical extravagance, is the presence of this idea of a redemption of the world, and the recognition, in a perverted form, of the person and work of Christ as taking part in this redemption.[2] And this indication of a partly

---

[1] Shelley, *Hellas*.
[2] See Dorner, *Person of Christ*, vol. I. Note *U* (Eng. Tr. p. 344).

Christian source of the system will also throw some light on the origin of the name by which it has been generally designated. Already in the LXX translation of the Old Testament, and still more clearly in the Apocryphal Book of Wisdom, the term γνῶσις had been employed to denote a knowledge of the true God or a knowledge especially given by Him;[1] and the same term was employed by the writers of the New Testament for that knowledge of God through Christ which is given by the Gospel. The mission of John the Baptist is prophetically declared by his father as to give *knowledge* of salvation to the Lord's people.[2] St Paul speaks of his Corinthian converts as enriched by Christ in all utterance and in all *knowledge*;[3] he enumerates among the gifts of the Spirit the word of *knowledge*;[4] he tells them again that God hath shined in our hearts to give the light of the *knowledge* of the glory of God in the face of Jesus Christ.[5] In like manner he speaks of casting down imaginations and every high thing that exalteth itself against the *knowledge* of God;[6] and says that he counts all things but loss for the excellency of the *knowledge* of Christ Jesus.[7] St Peter, in a like sense, exhorts the disciples to whom he writes to add to their faith virtue, and to virtue *knowledge*,[8] and bids them grow in grace and in the *knowledge* of our Lord and Saviour Jesus Christ.[9] Yet there are manifest indications of the existence, even in Apostolic times, of a system of false teaching which had usurped to itself especially the name of *knowledge*. Not to dwell now upon the pro-

---

[1] Ps. cxviii (cxix). 66; Prov. viii. 12, xxx. 3 (xxiv. 26 in *Vat.*); Eccl. ii. 26; Isa. xi. 2; Wisd. ii. 13, vii. 17, x. 10, xiv. 22. The term γνώστης is sometimes employed in the sense of a diviner or wizard: 1 Sam. xxviii. 3, 9; 2 Kings xxi. 6. See *Matter*, vol. I, p. 161.

[2] Luke i. 77.
[3] 1 Cor. i. 5.
[4] 1 Cor. xii. 8.
[5] 2 Cor. iv. 6.
[6] 2 Cor. x. 5.
[7] Phil. iii. 8.
[8] 2 Peter i. 5, 6.
[9] 2 Peter iii. 18.

bable meaning of the disputed passage in the eighth chapter of the First Epistle to the Corinthians, where the indifference as regards meats offered to idols is spoken of as the *knowledge* that puffeth up,[1] we have at least the unmistakeable and emphatic warning of the Apostle to Timothy, τὴν παρακαταθήκην φύλαξον, ἐκτρεπόμενος τὰς βεβήλους κενοφωνίας καὶ ἀντιθέσεις τῆς ψευδωνύμου γνώσεως,[2] a passage the point of which in relation to the texts previously quoted is obscured in our Authorised Version by the substitution of the word *science* for *knowledge*.

It is probable therefore, that the adoption of the terms *Gnosis* and *Gnostic*, as special designations of a philosophy and its professors, arose from the language of Christianity, and was intended to distinguish the Gnostic teaching as the rival and the assumed superior of the Christian Church. The former of these terms (γνῶσις), as we have seen, is contemporaneous with the teaching of St Paul; the latter (γνωστικός) is of later origin, and is said to have been first assumed towards the end of the first or beginning of the second century by the sect of the Ophites,[3] or according to another account by Carpocrates.[4] The distinction between the true and the false knowledge, between the knowledge claimed as the heritage of the Christian Church and the knowledge claimed by the rival systems which gloried in the name, is that which in all ages has distinguished the wisdom which is built on faith and received of God, from that which is built on doubt and invented by man. The knowledge professed by the Christian Church was a knowledge given by divine revelation and accepted in faith; whatever fuller insight into divine

---

[1] 1 Cor. viii. 1.
[2] 1 Tim. vi. 20.
[3] Hippolytus, *Ref. Hær.* v. 6.
[4] Irenæus, *Hær.* i. 25; cf. Eusebius, *H. E.* iv. 7, 9.

things could be attained by study or contemplation was admitted only in so far as it was in accordance with the revealed teaching, and, if not identical with it, at least a legitimate interpretation or explanation of it. The knowledge professed by the Gnostic teachers, on the other hand, was a knowledge designed to subordinate the revelation of Christ to the speculations of human philosophy—a curious inquiry, searching after an apprehension of God, not in what He has revealed of Himself, but in that which He has not revealed—an inquiry which, under the pretence of giving a deeper and more spiritual meaning to the Christian revelation, in fact uprooted its very foundations by making it subservient to theories incompatible with its first principles—theories of human invention, originating in heathen philosophies, and making those philosophies the criterion and end of revelation, instead of regarding revelation as the discovery by God of those truths which human wisdom had desired to see and had not seen. Such is the distinction with which St Paul combats the Gnostic systems in their germ and infancy. 'As ye have therefore received Christ Jesus the Lord, so walk in Him; rooted and built up in Him, and stablished in the faith, as ye have been taught, abounding therein with thanksgiving. Beware lest any man spoil you through philosophy and vain deceit, after the tradition of men, after the rudiments of the world, and not after Christ. For in Him dwelleth all the fulness of the Godhead bodily.'[1] And at the end of the second or beginning of the third century,[2] when the principal Gnostic systems had risen and flourished and were entering on the period of their decay, we find Clement of Alexandria adopting a similar

[1] Coloss. ii. 6–9.

[2] The *Stromateis* were certainly written after the death of Commodus (A.D. 193): see *Strom.* i. 21, p. 406 (Potter). Cave, *Hist. Lit.* p. 89, supposes the work to have been written in the same year.

criterion to distinguish between the true Gnostic or perfect Christian and the disciples of the false systems which laid claim to the name. 'That alone,' he says, 'is the proper and incontestable truth, in which we are instructed by the Son of God' .... 'That truth which the Greeks profess, though it partake of the same name, is divided from ours, as regards magnitude of knowledge and force of demonstration and divine power, and the like; for we are taught of God, instructed in truly sacred literature by the Son of God.'[1] 'Faith,' he says in the same book, 'is the first element of knowledge, as necessary to the true Gnostic as breathing is to life. As we cannot live without the four elements, neither can we attain to knowledge without faith.'[2] And again; 'That which we possess is the only true demonstration, being supplied by the sacred literature of the Holy Scriptures and by the heaven-taught wisdom, as the Apostle calls it (1 Thess. iv. 9). . . . But that demonstration which begets opinion and not knowledge is human, and is made by rhetorical argument and dialectical syllogisms; whereas the demonstration which is from above produces the faith of knowledge, by the comparison and interpretation of the Holy Scriptures, in the soul of those who are desirous of learning.'[3]

The Gnostics in fact regarded the Christian revelation as having a similar relation towards speculative philosophy to that in which the Jewish religion was regarded by Christians as standing towards their own belief. As the institutions of Judaism under type and symbol prefigured in the Christian belief the fuller revelation of Christ, so Christianity itself, in the estimation of the Gnostics, was but a figurative and symbolical exposition of truths; the

---

[1] *Strom.* i. 20, p. 376 (Potter). Cf. Bishop Kaye's *Clement of Alexandria* p. 124.

[2] *Ibid.* ii. 6, p. 445. Cf. Kaye, p. 136.

[3] *Ibid.* ii. 11, p. 454. Cf. Kaye, p. 139.

fuller meaning of which was to be supplied by philosophical speculation. Gnosticism revived the idea, familiar to heathen thought but wholly alien to the spirit of Christianity, of one religion designed for the wise and the initiated, and another for the ignorant and profane vulgar. Faith, the foundation of Christian knowledge, was fitted only for the rude mass, the ψυχικοὶ or animal men who were incapable of higher things. Far above these were the privileged natures, the men of intellect, the πνευματικοὶ or spiritual men, whose vocation was not to believe but to know.[1] How completely this distinction perverted the language of St Paul,[2] on which it was nominally founded, will appear in the subsequent course of our inquiry. Such a distinction, as Neander has well observed, was natural in the heathen systems of antiquity, because heathenism was destitute of any independent means, adapted alike to all stages of human enlightenment, for satisfying man's religious needs. Such a means however was supplied in Christianity by a faith in great historical facts, on which the religious convictions of all men alike were to depend. Gnosticism, by a reactionary process, tended to make religion forfeit the freedom gained for it by Christ, and to make it again dependent on human speculations. Christianity had furnished a simple and universally intelligible solution of every enigma which had occupied thinking minds—a practical answer to all the questions which speculation had busied itself in vain to answer. It established a temper of mind by which doubts that could not be resolved by the efforts of speculative reason were to be practically vanquished. But Gnosticism wished to make religion once more dependent

[1] See Neander, *Church History*, vol. II. p. 2 (ed. Bohn). Cf. Clem. Alex. *Strom.* ii. 3 (p. 433, Potter), τὴν μὲν πίστιν τοῖς ἁπλοῖς ἀπονείμαντες ἡμῖν, αὐτοῖς δὲ τὴν γνῶσιν (of the Valentinians).

[2] 1 Cor. ii. 14, 15.

on a speculative solution of these questions.¹ Religion was to be founded, not on historical facts, but on ontological ideas: through speculations on existence in general and its necessary evolutions, men were to be led to a comprehension of the true meaning of what Christianity represents under a historical veil. The motto of the Gnostic might be exactly given in the words of a distinguished modern philosopher, 'Men are saved, not by the historical, but by the metaphysical.'²

Two metaphysical problems may be particularly specified as those which Gnosticism borrowed from heathen philosophy, and to the solution of which the Christian revelation was made subordinate—the problem of Absolute Existence and the problem of the Origin of Evil. The two indeed, as we shall see hereafter, were by the Gnostics generalised into one; and this union may explain the language of Tertullian, Eusebius, and Epiphanius, all of whom speak of the origin of evil as the great object of heretical inquiry;³ but in themselves and in their historical relations, the two problems may be regarded as distinct, and each contributes its own ingredient to form the anti-Christian side of the Gnostic speculation. The search after an absolute first principle, the inquiry how the absolute and unconditioned can give rise to the relative and conditioned, is one which, when pursued as a theological inquiry, almost inevitably leads to a denial of the personality of God. Philosophy striving after a first

---

¹ Neander, *Church History*, vol. II. p. 4.

² 'Nur das Metaphysische, keineswegs aber das Historische macht selig'; Fichte, *Anweisung zum seligen Leben* (*Werke* v. p. 485).

³ Tertullian, *De Præscr. Hæret.* 7 'Eædem materiæ apud hæreticos et philosophos volutantur, iidem retractatus implicantur; Unde malum et quare?'; Eusebius, *H. E.* v. 27 περὶ τοῦ πολυθρυλλήτου παρὰ τοῖς αἱρεσιώταις ζητήματος, τοῦ Πόθεν ἡ κακία; Epiphan. *Hær.* xxiv. 6 Ἔσχε δὲ ἡ ἀρχὴ τῆς κακῆς προφάσεως τὴν αἰτίαν ἀπὸ τοῦ ζητεῖν καὶ λέγειν, Πόθεν τὸ κακόν; Cf. Baur, *Die Chr. Gnosis* p. 19.

principle which shall be one and simple and unconditioned, and incapable of all further analysis in thought, is naturally tempted to soar above that complex combination of attributes which is implied in our conception of personality, and in endeavouring to simplify and purify our representation of the Divine nature, ends by depriving it of every attribute which can make God the object of any religious feeling or the source of any moral obligation. Instead of a religious relation between God and man, the relation of a person to a person, this philosophy substitutes a metaphysical relation between God and the world, as absolute and relative, cause and effect, principle and consequence— happy if it stops short at this error only, and does not find itself compelled by the inexorable laws of its own logic to identify God with the world. And when the standpoint of philosophy is thus removed from a moral to a metaphysical aspect of God, the other great problem, the Origin of Evil, naturally assumes a similar character. Evil no longer appears in the form of *sin*, as a transgression on the part of a moral agent against the laws and will of a moral Governor. The personality of God having disappeared, the personality of man naturally disappears along with it. Man is no longer the special subject of relations towards God peculiar to himself by virtue of that personal and moral nature in which he alone of God's earthly creatures bears the image of his Maker: he is viewed but as a portion of the universe, an atom in that vast system of derived existence which emanates from the one First Principle.[1] The course of the world is his course as a part of the world; the laws of the world are his laws also, and the one pre-eminence of man among creatures, the one attribute which constitutes him a person and not a thing—the attribute of Free-Will—is swallowed up in the depths and

[1] Cf. Baur, *Die Chr. Gnosis* p. 67.

carried along with the stream of the necessary evolution of being. Contemplated from this point of view, evil is no longer a moral but a natural phenomenon; it becomes identical with the imperfect, the relative, the finite; all nature being governed by the same law and developed from the same principle, no one portion of its phenomena can itself be more evil, more contrary to the law, than another; all alike are evil only so far as they are imperfect; all alike are imperfect, so far as they are a falling off from the perfection of the absolute.[1] Thus contemplated, the problem of the origin of evil is identified with that of the origin of finite and relative existence; the question how can the good give birth to the evil, is only another mode of asking how can the absolute give birth to the relative; the two great inquiries of philosophy are merged into one, and religion and morality become nothing more than curious questions of metaphysics.

And such, as we shall see, was the actual course of the Gnostic speculations; and this circumstance will serve to explain the earnest abhorrence, the strong feeling of irreconcilable hostility, with which this teaching was regarded by the Apostles and Fathers of the Church. It was not merely an erroneous opinion on certain points of belief that they were combating; it was a principle which destroyed the possibility of any religion at all; which, in setting aside the personality of God and the personality of man, struck at the root and basis of all natural religion; which, by virtually denying the existence of sin and consequently of redemption from sin, took away the whole significance of the revelation of Christ. With this view of the spirit of the Gnostic teaching, we may the more readily believe the tradition of the vehement language of St John, 'Let us fly, lest the bath fall in, while Cerinthus the enemy of

[1] Cf. Baur, *Die Chr. Gnosis* p. 20.

the truth is in it'[1]—language which yet is hardly stronger than his own recorded words, 'Who is a liar but he that denieth that Jesus is the Christ? He is antichrist that denieth the Father and the Son.'[2] We may understand the zealous horror with which St Polycarp, the disciple of St John, addressed the Gnostic Marcion, 'I know thee the firstborn of Satan.'[3] This very charge of destroying the free will of man and subverting the distinction between right and wrong is made in express terms by Clement of Alexandria against the doctrines of Basilides and the Valentinians; and his argument may be extended beyond the point of view in which he has stated it, to the whole sphere of man's moral and religious action. 'Faith,' he says, 'if it be a natural privilege, is no longer a voluntary right action; nor can the unbeliever be justly punished, not being the cause of his own unbelief, as the believer is not the cause of his own belief. Moreover, if we rightly consider, the whole distinctive character of belief and unbelief cannot be liable to praise or blame, being preceded by a natural necessity sprung from Him who is all-powerful.'[4]

This feature of the controversy is not without interest to us in this present day; for, however different may be the premises of the popular philosophy of our own time, it conducts us to precisely the same conclusion. In this common error the most opposite extremes meet together; the transcendental metaphysics of the Gnostic philosophy and the grovelling materialism of our own day join hands together in subjecting man's actions to a natural necessity, in declaring that he is the slave of the circumstances in which he is placed; his course of action being certainly determined by them as effect by cause and

---

[1] Irenæus, *Hær.* iii. 3; cf. Eusebius, *H. E.* iv. 14.
[2] 1 John ii. 22.
[3] Irenæus, *l. c.*; Eusebius, *l. c.*
[4] *Strom.* ii. 3 (p. 434, Potter).

consequent by antecedent. Merged in the intelligible universe by the Gnostic of old, man is no less by modern 'science falsely so called' merged in the visible universe; his actions or volitions are moral effects which follow their moral causes 'as certainly and invariably as physical effects follow their physical causes.'[1] Under this assumption the distinction between moral evil and physical entirely vanishes. A man, however inconvenient his actions may be to his neighbour, is no more to blame for committing them than is a fire for consuming his neighbour's house or a sickness for destroying his life. Man cannot offend against any law of God; for his actions are the direct consequence of the laws which God (if there be a God) has established in the world; he is subject, to repeat the words of Clement, to a natural necessity derived from Him who is all-powerful. The consciousness of freedom is a delusion; the consciousness of sin is a delusion; the personality of man disappears under the all-absorbing vortex of matter and its laws. How long, we may ask, will it be before the personality of God disappears also, and the vortex of matter becomes all in all?

Δῖνος βασιλεύει, τὸν Δί᾽ ἐξεληλακώς.[2]

---

[1] Mill, *Examination of Sir W. Hamilton's Philosophy* p. 501.
[2] Aristophanes, *Nub.* 1471.

LECTURE II.

SOURCES OF GNOSTICISM.

In my last lecture I mentioned two problems borrowed from heathen philosophy, and intruded by Gnosticism on the Christian revelation—the problem of Absolute Existence and the problem of the Origin of Evil. These two problems, as we have seen, were by the Gnostics merged into one; but they came to them from different sources, and their previous history to some extent belongs to different systems of philosophy. The problem of the Absolute was handed down to them from Plato, through the medium of the Græco-Jewish school of Alexandria represented by Philo. Plato, towards the end of the sixth Book of the Republic, had described the endeavour of philosophy to ascend *as far as the unconditioned* (μέχρι τοῦ ἀνυποθέτου)[1] to the first principle of the universe, and had spoken of this first principle or ideal good as being something transcending all definite existence (οὐκ οὐσίας ὄντος τοῦ ἀγαθοῦ, ἀλλ' ἔτι ἐπέκεινα τῆς οὐσίας πρεσβείᾳ καὶ δυνάμει ὑπερέχοντος).[2] From this language, coupled with a perverted interpretation of the Platonic cosmogony, as represented in the Timæus, Philo elaborated a theory for the interpretation of the Jewish Scriptures, according to which the God who made and who governs the world, the God whose personal intercourse with His chosen people is conspicuous through-

[1] *Resp.* vi. p. 511.　　　[2] *Ibid.* p. 509.

out the whole teaching of the Old Testament, is distinguished from the absolute first principle, which, as being beyond personality and beyond definite existence, is immutable and incapable of relation to finite things. This latter—the supreme God—is absolute and simple existence, without qualities, and not to be expressed in speech.[1] The former—the Logos or mediator between the supreme God and the world—is invested with those personal attributes which characterize the God of the Hebrew Scriptures, and to him are referred those several passages of Scripture in which God is spoken of as holding direct intercourse with man.[2] Whether Philo really intends to represent the supreme God and the Logos as two numerically distinct beings, is a matter of dispute among his commentators,[3] and indeed in the case of a writer so extremely fanciful and unsystematic it is difficult to say whether he had any definite theory on this subject at all. The same may be also said of his description of the Divine powers or δυνάμεις, which are sometimes described in language which seems to represent them as distinct personal beings, sometimes appear to be merely poetical personifications of the several attributes of God, as manifested in relation to the world.[4] But it must at least be admitted that his language is such as to suggest to subsequent speculators, aided, as we shall see, by

[1] *Legis Alleg.* i. c. 13, p. 50 ἄποιος ὁ θεός: *Ibid.* c. 15, p. 53 δεῖ γὰρ ἡγεῖσθαι καὶ ἄποιον αὐτὸν εἶναι καὶ ἄφθαρτον καὶ ἄτρεπτον: *De Somn.* i. 39, p. 655, λέγεσθαι γὰρ οὐ πέφυκεν, ἀλλὰ μόνον εἶναι τὸ ὄν. Cf. *De Vit. Contempl.* c. 1, p. 472; *Quod Deus Immut.* c. 11, p. 281.

[2] Cf. Kitto's *Cyclopedia* (3rd edit.), Art. 'Philosophy,' p. 526, and the references there given.

[3] The negative is maintained by Burton, *Bampton Lectures* Note 93, and by Dorner, *Person of Christ* i. p. 27 (Eng. Trans.) and Note *A*, against Gfrörer, Dähne, Lücke, and the majority of recent critics. An intermediate view is taken by Zeller, *Philosophie der Griechen*, III. 2, p. 324, and to some extent by Professor Jowett, *Epistles of St. Paul*, I. p. 484 (2nd edit.).

[4] Cf. J. G. Müller, Art. 'Philo' in Herzog, vol. XI. p. 589; Gfrörer *Philo*, vol. I. pp. 151, 155 *seq.*

similar ideas borrowed from other sources, the theory of a series of intermediate spiritual beings interposed between the supreme God and the visible world, beginning with the Logos, as the highest, but extending itself through a succession of subordinate powers of no definite number or relation to each other, but capable of increase *ad libitum* according to the fancy of the philosopher for the time being, or the exigencies of the theory which he may happen to be occupied with.[1]

But the Gnostic philosophers differed from Philo in one important particular. Philo, as a Jew, had merely to adapt his system to the interpretation of the Old Testament: the Gnostics, dealing with the Christian revelation, had to extend the theory so as to connect it with some kind of an acknowledgment of the person and work of Christ. The Gnostics professed to acknowledge Christ as in some manner the Redeemer of the world; but from what does he redeem it? Not from sin in the proper sense of the term; not from the evil entailed upon man by his own voluntary transgression of God's law, for, under the Gnostic hypothesis, there is no free will in man, and therefore no voluntary transgression. The evil from which Christ redeems must therefore be evil of another kind—something not introduced into the world by man's disobedience, but something inherent in the constitution of the world itself. The evil that is in the world must therefore be due to the Creator of the world; it must be inherent in the world from the beginning—the result of some weakness at least, or some ignorance, if not of some

[1] Thus in the *De Cherub*. c. 9, we have three powers all distinct from the supreme God, symbolized by the two cherubim and the flaming sword. In *De Abrahamo* c. 24, there are three powers (the three beings who appeared to Abraham at Mamre), one of whom is identified with the supreme God. In *De Mut. Nom.* c. 4, we have a $\delta \acute{v} \nu a \mu \iota s$ $\epsilon \mathring{v} \epsilon \rho \gamma \epsilon \tau \iota \kappa \acute{\eta}$ added to the $\beta a \sigma \iota \lambda \iota \kappa \acute{\eta}$ and $\pi o \iota \eta \tau \iota \kappa \acute{\eta}$. In *De Prof.* cc. 18, 19, six powers are invented to answer to the six cities of refuge.

positive malignity concurring in its first formation. The Demiurge is thus necessarily lowered from the position which he holds in the system of Philo, as next to, if not one with, the supreme God. The Redeemer of the world must stand higher than the Creator; for he is sent to remedy the imperfection of the Creator's work: there will be a gulf between them of greater or less extent, according to the amount of evil which the philosopher may believe himself to have discovered in the world, and the consequent amount of imperfection which he may think proper to attribute to its maker, and this gulf may be filled up by any number of intermediate beings, forming so many successive links in the chain of descent from good to evil. It is obvious that under a theory of this kind the Jewish religion and the Scriptures of the Old Testament may be regarded as standing in either of two different relations towards Christianity, or rather towards the philosophy which takes the place of Christianity. The Creator of the world, the God of the Jewish people, may be regarded merely as an imperfect, or as a positively malignant being. He may be an emanation from the supreme God, imperfect in proportion to his remoteness from the source of existence, but still a servant of God, working under the Divine law and accomplishing the Divine purpose (if we may venture allusively to employ the term purpose in relation to an impersonal being)—accomplishing the Divine purpose it may be blindly and ignorantly, yet in subordination to a higher and better power. Or, on the other hand, he may be a being hostile to God; either the offspring of some power alien from God, and acting in opposition to the Divine purpose—of an original evil principle, the head of a kingdom of darkness in antagonism to the kingdom of light; or at least one so far degenerated from the original source of good that his imperfection becomes in result an actual contrariety to good.

Two opposite views may thus be taken of the Jewish religion. It may be an imperfect preparation for a Christian philosophy, which the latter is designed to supersede by completing, or it may be a system fundamentally hostile to Christianity, which the latter is designed to combat and overthrow. On account of this difference, the Gnostic schools have sometimes been divided into the two classes of Judaizing and anti-Jewish Gnostics; the one regarding it as the mission of Christ to complete an imperfect revelation, the other supposing Him to be sent to deliver the world from the bondage of an evil creator and governor. How far this distinction may be considered as furnishing the ground for an accurate classification of the several Gnostic systems, will be considered hereafter. At present we must endeavour to complete our sketch of the philosophical sources of Gnosticism, by recurring to the second great problem, which its professors applied to the interpretation of Christianity—the problem of the Origin of Evil.

The origin of evil holds a very subordinate place, if indeed it can be said to have been considered at all, in the philosophy of Greece. The Greek mind was rather disposed to view the world in the light of an evolution from below, than in that of an emanation and descent from above.[1] This may be seen not only in the poetical cosmogonies and theogonies which preceded philosophy proper, evolving the world and even the gods from a primitive chaos and darkness, but also in the first efforts of philosophy itself— in the hylozoism of the early Ionians, evolving the higher forms of existence from the action of some primitive material element, and again, after this view had been

[1] Cf. Baur, *Die Chr. Gnosis* p. 30.

superseded by the influence of the mathematical and metaphysical abstractions of the Pythagoreans and Eleatics, in its revival in a modified form in later theories, in the four elements of Empedocles, in the ὁμοῦ πάντα of Anaxagoras, in the atoms of Leucippus and Democritus. Even the metaphysical schools of Greek philosophy, commencing their speculations with the highest and purest abstractions, cannot be said to have in any way grappled with the problem of the existence of evil. The Eleatics contented themselves with little more than the dogmatic assertion that the One alone exists, and that plurality and change have no real being. Plato, though taking a transient glance at the problem in that passage of the Republic where he lays it down as a rule of teaching concerning God, that he is not the cause of all things, but only of those things that are good,[1] and again in the mythical utterance of the prophet of destiny towards the close of the book, αἰτία ἑλομένου, θεὸς ἀναίτιος,[2] cannot be said to have fairly grappled with the positive side of the question, what is the cause of evil, and how can it come into the world against the will of God? In the cosmogony of the Timæus, though the Demiurge is represented as forming the world out of pre-existing matter, yet this matter itself is so little regarded as a cause of evil, as something in its own nature hostile to the Deity, that on the contrary we are told that the world, as thus made, was an image of the eternal gods, and that the Father who made it admired it and was rejoiced.[3] In other passages, it is true, a darker side of the world makes its appearance. God is said to complete the idea of good in the world *as far as is possible*;[4] a

---

[1] *Resp.* ii. p. 380, μὴ πάντων αἴτιον τὸν θεόν, ἀλλὰ τῶν ἀγαθῶν.
[2] *Ibid.* x. p. 617.
[3] *Timæus* p. 37.
[4] *Ibid.* p. 30 A: cf. p. 46 C.

struggle is intimated as having taken place between reason and necessity, the actual constitution of the world being compounded of both.[1] In other dialogues[2] mention is made of a *something* in the world which must always be opposed to good,[3] and of the bodily element in the composition of the world which was disorderly before it entered into this present world, and hinders it from perfectly accomplishing the teaching of its Maker and Father. But such hints as these, scattered and incidental as they are, though they gave occasion to Aristotle to say that Plato regarded matter as a source of evil,[4] show that the problem was one which the mind of the philosopher only glanced at transiently and unwillingly, which he was glad to keep as far as possible in the background of his teaching, and of which he never attempted a systematic solution. Aristotle, while acknowledging the existence of evil as a fact, and dealing with it practically in his ethical doctrines and precepts, pays but little attention to the metaphysical problem of its origin. Neither in the list of questions which he proposes to discuss in his Metaphysics, nor in the body of the work, does this inquiry appear; and his conception of matter as of a merely potential and passive nature is remote from that point of view in which it is contemplated as an actual cause of evil. The Stoics indeed may be said to have partially considered the question from their own point of view; but their pantheism, and their theory of the perfection of the world as a whole, compelled them to treat it only in a partial and superficial aspect. Their

[1] *Timæus* p. 48 A.
[2] *Theætetus* p. 176 A.
[3] *Politicus* p. 273 A. Cf. Zeller, II. 1, p. 487.
[4] *Metaph.* i. 6 ἔτι δὲ τὴν τοῦ εὖ καὶ τοῦ κακῶς αἰτίαν τοῖς στοιχείοις ἀπέδωκεν ἑκατέροις ἑκατέραν. We omit those passages in which Plato speaks of the human body as the cause of the evil of the soul (*e.g. Phædo* pp. 66, 79). These do not refer to the origin of evil in general, but to its particular working in a definite organization.

LECT. II.   *SOURCES OF GNOSTICISM.*   23

inquiries were not so much directed to an explanation of the origin of evil, as to attempts to reconcile the fact of its existence with the supposed perfection of the universe, and their conclusions were for the most part such as the principles of their philosophy would naturally suggest and which modern writers have sometimes borrowed without being fully aware of their tendency—namely, that the imperfection of part is necessary to the perfection of the whole;[1] that some things which appear to be evil are not so in reality;[2] that evil is necessary to the existence of good, because one of two contraries cannot exist without the other.[3] In such positions as these, we see the germ of the questions discussed in works like Leibnitz's Théodicée, or Pope's Essay on Man. They are not philosophical inquiries intended to explain how evil came into the world, but examinations of difficulties occasioned by the fact of its existence when viewed in relation to other facts or doctrines.

The slight and cursory notice which this question received in Greek philosophy may to some extent be accounted for by the character of the national mind. The Greek was of all men least disposed to look on the gloomy or the negative side of the visible world: his feelings opened themselves to all that was bright and beautiful

---

[1] So Chrysippus in Plutarch, *De Stoic. Rep.* c. 44 τέλεον μὲν ὁ κόσμος σῶμά ἐστιν, οὐ τέλεα δὲ τὰ τοῦ κόσμου μέρη, τῷ πρὸς τὸ ὅλον πως ἔχειν καὶ μὴ καθ' αὑτὰ εἶναι. Cf. Zeller, III. 1, p. 160. So Pope, *Essay on Man*:

'All discord, harmony not understood;
All partial evil, universal good.'

[2] *e.g.* pain and physical evil in general. Cf. Seneca, *Epist.* 85, 30 'Dolor et paupertas deteriorem non faciunt; ergo mala non sunt'; and the theological application of the same position by M. Aurelius, ii. 11.

Cf. Zeller, III. 1, p. 199.

[3] Chrysippus in Plutarch, *De Stoic. Rep.* c. 35 Ἡ δὲ κακία πρὸς τὰ δεινὰ συμπτώματα ἴδιόν τινα ἔχει λόγον. γίνεται μὲν γὰρ καὶ αὐτή πως κατὰ τὸν τῆς φύσεως λόγον καὶ, ἵν' οὕτως εἴπω, ἀχρήστως γίνεται πρὸς τὰ ὅλα, οὔτε γὰρ τἀγαθὰ ἦν: Chrysippus in A. Gell. vi. 1 'Nam cum bona malis contraria sunt, utraque necessarium est opposita inter se et quasi mutuo adverso quæque fulta nisu consistere: nullum adeo contrarium est sine contrario altero.'

and beneficial in nature; his creative fancy imagined gods for itself in the sun and moon and stars of heaven, in the mountains and groves and streams of his native land, in the corn and wine and fruits of the earth which contributed to his enjoyment.[1] Such a temperament was not likely to be impressed with an overwhelming sense of the evil that is in the world, nor to tinge the national philosophy with dark representations of the inherent malignity of matter.

Very different was the tone of thought in the East, where philosophy, far more than in Greece, was identified with religion; where, consequently, the presence of evil was more keenly felt, and theories concerning its nature and origin formed the very keynote of philosophical speculation. Two principal theories may be specified as endeavouring in different ways to account for the existence of such a phenomenon: the dualistic theory, which proceeded on the hypothesis of an original struggle between two antagonistic principles of good and evil, and the emanation theory, which supposes a gradual deterioration by successive descents from the primitive source of good. The former may be distinguished as the Persian,

[1] Da der Dichtung zauberische Hülle
Sich noch lieblich um die Wahrheit wand,
Durch die Schöpfung floss da Lebensfülle
Und was nie empfinden wird, empfand.
An der Liebe Busen sie zu drücken,
Gab man höhern Adel der Natur,
Alles wies den eingeweihten Blicken,
Alles eines Gottes Spur.

Wo jetzt nur, wie unsre Weisen sagen,
Seelenlos ein Feuerball sich dreht,
Lenkte damals seinen goldnen Wagen
Helios in stiller Majestät.
Diese Höhen füllten Oreaden,
Eine Dryas lebt' in jenem Baum,
Aus der Urnen lieblicher Najaden
Sprang der Ströme Silberschaum.
SCHILLER, *Die Götter Griechenlands*.

the latter as the Indian theory. I do not mean that the emanation doctrine is peculiar to India; on the contrary, it holds a prominent position in the Persian religious philosophy likewise, as indeed in most speculations of Oriental origin;[1] but in the Persian philosophy the hypothesis of emanations appears as a consequence of the existence of evil, while in the Indian philosophy it is the cause of it. The one assumes the existence of two conflicting powers of good and evil, each of which gives rise to subordinate beings of similar nature assigned to assist in the conflict. The other supposes one original existence, of the highest and most abstract purity, and represents the origin of evil as the final result of successive degrees of lower and less perfect being.

The Zoroastrian religious system, which, commencing according to tradition in Bactria, one of the eastern provinces of the Persian empire, became ultimately the received religion of Persia in general, is involved in much obscurity as regards the period, as well as the manner of its origin. Whether Zoroaster (Zerdusht or Zarathustra), its reputed founder, was a historical or a mythical personage,[2] whether he flourished, according to one favourite opinion, in the reign of Darius Hystaspis, or, as others maintain, at a much earlier period,[3] whether his religious system was wholly original or the reformation of a previous belief, are points still under controversy, and about which it is unsafe to pronounce any decided opinion.[3] But the system itself, according to what appears to have been its earliest form, was based on the assumption of the existence of two original and independent powers of good

[1] Cf. Baur, *Die Chr. Gnosis* p. 30.
[2] Niebuhr (*Kleine Schriften*, vol. I. p. 200) regards him as mythical. See Art. 'Zoroaster' in Smith's *Dict. of Biography*.
[3] For different theories concerning the age and work of Zoroaster see Milman, *Hist. of Christianity*, vol. I. p. 63 *seq.*

and evil, or light and darkness—Ormuzd (*Ahura Mazda*, the wise Lord) and Ahriman (*Angra Mainyus*, the wicked spirit). Another account of the doctrine represents both these beings as the offspring of a higher principle called Zarvana Akarana ('boundless time'), but this appears to be a later refinement of the theory which originally regarded the two principles as co-existent from the beginning in eternal antagonism.[1] Each of these hostile powers is of equal strength, each supreme within his own domain. Ormuzd dwells in the region of perfect light, Ahriman in that of perfect darkness, and between them is an interval of empty space, separating the one from the other. Each becomes at length aware of the other's existence, and of the necessity of a contest between them. For three thousand years each is occupied in the creation of subordinate powers to assist him in the struggle.[2] Thus there arose from Ormuzd three orders of pure spirits: first, the six *Amshaspands* who surround his throne, and are his messengers to inferior beings; then the twenty-eight *Izeds*, together with their chief Mithra; and finally, the innumerable host of *Fervers*, a kind of personification of the creative ideas, the archetypes of the sensible world.[3] In opposition to these, Ahriman produces an equal number of Devs or evil spirits. After these creations Ormuzd is represented as having artfully induced Ahriman to agree to a further truce, in consequence of which the latter subsides into complete inactivity for three thousand years longer, during which time Ormuzd, with the assistance of his subordinate powers,

---

[1] Spiegel, Art. 'Parsismus' in Herzog's *Encyklopädie*, XI. pp. 117, 119, and cf. Milman, *Hist. of Christianity*, vol. I. p. 69.

[2] *Ibid.*

[3] See Matter, *Hist. de Gnosticisme*, vol. I. p. 117. The six Amshaspands, together with Ormuzd and Mithra, seem to correspond to the Valentinian Ogdoad. The twenty-eight Izeds, with Ormuzd and Mithra, answer to the thirty Æons.

proceeds to create the material world—first the heavens, then water, then the earth, then the trees, then cattle, and finally men. The earth is situated in the intermediate space between the kingdoms of light and darkness, and becomes ultimately the battle-field of the strife between the two powers. At the end of the three thousand years of inaction, Ahriman obtains a footing on the earth, and attempts to counteract the work of Ormuzd by producing creatures of a contrary kind, noxious animals and poisonous plants. He also led away from their allegiance the first pair of mankind, and inflicted upon them various evils, such as hunger, sleep, age, sickness, and death. This struggle between good and evil upon the earth is to continue for six thousand years, during which the lower order of the material creation, inanimate as well as animate, are good or evil of necessity, according to the source from which they spring. Man alone has the power of choosing for himself the one side or the other, and partaking of good or evil, of reward or punishment, according to his choice.[1]

In reading the above cosmogony it is impossible not to be struck with the resemblance of many of its details to the Mosaic narrative of the Creation and the Fall,[2] notwithstanding the wide departure of its dualistic hypothesis from the pure monotheism of the Hebrew faith. The creation of the world by the good spirit; the order of creation in its several parts, ending with man; the subsequent intrusion of the spirit of evil; his seduction of the first pair of human beings; the evils which he brings upon the earth and upon men; are points of resemblance which seem to warrant the conclusion that a

[1] Spiegel, Art. 'Parsismus,' in Herzog's *Encyklopädie* p. 118. The account is chiefly taken from the Persian work called *Bundehesh*, a treatise on the creation, government, and end of the world.

[2] Cf. Franck, *La Kabbale* p. 359 seq.

modification at least, if not the original formation of the Zoroastrian system, is due to a period subsequent to the intercourse between the two nations brought about by the Jewish captivity. Whatever antiquity different critics may be disposed to ascribe to the oral traditions on which the religion of the Zendavesta is based, it is admitted that the written records in which it is now contained cannot for the most part claim a higher antiquity than the rise of the Sassanid dynasty in the third century after Christ.[1] How much of the earlier tradition is primitive, and what accretions it may have received in the course of time, it is impossible, in the absence of written documents, to decide with any certainty; but perhaps the different theories concerning the age of Zoroaster and the introduction of his religious system may be in some degree reconciled with each other, if we suppose a reformation of the religion to have taken place in the reign of Darius Hystaspis,[2] a supposition which will help to conciliate the traditions of the antiquity of the first origin of the religion with the traces which it bears in its later form of the influence of the sacred books of the Hebrew captives.

This suspicion receives some confirmation when we compare the Persian system with one to which in its original form it was probably nearly related—the religious philosophy of India. If the affinity between the Zend and the Sanscrit languages, and the similarity in some of the legends and traditions of the two nations, indicate

[1] According to the Persian tradition, Alexander caused most of their earlier sacred books to be translated into Greek, and then destroyed the originals. It is probable at least, that a great part of them were lost after Alexander's conquest. See Spiegel, p. 127. The collection which constitutes the present written text of the Avesta is not earlier than the time of Ardeshir I (Bleeck, *Avesta*, Introduction p. x; Erskine quoted by Milman, I. p. 65), though the document from which it was compiled may be older in writing as certainly in oral tradition. The other books are mostly later. See Spiegel, p. 128.

[2] See Milman, *Hist. of Christianity*, vol. I. p. 64.

a common origin of their religious beliefs,[1] the differences between these two beliefs in their more developed stages no less indicate a considerable change in one or the other at a later period. The Persian system, as we have seen, is dualistic; the Indian is a monotheism, pushed to the extreme of pantheism, and even (strange as such a development may seem) of atheism. In the Persian scheme the source of evil is spiritual; in the Indian it is material. Evil itself in the one is a terrible reality; in the other, as in all consistent pantheistic schemes, it is a mere appearance and an illusion. In the Persian doctrine matter itself is not essentially evil; it is the production of a beneficent being, and the object into which it enters may be good or evil according to the power by which they are produced. In the Indian system matter is the root of all evil, and the great aim of religion is to free men from its contamination, even at the cost of annihilation itself.

Of the two great divisions of the Indian religion, Brahmanism and Buddhism, the latter is that with which we are chiefly concerned as the channel through which Indian belief and speculation obtained an influence in other countries. The Brahmanical religion was founded upon the total isolation of the Indian people and its castes, and admitted of no communion with other nations; the Buddhist faith was designed for all mankind, and its disciples were zealous and successful propagandists.[2] The principal points of contact however between Indian philosophy and Gnosticism may be regarded as common to both branches of the former. These are, (1) the doctrine of the emanation of the world from the one absolute ex-

[1] Bleeck, *Avesta*, Introduction pp. ix, x; cf. Milman, *Hist. of Christianity* I. p. 66.

[2] Cf. Ritter, *Hist. of Philosophy* I. p. 63; M. Müller, *Buddhism and Buddhist Pilgrims* p. 22.

istence, and of its final reabsorption into that existence;[1] (2) the doctrine of the inherent evil, and at the same time of the unreality of matter;[2] (3) the doctrine of the antagonism between spirit and matter, and the practical consequence, that the highest aim of religion is to free the soul from the contamination of matter, and to raise it to a final absorption in the being of the absolute.[3] The Buddhist however carried his metaphysical abstraction to a higher point even than the Brahman. While the Brahm of the orthodox Hindu philosophy, the one sole absolute substance, the ground and reality of all things, is represented as simple existence,[4] the first principle of the Buddhist religion is carried a step higher still in abstraction, and identified with pure nothing. According to the Buddhist creed nothing is, and all seeming existence is illusion, the offspring of ignorance, which true knowledge resolves into nothing.[5] The highest end of human life is to escape from pain by annihilation; the highest virtue is that which prepares the soul for the knowledge which is to end in annihilation.[6] In order to overcome ignorance, the cause of seeming existence, and desire, the cause of ignorance, the votary of Buddhism is bidden to practise the most rigid asceticism and to devote himself to the most intense meditation. By this process he is gradually to extinguish desire, sensation, thought, feeling, even consciousness itself, till he finally arrives at complete rest in complete extinction (*Nirvána*, literally 'blowing out') the soul being not even, as in the Brahman doctrine, absorbed as a drop in the ocean, but in the literal meaning

---

[1] Cf. Milman, *Hist. of Christianity* I. p. 62.

[2] Cf. Baur, *Die Chr. Gnosis* p. 54; Milman, vol. II. p. 34.

[3] *Ibid.* p. 58.

[4] 'Das leere Wesen.' Cf. Hegel, *Philos. der Religion* (*Werke*, XI. p. 35). See St. Hilaire as quoted by Max Müller, *Buddhism* etc. p. 20.

[5] M. Müller, *Buddhism* etc. pp. 14, 19.

[6] *Ibid.* p. 15.

of the phrase, blown out like a lamp.[1] The Gnostic systems fall far short of this gigantic heroism of absurdity; yet its influence in a diluted form may undoubtedly be traced in the antagonism which they maintained to exist between matter and spirit, in the deliverance of spirit by asceticism, and in the contrast between ignorance and knowledge, the one the source of illusion and misery, the other the sole means of obtaining deliverance and repose.[2]

The influence of the Persian religious philosophy may be most clearly traced in those forms of Gnosticism which sprang up in Syria, a country which both from geographical position and historical circumstances must have had frequent means of communication with the head-quarters of the Magian system.[3] The sects which sprang up in this country chiefly based their teaching on the dualistic assumption of an active spiritual principle and kingdom of evil or darkness, opposed to the kingdom of goodness or light. The Indian influence in a modified form may chiefly be traced in those forms of Gnosticism which sprang up in Egypt, which appears to have been visited by Buddhist missionaries from India within two generations from the time of Alexander the Great,[4] and where we may find permanent traces of Buddhist influence, established at all events before the Christian era. The Therapeutæ or contemplative monks of Egypt, described by Philo, whom Eusebius by an anachronism confounds with the early Christians, appear to have sprung from an union of the Alexandrian Judaism with the precepts and modes of life of the Buddhist devotees, and though their asceticism fell

[1] M. Müller, *Buddhism* etc. pp. 19, 46.
[2] Cf. King, *The Gnostics and their Remains* p. 21.
[3] Cf. Gieseler, *Church History*, vol. I. p. 138; Neander, *Church History*, vol. II. p. 13.
[4] See King, *The Gnostics and their Remains* p. 23. The King to whom the mission is attributed is Asoka, the grandson of Chandragupta (Sandracottus), the contemporary of Alexander.

short of the rigour of the Indian practice, as their religious belief mitigated the extravagance of the Indian speculation, yet in their ascetic life, in their mortification of the body and their devotion to pure contemplation, we may trace at least a sufficient affinity to the Indian mystics to indicate a common origin.[1]

The principal sources of Gnosticism may probably be summed up in these three. To Platonism, modified by Judaism, it owed much of its philosophical form and tendencies. To the Dualism of the Persian religion it owed one form at least of its speculations on the origin and remedy of evil, and many of the details of its doctrine of emanations. To the Buddhism of India, modified again probably by Platonism, it was indebted for the doctrines of the antagonism between spirit and matter and the unreality of derived existence (the germ of the Gnostic Docetism), and in part at least for the theory which regards the universe as a series of successive emanations from the absolute Unity. Other supposed sources, to which Gnosticism has with more or less probability been sometimes referred, will be noticed in my next lecture.

[1] On the connection of the Therapeutæ with the Indian mysticism, see Milman, *Hist. of Christianity*, vol. II. pp. 37, 41. On its connection with the Jewish-Alexandrian philosophy, see Dähne, *Jüdisch-Alex. Religions-Philosophie*, vol. I. p. 453.

LECTURE III.

SOURCES OF GNOSTICISM—CLASSIFICATION OF GNOSTIC SECTS.

IN addition to the three sources to which in my last lecture I endeavoured to trace the origin of the Gnostic systems, namely, the Græco-Jewish philosophy of Alexandria and the religious systems of Persia and India, other countries and systems have been occasionally named as probable tributaries to the stream. Egypt, Phœnicia, China, have all been enumerated by modern critics among the precursors of Gnosticism;[1] but it may be doubted whether anything can be produced from the philosophy or religion of these countries which may not be derived more directly and with more probability from the sources previously mentioned. There remains however at least one system of religious philosophy, which, on account of its close affinity to the Gnostic theories and the possibility, to say the least, of an actual historical connection between it and them, cannot be passed over without a special examination —I mean the Kabbala, or secret teaching of the Jews.

The word *Kábbala* (if we may adopt a pronunciation which, though not strictly accurate, has at least been naturalised in English)[2] literally means *reception* or *received doctrines*, and, substituting the active for the passive relation, may be perhaps fairly rendered *tradition*, a

---

[1] See Matter, *Hist. du Gnosticisme*, livre i. ch. v, vii, ix.

[2] Heb. קַבָּלָה. Scott, in the *Lady of the Lake*, has

'Eager he read whatever tells
Of magic, *cabala*, and spells.'

word more exactly corresponding to the Hebrew *Massorah*.[1] In actual use it designates a system of traditional and partially at least of esoteric or secret teaching, which has not inaptly been called the Jewish Metaphysic,[2] and which may be compared to the Jewish philosophy of Alexandria, as being, like it, an attempt to combine the theology of the Old Testament with a philosophical speculation derived from foreign sources. But while the Alexandrian philosophy was cultivated by Hellenistic Jews and published entirely in the Greek language, the Kabbalistic doctrines, if we allow them the same antiquity, must be regarded as the peculiar study of the Jews of Palestine,[3] and as confined with equal exclusiveness to the Hebrew language.[4] The principles also of the two systems, notwithstanding some resemblances in matters of detail,[5] must be regarded as fundamentally different. While the Platonic philosophy, which was the chief source of the speculations of Philo, is, in principle at least, a dualism, recognising an original distinction, and even opposition, between the maker of the world and the matter out of which it is made,[6] the philosophy which the Kabbalists attempted to blend with the belief of their fathers is in principle a pure pantheism, adopting as its foundation the hypothesis of an absolute unity—a God who is at the same time the cause, the substance, and the form of all that exists and all that

---

[1] מסורה. Cf. Franck *La Kabbale*, Préface p. 1; Ginsburg, *The Kabbalah* p. 4.

[2] Reuss, Art. 'Kabbala,' in Herzog's *Encyklopädie*, VII. p. 195.

[3] Cf. Franck, *La Kabbale* p. 270.

[4] *i.e.* the dialect of Jerusalem Chaldee modified by Hebrew. Cf. Franck, *l. c.* p. 103.

[5] *e.g.* the theory of ideas, the pre-existence and the transmigration of souls. See Franck, pp. 241, 262.

[6] Strictly speaking, the Platonic philosophy recognises three independent principles, the Demiurge, the ideal world, and the primitive matter. But the ideal world, which was also in its own way recognised by the *Kabbala*, does not bear upon our present comparison, and was, by the later Platonists at least, not regarded as an independent world, but as existing in the mind of the Deity.

LECT. III.   *CLASSIFICATION OF GNOSTIC SECTS.*   35

can exist.¹ The Kabbala has been asserted to be the parent of the philosophy of Spinoza;² and whatever may have been the historical connection between the two, the similarity of their principles can hardly be denied. In the place of the personal God, distinct from the world, acknowledged in the Old Testament, the Kabbala substitutes the idea of an universal and infinite substance, always active, always thinking, and in the process of thought developing the universe. In the place of a material world, distinct from God and created from nothing, the Kabbalist substitutes the idea of two worlds, the one intelligible, the other sensible, both being, not substances distinct from God, but forms under which the divine substance manifests itself.³ Here we have under one aspect, that of the universal substance, the principle of Spinoza, under another, that of the universal process, the principle of Hegel.⁴ The doctrines of the Kabbala are chiefly contained in two books, known as the 'Sepher Yetzirah'⁵ or 'Book of Creation,' and the book called 'Zohar'⁶ or 'Light.' The former professes to give an account of the creation of the visible world; the latter, of the nature of God and of heavenly things—in short, of the spiritual world.⁷ Both proceed from the same pantheistic point of view, though differing in the details of their contents.⁸ The former pretends to be a monologue of the patri-

¹ Franck, *La Kabbale* p. 263.
² By Wachter, who afterwards retracted the charge. Cf. Franck, p. 25. Leibnitz, in his *Animadversions* on Wachter's book (published in 1854 by M. Foucher de Careil under the title *Réfutation inédite de Spinoza par Leibnitz*), partly, though not entirely agrees with Wachter's first view. See also his *Théodicée* § 372 (*Opera*, Erdmann, p. 612). For a parallel between the Kabbala and Spinoza, see Ginsburg, p. 95.

³ Franck, *La Kabbale* p. 258. Cf. Reuss in Herzog, Art. 'Kabbala,' p. 197.
⁴ On Hegelianism in the Kabbala cf. Franck, pp. 162, 186, 193; and Milman, *Hist. of the Jews* III. p. 433.
⁵ סֵפֶר יְצִירָה.
⁶ סֵפֶר הַזּוֹהַר: a name taken from Dan. xii. 3, or more commonly זֹהַר.
⁷ Franck, p. 74.
⁸ Reuss in Herzog, Art. 'Kabbala,' p. 197.

arch Abraham, and professes to declare the course of contemplation by which he was led from the worship of the stars to embrace the faith of the true God.[1] It consists of a scheme of cosmogony and anthropogony, running parallel to each other, man being regarded as the microcosm, or image in miniature of the world, exhibiting in his constitution features analogous to those of the universe. The method reminds us of Thales and Pythagoras together; the letters of the Hebrew alphabet, together with their numerical powers, being employed as symbols to represent the material elements of the world regarded as emanations or developments of the one divine substance or spirit.[2] For the purpose of our present inquiry however, this work is of little importance compared with the other Kabbalistic book, the Zohar, in which, if at all, the traces of a connection between Kabbalism and Gnosticism will be found.

The theory of the Zohar is an attempt to exhibit all definite existences, spiritual and material, as a series of emanations, more or less remote, from a primitive abstraction called *En Soph* (אין סוף, τὸ ἄπειρον, 'that which has no limits'). This *En Soph* is the highest of all possible abstractions, an incomprehensible unity, having no attributes and no definite form of existence, and which therefore may be regarded as, in a certain sense, non-existent.[3] At the same time, it virtually comprehends within itself all existence; for all that is emanates from it, and is contained in it; for, as it is infinite, nothing can exist beyond it. The first order of emanations, by which the primitive infinite becomes known, consists of *the Sephiroth* (ספירות), a word which has been sometimes explained by *Intelligences*, but which may more probably be identified in

---

[1] Ginsburg, *The Kabbalah* p. 65.
[2] For a complete analysis of this book, see Franck, 2ᵐᵉ *Partie* ch. i, and Ginsburg, p. 65 *seq*.
[3] Franck, p. 177; Ginsburg, p. 6 (cf. p. 99).

meaning with its root סָפַר, 'to number,' and with the verbal סְפָר, 'a numbering,'[1] which is by some supposed to be the origin of our word *cipher*.[2] These ten Sephiroth are the attributes of the infinite Being, having no reality in themselves, but existing in the divine Being as their substance, while he (or rather it) is wholly manifested in each one of them, they being but different aspects of one and the same reality.[3] They are divided into three pairs, represented as male and female, with three combining principles, and a final emanation uniting the whole.[4] This system of the ten primitive Sephiroth is arranged in a form bearing a fanciful resemblance to the human body, and their combination is from this point of view called by the name of *Adam Kadmon*, the primordial or archetypal man; a figurative expression of the theory which regards man as the microcosm, as the miniature representation not only of the sensible world, but of the intelligible systems of which the sensible world itself is a further development. The division of these principles into male and female was considered by the Kabbalists as essential to the production and conservation of all that is derived from them;[5] and this fancy reappears, as we shall hereafter see, in some of the Gnostic systems. From the conjunction of the Sephiroth[6] emanated directly or remotely three worlds; two called the worlds of *creation* and of *formation*, being spiritual, though of different degrees of purity, and inhabited by spiritual beings; the last, called the world of *action*, being material, subject to change and corruption, and inhabited by the evil spirit and the hosts subordinate to him.[7] The final destiny

---

[1] Franck, p. 147; Reuss, p. 199.
[2] Menage, as cited in Richardson's *Dictionary*, Art. 'Cipher.'
[3] Franck, p. 178; Ginsburg, p. 15.
[4] Ginsburg, pp. 9, 19.
[5] Ginsburg, pp. 9, 20; Franck, p. 188.
[6] For the details of this conjunction, see Franck, p. 200 *seq.*, Ginsburg, p. 19 *seq.*
[7] Ginsburg, pp. 23, 25.

however of these worlds, as of all finite existence, is to return to the infinite source from which they emanated. Even the evil spirit himself will ultimately become once more an angel of light. The souls of men however will not return to the infinite till they have developed all the perfections of which they are capable, and if this is not effected in a single life, the soul must migrate into another body until the development is complete. Sometimes two souls are sent into the same body, that the stronger may help the weaker.[1]

The resemblance of this strange theory to some of the Gnostic speculations is undeniable, but the question as regards the actual historical relation between the two systems is involved in considerable chronological difficulties. If indeed we were to listen to the claims of some of the Kabbalists themselves, there would be no difficulty, so far as its antiquity is concerned, in supposing their doctrine to have influenced every school of philosophy from the creation downwards; for the Kabbala, we are told, was studied by angels in Paradise, who communicated it to Adam after the fall, as a means of restoration to his lost happiness.[2] Even one of its written documents, the Book of Creation, was supposed by admiring commentators to have proceeded from the pen of the patriarch Abraham, whose meditations it records.[3] The most popular tradition however confines itself within much more modest limits, attributing the composition of the Book of Creation to Rabbi Akiba, the standard-bearer of the insurgent Barcochab, who was put to death by the Romans after the suppression of the rebellion (A.D. 135), while the book Zohar is popularly ascribed to Rabbi Simon ben Jochai, a few years later. There are not

[1] Cf. Ginsburg, p. 64; Franck, p. 217.
[2] Ginsburg, p. 2.
[3] Franck, p. 86.

wanting however other eminent critics who maintain an internal evidence that the Book of Creation cannot have been written earlier than the ninth century of our era;[1] while the Book of Light is brought down to a still later date, and regarded as the composition of a Spanish Jew in the latter part of the thirteenth century.[2] It is admitted on all hands that there are portions of the book which must be regarded as comparatively modern interpolations; and even those critics who contend for the antiquity of the doctrines allow that the book in its present form cannot have been completed earlier than the end of the seventh, or beginning of the eighth century.[3] But it is probable that some at least of the doctrines existed in a traditional form long before the date of the written authorities. Notwithstanding the fundamental antagonism between the monotheism or rather pantheism of the Kabbala and the dualism of the Zoroastrian religious philosophy, the numerous resemblances of detail which exist between the two systems seem to warrant the conclusion that the remote origin of the Kabbalistic traditions must be referred to the period of the Captivity, and to the influence upon the Jewish mind of the philosophy of their Persian masters.[4] Many of these resemblances refer to points which have no direct relation to our present subject; but the parallel between the *En Soph*, the abstract Infinite of the Kabbala, and the *Boundless Time* which stands as a first principle in one form at least of the Persian doctrine, as well as that between the

---

[1] Zunz in Ginsburg, p. 77. Franck on the other hand asserts that the language of the book shows that it must have been written not later than the middle of the first century, if not earlier; *La Kabbale* pp. 80, 91.

[2] Moses de Leon, who died in 1305. See Ginsburg, p. 90.

[3] Franck, p. 135; Reuss in Herzog, p. 196; Milman, *Hist. of the Jews* III. p. 431.

[4] See Franck, pp. 353–390; Milman, *Hist. of the Jews* III. p. 432; Matter, I. p. 136.

six Amshaspands or first emanations of the one doctrine and the ten Sephiroth of the other,[1] with the innumerable subordinate developments of spiritual beings in each, constitute a similarity of first principles which can hardly be explained except on the supposition of a common origin. The very similarity however of the two systems makes it difficult to decide whether the Gnostic theories were in any degree directly influenced by the early traditions of the Kabbala, or whether the relation between them may not be accounted for by their common descent from a Persian source. Matter, the learned historian of Gnosticism, propounds this question without venturing to give a decisive answer to it;[2] and it may be doubted whether we are in possession of sufficient materials for a complete investigation of the case. Yet though the direct influence of the Persian doctrines must be recognised in some portions at least of the Gnostic teaching, there are others in which it seems more probable that the influence has been conveyed through a Hebrew channel. Such, for instance, is the division of the supreme emanations into pairs as male and female, a representation which, if it appears at all in the original Persian theory, occupies at least a very subordinate place,[3] while in the Kabbalistic teaching it is made essential to the production of an enduring offspring in the inferior emanations. The same distinction appears at the very beginning of the Gnostic teaching. Simon Magus, who, if not, as he is usually considered, the founder, must at least be regarded as the precursor of the Gnostic heresies, and who professed to be

---

[1] That the Persian Amshaspands, like the Jewish Sephiroth, are but allegorical names for the attributes of the Deity, see *Quarterly Review* for October, 1867, p. 456.

[2] *Histoire Critique du Gnosticisme* I. p. 141.

[3] Matter, vol. I. p. 117, says, 'Les Amshaspands sont des deux sexes.' But in the *Zend Avesta* one only of the six is female, and the sexual distinction is not connected with any theory of generation. See Bleeck's *Avesta*, Part ii. p. 29.

'the great Power of God,'[1] is described as carrying about with him a certain woman named Helena, 'of whom he said that she was the first conception of his mind, the mother of all things, by whom in the beginning he conceived the idea of making the angels and archangels; for that this conception (*hanc ennoian*) proceeded forth from him, and knowing her father's wishes, descended to the lower world, and produced the angels and powers by whom the world was made.'[2] The relation thus profanely asserted to exist between Simon himself claiming to be the first power or emanation from God, and his female companion announced as his own first *ennoia* or conception, almost exactly corresponds to the Kabbalistic account of the highest pair of Sephiroth, proceeding from the crown or primordial emanation. At first there proceeded forth a masculine or active potency designated *Wisdom* (חָכְמָה). This *Sephira* sent forth an opposite, *i.e.* a feminine or passive potency, denominated *Intelligence* (בִּינָה), and it is from the union of these two, which are called the *Father* and *Mother*, that the remaining seven *Sephiroth* proceeded.[3] Another remarkable parallel may be found in the language of Irenæus with regard to a later school of Gnostics—the Marcosians, or disciples of Marcus, a follower of Valentinus. 'Some of these,' he says, 'prepare a bridal chamber, and perform certain mystic rites of initiation with incantations addressed to the persons being initiated. This ceremony they say is a spiritual marriage after the similitude of the celestial unions (κατὰ τὴν ὁμοιότητα τῶν ἄνω συζυγιῶν). Others bring their disciples to the water, and baptize them with the following form of words: *Into the name of the unknown Father of the*

---

[1] Acts viii. 10.
[2] Irenæus, i. 23. Cf. Burton, *Bampton Lectures* p. 390.
[3] Ginsburg, *The Kabbalah* p. 8. Cf. Franck, p. 343.

universe, and into truth, the mother of all things, and into him who came down upon Jesus, and into unity, and redemption, and communion of powers. Others repeat Hebrew words over the initiated, the more to amaze them.'[1] The words themselves are given by Irenæus in the continuation of the passage, but the text is so corrupt that hardly any sense can be made of them.[2] Yet the mention of the *celestial unions* and of the *father and mother of all things*, as well as the employment of Hebrew words in their incantations, seem to indicate not only that these heretics had, in common with other Gnostics, adopted a classification of divine emanations as male and female, but also that they had derived their classification from some source in which the language employed was the same as that of the Jewish Kabbala.[3]

Other parallels will come before us when we proceed to treat of the details of the several Gnostic sects. At the present stage of the inquiry it will be more appropriate to sum up the results in a general and provisional form, which we may do by borrowing the language of the learned French expositor of the Kabbala. Of the two most distinguished leaders of the Gnostic schools, Basilides and Valentinus, M. Franck remarks: 'In the remains which have descended to us of these two celebrated heresiarchs we can without difficulty detect the presence of the most characteristic elements of the Kabbala; such as the unity of substance, the formation of things first by concentration, then by gradual expansion of the Divine light, the theory of pairs and of the four worlds, the two Adams, the three souls, and even the symbolical language of numbers, and of the letters of the alphabet. . . . We

---

[1] Irenæus, i. 21. 3. Cf. Eusebius, *H. E.* iv. 11, and Theodoret, *Hær. Fab.* i. 14, who notices the use of Hebrew terms by the Gnostics. See Burton, *Bampton Lectures* p. 305.

[2] Cf. Massuet's note on this passage of Irenæus.

[3] Cf. Matter, vol. I. p. 141.

have already shown that the metaphysical ideas which form the basis of the Kabbala are not borrowed from the Greek philosophy; that, far from having been the native products of either the Pagan or the Jewish school of Alexandria, they were imported into those schools from Palestine; and finally we have shown that Palestine, or at least Judea properly so called, is not even itself the cradle of the doctrines; for, notwithstanding the impenetrable mystery with which they were surrounded by the doctors of the synagogues, we find them, though in a form less abstract and less pure, in the unbelieving capital of the Samaritans, and among the heretics of Syria. . . . The foundation of these ideas remains always the same; nothing is changed in the relations between them or in the formulas in which they are clad or in the strange traditions which accompany them.'[1]

I shall conclude this lecture with a brief account of the various attempts that have been made in modern times (the early authorities in this respect are altogether deficient) to form something like a classification or systematic arrangement of the several Gnostic schools, so as to exhibit the scattered notices which we possess of their several tenets with some regard to their philosophical affinity and connection with each other. It must be premised however, that all such attempts coming as preliminaries to an account of the details of the different systems must be regarded as merely general and provisional. The grounds which may be alleged in justification or in condemnation of one or another cannot be fully understood till the details themselves are before us; and though a preliminary account of these classifications is of interest in itself, and may help to throw light on what is

[1] *La Kabbale* p. 350 *seq*. For the Adam Kadmon of the Kabbala in Gnosticism, see Burton, *Bampton Lectures* p. 305.

to follow, we are not yet in a position to judge between the several principles, and to decide which is best supported by the actual features of the several systems with which they attempt to deal. Nevertheless, as such classifications have occupied the attention of some of the most learned and acute inquirers of modern times, and as most of the recent writers on the subject have attempted something of the kind as a preliminary to a more detailed examination, I shall venture in this respect to follow their example by giving a short statement of what has hitherto been done in this province.

The first writer who attempted to classify the Gnostic systems on any other ground than that of mere chronological sequence, is the learned Mosheim, briefly in his 'Ecclesiastical History,' and more fully in his 'Commentaries on the Affairs of the Christians before the time of Constantine the Great.' 'It will be easily perceived,' he says in the latter work, 'by any one who shall have carefully investigated the account here given of the sects called *Gnostic*, that there is this principal point of difference between them; namely, that while some retained whole and entire the ancient Oriental doctrine of two principles of things, others subtracted something from it and supplied the deficiency by foreign inventions. All agree in admitting the existence from all eternity not only of God, but of a matter containing the cause of all depravity and evil. . . . But those who sprang up in Syria and Asia assigned to this eternal matter a special Lord and Master, either self-existent or sprung from matter itself; thus recognising, in addition to the good principle, an evil principle, which however was regarded as distinct from the Creator of the world. Those on the other hand who sprang up in Egypt, such as Basilides, Valentinus, and others, know nothing of this Prince of matter, though they added to the Oriental teaching various fancies and inventions of Egyptian origin.'[1] A similar principle of classification is adopted by another learned German Church historian, Gieseler, who however finds it necessary to add to the Egyptian and Syrian schools a third class comprising Marcion and his followers.[2] A more philosophical principle of arrangement has been suggested by Neander, who distinguishes the Gnostic sects into two classes according to the relation which Christianity, in their conception of it, is supposed to bear to the Jewish religion and to the God of the Old Testament. All the Gnostic systems had one feature in common; namely, that they regarded the Old and the New Testament as revelations of two different Gods, and considered the mission of Christ to proceed from a higher power than the God of the Jewish religion, who was identified with the Demiurge or Maker of the world. But under this common assumption there was room for two very opposite estimates of the older revelation and of the God whom it reveals. Some of the Gnostic sects regarded the Demiurge as a being altogether alien from and opposed to the Supreme God; others considered him merely as a subordinate power, inferior but not hostile to the Supreme God, and acting, before the coming of a more perfect revelation, as his unconscious organ.[3] By the former, Judaism was regarded as a religion wholly antagonistic to Christianity, and which the higher revelation was designed to destroy. The latter regarded it as an imperfect preparation for Christianity, which the higher revelation was designed to complete. From this point of view the Gnostic schools may be divided into two classes, those hostile to and those

[1] *De Rebus Christ. ante Const.* p. 410.
[2] Gieseler, *Eccl. Hist.* vol. I.
§§ 45–47.
[3] Neander, *Church History*, II. p. 39 (ed. Bohn).

comparatively favourable to Judaism. Under the former head Neander classes the Ophites, as well as the schools of Carpocrates, Saturninus, and Marcion. Under the latter he reckons Cerinthus, Basilides, Valentinus and his followers, and Bardesanes. As Mosheim's classification was supplemented by Gieseler, so that of Neander has been supplemented by Baur, who adds Heathenism to Judaism as two religions whose relations to Christianity and to each other were contemplated from different points of view, and thus he recognises three principal forms of Gnosticism. The first, which embraces most of the earlier sects, including the schools of Basilides, Valentinus, the Ophites, Saturninus, and Bardesanes, regarded the pre-Christian forms of religion, the Heathen no less than the Jewish, as preparations for Christianity and partial discoveries of the truth. The second, represented by Marcion, regarded Christianity in the light of a system wholly antagonistic both to Judaism and Heathenism; while the third, to which belongs the system of the Clementine Homilies, and perhaps that of Cerinthus, endeavoured to unite Judaism and Christianity together in a common antagonism to Heathenism.[1] In opposition to these attempts at philosophical classification, the historian of Gnosticism, Matter, considers the only true classification to be that which exhibits the succession of events and points out the principal schools according as they arose in different countries. From this point of view he recognises three principal centres of Gnosticism, Syria, Egypt, and Asia Minor, and classifies the different sects according as they were formed under influences emanating from one or other of these localities. Under this classification the Syrian Gnosticism is represented by the schools of Saturninus and Bardesanes; the Egyptian by those of Basilides,

[1] See Baur, *Die Chr. Gnosis* pp. 114–121.

Valentinus, and the Ophites, with some minor sects; and the Gnosticism of Asia Minor by Cerdon, Marcion, and their successors.[1]

In the midst of these conflicting opinions concerning the true method of classification, it would be dangerous, at any rate at the present stage of our inquiry, to attempt anything like a philosophical division of the Gnostic sects, a task which is rendered more difficult by the variety of the influences under which the different systems were formed. For the present I shall endeavour to confine myself as nearly as possible to a chronological order of events, commencing with a question in itself the most interesting, and to be answered from sources with which we are most familiar, that of the traces of the existence of an early Gnosticism to be discovered in the books of the New Testament. This inquiry will be prosecuted in my next lecture, from which we shall afterwards proceed to those later developments which manifested themselves subsequently to the close of the Canon of Scripture.

[1] Matter, *Hist. Critique du Gnosticisme* I. p. 323 *seq.*

LECTURE IV.

NOTICES OF GNOSTICISM IN THE NEW TESTAMENT.

On the mention of Gnostic teachers contemporaneous with the Apostles and alluded to in the New Testament, we are naturally disposed in the first instance to turn to the account given in the Acts of the Apostles concerning Simon Magus, who by general consent, at least of the early authorities, has been selected as the father and first representative of the Gnostic heresies. Yet with the exception of the expression 'the great Power of God,' which we shall have occasion to consider hereafter, the narrative of the Acts throws no light on the peculiar character of Simon's teaching, the particulars of which must chiefly be gathered from later and uninspired authorities. The earliest distinct indications of a Gnostic teaching contemporary with the Apostles is to be found in the Epistles of St. Paul; chiefly, as might naturally be expected, in those addressed to churches, or persons presiding over churches, in Asia, one of the early centres of the Gnostic teaching; to which must be added those addressed to the city of Corinth, whose commercial activity and constant intercourse with other centres of civilisation rendered it easily accessible to the influences of Asiatic and Alexandrian teaching. In fact the two Epistles to the Corinthians are the earliest in point of time of the Apostolic writings in which we can with any probability recognise an allusion to the germs of a teaching which afterwards developed itself in the Gnostic schools.[1] Here we have the earliest instance of the use of the word γνῶσις in a depreciatory sense, ἡ γνῶσις φυσιοῖ, ἡ δὲ ἀγαπὴ οἰκοδομεῖ,[2] and the occasion on which these words are used is such as to warrant us with some probability in interpreting the term in the same technical and peculiar sense in which it was afterwards so constantly employed. The question to which the words relate is the lawfulness of eating meats which had been offered to idols; and we have evidence that the lawfulness of partaking of these sacrifices was distinctly maintained, not merely by the later Gnostics, but by their precursor Simon Magus, who, under the pretence of superior knowledge, indulged in this respect in the utmost licence of practice, maintaining that to those who knew the truth idolatry was a thing wholly indifferent, and that whether they partook of the heathen sacrifices or not was a thing of no consequence in the sight of God.[3] The context of the passage seems to support this interpretation. The words of the next verse, εἰ δέ τις δοκεῖ εἰδέναι [al. ἐγνωκέναι] τι, οὐδέπω οὐδὲν ἔγνωκεν κάθως δεῖ γνῶναι, εἰ δέ τις ἀγαπᾷ τὸν Θεόν, οὗτος ἔγνωσται ὑπ' αὐτοῦ, read like a direct rebuke of that pretension to a perfect knowledge of God and divine things which forms the basis of the whole Gnostic teaching; to which it may be added that Irenæus, who wrote at a time when the Gnostic systems were still in existence, and who entitled his work, 'The Detection and Overthrow of Knowledge falsely so called,' expressly cites these words of St. Paul as having reference to the Gnostic doctrine. 'On this account,' he says, 'Paul declared that knowledge puffeth up

---

[1] Assuming the probable date of the two Epistles to the Corinthians as A.D. 57.

[2] 1 Cor. viii. 1.

[3] Cf. Burton, *Bampton Lectures* p. 100, and note 64. His authority is Origen, *c. Cels.* vi. 11, καίτοι γε ὑπὲρ τοῦ πλείονας ὑπαγαγέσθαι ὁ Σίμων τὸν περὶ τοῦ θανάτου κίνδυνον, ὃν Χριστιανοὶ αἱρεῖσθαι ἐδιδάχθησαν, περιεῖλε τῶν μαθητῶν, ἐναδιαφορεῖν αὐτοὺς διδάξας πρὸς τὴν εἰδωλολατρίαν.

but charity edifieth; not as blaming the true knowledge of God, for then he must first have accused himself; but because he knew that certain men, elated by the pretence of knowledge, were falling away from the love of God, and while deeming themselves to be perfect, imagined an imperfect creator of the world.'[1] We may infer also from other passages in these Epistles that among the opponents of St. Paul in the Corinthian Church were some who endeavoured to disparage the authority of the Apostle on the ground of their own superior *knowledge*; and when we find St. Paul, in writing to this church, both vindicating his own claim to knowledge so far as such a claim could be justly made by man, εἰ δὲ καὶ ἰδιώτης τῷ λόγῳ, ἀλλ' οὐ τῇ γνώσει,[2] and at the same time reminding his readers that all human knowledge is but in part, and shall vanish away when that which is perfect is come,[3] these words acquire a fuller significance if we recognise in the Corinthian opponents of the Apostle's authority the precursors of those Ebionite Gnostics who at a later period calumniated him as an apostate from the Law.[4]

It is not improbable that Gnostic doctrines are at least partially and indirectly combated, along with other errors of a similar character, in the Apostle's elaborate and triumphant argument for the resurrection of the body in the fifteenth chapter of the First Epistle.[5] It is true that this article of the Christian faith was so entirely opposed to all the schools of heathen philosophy (as may be seen from St. Paul's dispute on the same topic with the Epicureans and the Stoics at Athens), that it is difficult to select any one school of heathen thought as peculiarly or especially referred to. But we shall see a little later how the pe-

---

[1] Irenæus, *c. Hær.* ii. 26.
[2] 2 Cor. xi. 6.
[3] 1 Cor. xiii. 8, 10.
[4] Cf. Neander, *Church Hist.* I. p. 479.
[5] Cf. Burton, *Bampton Lectures* p. 183.

culiarly Gnostic form of this error appears in the teaching of St. Paul's subsequent opponents, Hymenæus and Philetus; and we may reserve what has to be said on this point till we come to speak of the Epistle in which their heresy is mentioned.[1]

Passing over the very doubtful allusions to Gnosticism which some have supposed to exist in the Epistle to the Romans,[2] we come next in order to the letters addressed to the two Asiatic churches of Ephesus and Colossæ. Here we are in one of the chief centres of Gnostic influences, both as regards philosophical teaching and practical addiction to magic arts and enchantments;[3] and here, accordingly, we find allusions to the Gnostic teaching more frequent and more distinct. When the Apostle prays that his Ephesian converts may know the love of Christ which passeth knowledge (τὴν ὑπερβάλλουσαν τῆς γνώσεως ἀγάπην τοῦ Χριστοῦ),[4] we are reminded of that contrast between knowledge and love, on which he had previously insisted in his advice to the Corinthians; and when he adds 'that ye may be filled with all the fulness of God' (ἵνα πληρωθῆτε εἰς πᾶν τὸ πλήρωμα τοῦ Θεοῦ),[5] we are at least conscious of the use of a current term in Gnostic phraseology, though the verse does not, taken by itself, necessarily imply an allusion to Gnostic theories.[6] But when in two other

---

[1] Burton, *Bampton Lectures* p. 84, seems to allow a possible allusion to Gnosticism in the *wisdom* censured by St. Paul, 1 Cor. i. 21, ii. 6. But these passages may as probably refer to Greek philosophy.

[2] Burton, p. 96, supposes a reference of this kind in Rom. xvi. 17–19, which he allows to be the only one.

[3] Acts xix. 19. Cf. also the 'Ephesian letters,' for which see Matter, I. p. 204, Burton, *Bampton Lectures* p. 83.

[4] Ephes. iii. 19.

[5] *Ibid.* Cf. Burton, B. L. p. 83.

[6] The literal meaning of πλήρωμα is either 'id quod impletum est,' or 'id quo res impletur'; and the passage may mean, 'up to the measure of that which is filled with God,' *i.e.* 'so as yourselves to be thoroughly filled with God,' or 'up to the measure of that with which God is filled,' *i.e.* 'so as to be full of the spiritual perfections with which God is filled.' Ellicott and Alford seem to adopt the latter sense, but the former best suits the use of πλήρωμα in the other pas-

passages of the same Epistle we find the Church spoken of as the body of Christ, 'the fulness (τὸ πλήρωμα) of Him that filleth all in all,'[1] and when the Christian is spoken of as coming 'unto a perfect man, unto the measure of the stature of the fulness (τοῦ πληρώματος) of Christ,'[2] though the word in all these passages is used in a different sense from that in which it held so conspicuous a place in the Gnostic teaching, we are tempted at first sight to assent to the surmise that the choice of this term may have been dictated by a desire to turn the minds of his readers from the false to the true use of it, to remind them that the true Pleroma, the place of those united with God, was not in that mystic region of spirits where the Gnostics placed it, nor to be attained to, as they asserted, by knowledge only; that the body of Christian believers was the true Pleroma of God—the place which God fills with His presence; and that the bond of union which raised man to it was not knowledge, but love.[3] And this surmise is perhaps confirmed by the words which follow the last of these passages, and which seem distinctly to point to a false teaching which it is designed to correct: 'That we henceforth be no more children, tossed to and fro, and carried about with every wind of doctrine, by the sleight of man, and cunning craftiness, whereby they lie in wait to deceive.'[4] The interpretation however of these passages must be admitted to be very doubtful; and it is at least an open question whether the use of the term πλήρωμα was

---

sage. Philo, *De Præm. et Pœn.* 11 (p. 418 M), uses it of the human soul, γενομένη πλήρωμα ἀρετῶν ἡ ψυχή; and this seems to correspond to its application to God as *filled with* all excellencies. Cf. Olshausen on Ephes. i. 23.

[1] Ephes. i. 23.

[2] Ephes. iv. 13.

[3] Cf. Burton, *Bampton Lectures* pp. 125, 6.

[4] Ephes. iv. 14. The last words, ἐν πανουργίᾳ πρὸς τὴν μεθοδείαν τῆς πλάνης, may be more literally rendered, 'in craftiness tending to the deliberate system of error.' See Ellicott.

suggested to St. Paul by Gnostic writers, or borrowed by them from the New Testament.

The Epistle to the Colossians, which was written at the same time with that to the Ephesians, contains however more distinct indications of the existence of Gnostic errors among those to whom it was addressed.[1] The false teaching which the Apostle denounces in this Epistle seems to have manifested itself in the form of a combination of Judaism with Gnosticism, such as was afterwards more fully developed in the teaching of Cerinthus; though the tradition which brings Cerinthus himself into personal collision with St. Paul will hardly bear the test of chronology.[2]

The characteristics of this teaching may be easily gathered from evidence furnished by the language of the Epistle. First; it pretended, under the plausible name of *philosophy*, to be in possession of a higher knowledge of spiritual things than could be obtained through the simple preaching of the Gospel. Secondly; it adopted the common tenet of all the Gnostic sects, that of a distinction between the supreme God and the Demiurgus or creator of the world. Thirdly; by virtue of its pretended insight into the spiritual world, it taught a theory of its own concerning the various orders of angels and the worship to be paid to them. And fourthly; in connection with these theories, it enjoined and adopted the practice of a rigid asceticism, extending and exaggerating the ceremonial prohibitions of the Jewish law, and probably connecting them with a philosophical theory concerning the evil nature of matter.[3]

---

[1] Probably from Rome, during St. Paul's first imprisonment, A.D. 61 or 62. Both Epistles were sent by the hands of Tychicus; Ephes. vi. 21, Coloss. iv. 7. Some consider them to have been written during the earlier imprisonment at Cæsarea from A.D. 58 to 60.

[2] Cf. Neander, *Planting of Christianity* p. 325 (ed. Bohn).

[3] See Neander, *Planting of Christianity* p. 321.

All these characteristics may be distinctly traced in the warning language of St. Paul. As regards the first, we find him bidding his readers to beware lest any man spoil them 'through philosophy and vain deceit, after the tradition of men, after the rudiments of the world, and not after Christ;'[1] and he speaks of the false teacher as 'intruding into things which he hath not seen, vainly puffed up by his fleshly mind.'[2] As regards the second, we find the Apostle exhausting every power of language in declaring that by Christ, 'the image of the invisible God,' 'all things were created, that are in heaven and that are in earth, visible and invisible, whether they be thrones or dominions or principalities or powers; all things were created by Him and for Him; and He is before all things, and by Him all things consist.'[3] As regards the third, the obscure text, 'Let no man beguile you of your reward in a voluntary humility and worshipping of angels,'[4] receives a satisfactory explanation if we suppose that the well-known doctrine of the early Gnostics, that the world was created by angels, had among the Judaizing Gnostics taken, as it naturally might, the form of a worship addressed to them as mediators between the supreme God and the world.[5] And

---

[1] Coloss. ii. 8. The expression τὰ στοιχεῖα τοῦ κόσμου seems to mean elementary teaching, sensuous rather than really spiritual, and so belonging to this world. Cf. Lightfoot and Ellicott on Gal. iv. 3.

[2] Coloss. ii. 18. On the retaining of the negative, ἃ μὴ ἑόρακεν, see Ellicott on this place, and Neander, *Planting* p. 327.

[3] Coloss. i. 16, 17. Cf. Burton, B. L. p. 113.

[4] Coloss. ii. 18. The word θέλων may be more literally rendered either 'purposing to beguile you'(see Ellicott here), or 'for his own arbitrary pleasure.' See Neander, *Planting* p. 327.

[5] Cf. Baur, *Die Chr. Gnosis* p. 49. Simon Magus held that the world was created by angels (Irenæus, i. 23). But Simon's anti-Judaizing tendency would lead him to regard these angels as governing ill, and to state his own mission as opposed to theirs (Irenæus, l. c.), though he seems to have used their names for magical purposes (Tertullian, *De Præscr.* c. 33). Judaizing Gnostics on the other hand, identifying the Demiurge with

finally, as regards the fourth characteristic, the spurious asceticism which manifests itself in subjection to ordinances of man's commanding, 'Touch not, taste not, handle not,' and the show of wisdom which consists in will-worship, and humility, and neglecting of the body, are contrasted with the true mortification of those who are dead to the world, and whose life is hid with Christ in God. 'Mortify therefore your members which are upon the earth: fornication, uncleanness, inordinate affection, evil concupiscence, and covetousness, which is idolatry.'[1]

The Gnostic term *pleroma* appears in this Epistle as well as in that to the Ephesians, and with very nearly the same significance. That which was before said of the Church, the body of Christ, 'the fulness of Him that filleth all in all,' is now said of Christ, the head of that body: 'It pleased the Father that in Him should all fulness dwell.'[2] But we may perhaps further remark that in the second of the two passages in this Epistle in which the word is used, ὅτι ἐν αὐτῷ κατοικεῖ πᾶν τὸ πλήρωμα τῆς θεότητος σωματικῶς,[3] the stress that is laid on this last word is designed to refute another error of the Gnostic teaching, arising from their hypothesis of the evil nature of matter—the denial of the real Incarnation of Christ. The Docetic heresy was one of the earliest forms of Gnosticism;[4] and we shall have occasion to show that, not very long after the time at which this Epistle was written, it came distinctly under the notice of St. Paul, and was the object of one of his most severe rebukes.

If teaching of this character had begun to corrupt the Ephesian Church at the time of St. Paul's first imprison-

---

the God of the O. T., would be likely to worship him and his assistant or subordinate angels.

[1] Coloss. ii. 20–23, iii. 3–5.
[2] Coloss. i. 18, 19.
[3] Coloss. ii. 9.
[4] See Burton, *B. L.* p. 158.

ment at Rome, when the Epistle to the Ephesians was written, we find further evidence that the evil had spread more widely, and taken root more deeply, at a somewhat later date, when the two Epistles were written to Timothy, the bishop of that Church. The first of these Epistles, together with that to Titus, was probably written some time after St. Paul's release from his first imprisonment, about A.D. 65; and the second, the latest of the Apostle's writings, during his second imprisonment, shortly before his martyrdom, probably A.D. 67. In the First Epistle the heretical teaching is distinctly mentioned under its own name—$\psi ευδώνυμος$ $γνῶσις$, 'knowledge falsely so called';[1] though it is doubtful whether the $ἀντιθέσεις$ ascribed to this false knowledge refer to the opposite principles recognised in most of the Gnostic systems, or simply to the opposition which these false teachers offered to the Gospel.[2] The latter seems on the whole to be the more simple and probable interpretation. As at the end of the Epistle St. Paul thus warns Timothy against the falsely-named knowledge, so at the beginning he bids him not to 'give heed to fables and endless genealogies, which minister questions, rather than godly edifying which is in faith';[3] a passage which the majority of commentators, ancient and modern, consider with reason as applying to the successive emanations of spiritual beings which were asserted in the Gnostic systems from the very beginning of their teaching. Nor does it in any way invalidate this interpretation, when we find these same genealogies mentioned in the contemporary Epistle to Titus together with

[1] 1 Tim. vi. 20.

[2] Cf. Burton, *B. L.* p. 80. For authorities for referring this text to the Gnostics, see *ibid.* note 37. Ellicott on this passage gives reasons for preferring the latter interpretation. For the former, see Matter, *Hist. du Gnost.* vol. I. p. 208.

[3] 1 Tim. i. 4, where $οἰκονομίαν$ should rather be read and rendered 'a dispensation.' The easier reading $οἰκοδομίαν$ is deficient in authority.

'strivings about the law' (μάχαι νομικαί),[1] while in the earlier part of the same Epistle there is a similar warning against 'Jewish fables' (μὴ προσέχοντες Ἰουδαϊκοῖς μύθοις),[2] for we have already seen in the Epistle to the Colossians how the Gnostic speculations at this time were accompanied by a spurious asceticism based on the Jewish law, such as to mark its teachers as men of Jewish origin and Judaizing tendencies, even if we do not admit an allusion (which is possible, though disputable on chronological grounds) to the genealogical emanations of the Jewish Kabbala.[3]

In the Second Epistle to Timothy, written probably about two years later than the First, we find an allusion to a definite feature of heretical teaching which there is little difficulty in connecting with Gnostic principles. The Apostle here writes, 'Shun profane and vain babblings, for they will increase unto more ungodliness, and their word will eat as doth a canker: of whom is Hymenæus and Philetus, who concerning the truth have erred, saying that the resurrection is passed already, and overthrow the faith of some.'[4] The Hymenæus here mentioned is probably the same person who in the former Epistle to Timothy is coupled with Alexander as having put away faith and a good conscience, and made shipwreck concerning the faith;[5] and a reference to the earliest form of Gnostic error will enable us to understand the exact nature of the false doctrine here reprehended. One of the fundamental tenets of Gnosticism from the beginning, and one which we have already seen manifested in the corruptions of the Church at Colossæ, was the doctrine of the evil nature of matter and of the material body. This

[1] Titus iii. 9.
[2] *Ibid.* i. 14.
[3] See Burton, *B. L.* p. 114. The same view is held by Vitringa; see Alford on 1 Tim. i. 4.
[4] 2 Tim. ii. 16–18.
[5] 1 Tim. i. 19, 20. Cf. Burton, *B. L.* p. 135.

led, as we have already observed, to a denial of the Incarnation of Christ; for a Divine being could not be supposed to assume a body made of evil matter. This heresy manifested itself in two forms: first, that of the Docetæ, who held the body of our Lord to be an immaterial phantom; and secondly, that of the Ebionites and others, who asserted that the spiritual being Christ was a distinct person from the man Jesus; that the former descended upon the latter at his baptism and left him before his crucifixion, never being united to him in one person. It is obvious at once how radically incompatible this theory must be with the central doctrine of the apostolic preaching—the bodily resurrection of Christ as the first fruits of them that slept, and through Christ the future resurrection to life of those that are Christ's at His coming. How to such a philosophy was it conceivable that 'Christ did truly rise again from death, and took again his body, with flesh, bones, and all things appertaining to the perfection of man's nature'? Or how could it be believed that hereafter 'at His coming all men shall rise again with their bodies'? Still the doctrine of the resurrection was too fundamental a point of the Christian faith to be openly and altogether denied by any having the slightest claim to be in any sense believers in Christ. If not openly repudiated, it must be evaded; it must be neutralised—to adopt a device not limited to the first century or to Gnostic heretics; it must be 'spiritually understood.' There is no doubt a resurrection, but it is a resurrection of the spirit, not of the flesh. The Gnostic, the man of religious knowledge emancipated from the dead letter and outward symbols of truth and admitted by wisdom to the higher mysteries beyond them, may be truly said to have passed from death to life, to have risen from the natural and put on the spiritual state. In this way it was maintained that 'the resurrection is past already,' being a spiritual process taking place during the present life.[1] That such a doctrine was actually held, not only by some of the later Gnostics, but also by the earliest disciples of the heresy, may be inferred from the language of Irenæus, who attributes to the Simonians, the followers of Simon Magus, as well as to the disciples of the later Carpocrates, the theory 'esse autem resurrectionem a mortuis agnitionem ejus, quæ ab eis dicitur, veritatis.'[2] It is probable that this error may be one of those to which St. Peter alludes, when he speaks of the unlearned and unstable wresting passages in St. Paul's Epistles to their own destruction;[3] for the heresy in question, though utterly contradicting the whole tenor of St. Paul's teaching, might have found an imaginary support in his language to the Romans and to the Colossians. 'Therefore are we buried with him by baptism unto death, that like as Christ was raised up from the dead by the glory of the Father, even so we also should walk in newness of life'; and again, 'Buried with him in baptism, wherein also ye are risen with him through the faith of the operation of God, who hath raised him from the dead.'[4]

I have reserved to the last place the Epistle to the Hebrews, on account of the doubts that have been raised as to its authorship. It is probable however, that under any circumstances the position now assigned to it, if not strictly in the order of chronology, will not be more than two or three years out of it. If, as I think on the whole the most probable, we consider this Epistle as written or at least superintended by St. Paul, the most natural date to assign to it will be the year 64 or 65, after the termina-

---

[1] On this doctrine as held by the Gnostics, see Burton, *B. L.* p. 134, and note 59. Cf. Alford and Ellicott on 2 Tim. ii. 18.

[2] Irenæus, ii. 31, 2. Cf. Tertullian, *De Resurr. Carnis* c. 19.

[3] 2 Peter iii. 16.

[4] Rom. vi. 4; Coloss. ii. 12.

tion of the Apostle's first imprisonment at Rome. It will thus only just precede the First Epistle to Timothy and that to Titus. If on the other hand we deny the Pauline authorship, we may possibly place it a short time after the Apostle's death, but at all events before the destruction of Jerusalem—probably therefore not later than 68 or 69.[1] The date of this Epistle will therefore very nearly coincide with the period which we have just been considering, and we may naturally expect to find allusions to the same phase of false doctrine. And in fact we may trace in this Epistle probable allusions to the two great errors which characterized Gnosticism from the beginning—the attempt to distinguish the supreme God, the Father of our Lord Jesus Christ, from the God of the Old Testament, and the denial of the real Incarnation of the Redeemer. In the opening words of the Epistle the writer confidently affirms that it is one and the same God who spake to the Jews by the prophets and who speaks now by Christ; 'God, who at sundry times and in divers manners spake in time past unto the fathers by the prophets, hath in these last days spoken unto us by His Son.'[2] And in a subsequent passage the Incarnation of Christ is asserted in terms which seem to have direct reference to some of the Docetic theories: 'Forasmuch then as the children are partakers of flesh and blood, he also himself likewise took part of the same; that through death he might destroy him that hath the power of death, that is, the devil. . . . For verily he took not on him the nature of angels, but he took on him the seed of Abraham. Wherefore in all things it behoved him to be made

---

[1] Timothy seems to have been just set at liberty when this Epistle was written (Heb. xiii. 23). If this event occurred after St. Paul's death, the most probable time of its occurrence will be immediately after the death of Nero in A.D. 68.

[2] Heb. i. 1, 2. Cf. Burton, B. L. p. 128.

like unto his brethren.'¹ The occurrence of these allusions to Gnosticism seems to strengthen the supposition that this Epistle was addressed, if not to the Jewish Christians at Jerusalem (which on the whole the language in which it is written renders improbable ²), at least to that other seat of Judaism and Jewish worship, Alexandria, one of the chief centres from which Gnostic doctrines emanated. If this hypothesis be tenable, it is, to say the least, a noteworthy coincidence, that of all the early Christian Churches that of Alexandria is the one which has most positively and consistently affirmed the Pauline authorship of the Epistle.³

A separate consideration must be given to a few passages from these Epistles, which are sometimes cited as containing allusions to the Gnosticism of this period, but which labour under some peculiar difficulties, both chronological and exegetical. I mean those texts in which the word *Æon* occurs either in the singular or the plural number. In the midst of numerous passages of the New Testament in which this word is undoubtedly used without any reference to its Gnostic signification, two have been selected in which the term has by some critics been interpreted in a personal sense as meaning one of the spiritual beings of the Gnostic mythology.⁴

The first of these is in the Epistle to the Ephesians (ii. 2), [ταῖς ἁμαρτίαις] ἐν αἷς ποτε περιεπατήσατε κατὰ τὸν αἰῶνα τοῦ κόσμου τούτου, κατὰ τὸν ἄρχοντα τῆς ἐξουσίας τοῦ ἀέρος, where our translation renders 'according to the *course* of this world,' which is probably the true meaning. The

---

¹ Heb. ii. 14, 16, 17. Cf. Burton, *B. L.* p. 167.

² Unless we accept the tradition of a Hebrew original of this Epistle asserted by Clement of Alexandria, Eusebius, Jerome, and others. Cf. Euseb. iii. 30, vi. 14; Hieron. *Cat. Script. Eccles.* c. 5.

³ See the Alexandrian evidence on this point in Alford's *Prolegomena*; who however himself holds a different view.

⁴ Cf. Burton, *B. L.* pp. 111, 115.

Gnostic sense is open to the objection that it makes the Apostle himself in some degree sanction the Gnostic mythology, as well as that it is opposed to St. Paul's constant use of the term αἰών in other places.[1] The second passage is that in the beginning of the Epistle to the Hebrews, δι' οὗ καὶ τοὺς αἰῶνας ἐποίησεν, where again our English translation, 'he made *the worlds*,' is more accurate than that which supposes a Gnostic sense. The latter interpretation is refuted by the parallel passage in the beginning of the eleventh chapter, πίστει νοοῦμεν κατηρτίσθαι τοὺς αἰῶνας ῥήματι Θεοῦ, εἰς τὸ μὴ ἐκ φαινομένων τὰ βλεπόμενα [al. τὸ βλεπόμενον] γεγονέναι, where the explanation of τοὺς αἰῶνας by τὰ βλεπόμενα (or τὸ βλεπόμενον) precludes the possibility of an allusion to the Gnostic Æons. But a more general objection may be found in the chronology of the Gnostic language. Though the term *Æon* is known to have been used by Valentinus and others of the second century to express their emanations of spiritual beings, there is not sufficient evidence to show that the word was so used as early as the time of St. Paul, or rather there is some evidence to the contrary. In a curious fragment from a work of Simon Magus which has been preserved by Hippolytus, the term occurs apparently in a different sense;[2] and the language of Hippolytus himself in a subsequent passage seems to imply that the term *Æons* was first introduced by Valentinus as an innovation on the language of Simon.[3]

---

[1] See especially Gal. i. 4 ἐκ τοῦ ἐνεστῶτος αἰῶνος πονηροῦ, 'from this present evil world' or 'course of things.'

[2] Simonis 'Απόφασις Μεγάλη in Hippol. *Ref. Hær.* vi. 18, p. 250 (ed. Duncker), δύο εἰσὶ παραφυάδες τῶν ὅλων αἰώνων, where the term αἰῶνες seems to mean the first principle of all things. Cf. Harvey's *Irenæus*, Introd. p. lxvii.

[3] Hippol. *R. H.* vi. 20, p. 258 (Duncker), Οὗτος δὴ καὶ ὁ κατὰ τὸν Σίμωνα μῦθος, ἀφ' οὗ Οὐαλεντῖνος τὰς ἀφορμὰς λαβὼν ἄλλοις ὀνόμασι καλεῖ. ὁ γὰρ νοῦς καὶ ἡ ἀλήθεια, καὶ λόγος καὶ ζωή, καὶ ἄνθρωπος καὶ ἐκκλησία, οἱ Οὐαλεντίνου αἰῶνες, ὁμολογουμένως

Thus far we have examined the traces of early Gnosticism furnished by the Scriptures of the New Testament down to the death of St. Paul. We must postpone to another lecture the examination of the evidence furnished by later writings, particularly those of St. John.

εἰσὶν αἱ Σίμωνος ἐξ ῥίζαι, νοῦς, ἐπίνοια, φωνὴ, ὄνομα, λογισμὸς καὶ ἐνθύμησις. Cf. Matter, I. p. 303.

LECTURE V.

NOTICES OF GNOSTICISM IN THE NEW TESTAMENT.

OUR last lecture was occupied with an examination of those notices of Gnostic doctrines or practices which are to be found in the Scriptures of the New Testament down to the death of St. Paul, a date not more than three years earlier than the destruction of Jerusalem. Before proceeding to examine the later historical notices of the same errors which are to be found in those portions of the sacred writings which belong to the last thirty years of the century, it may be well to call your attention for a short time to some passages of the earlier Scriptures in which the Gnostic teaching appears to be noticed, not by way of historical reference to that which was already in existence, but by way of prediction of that which was to come. Three passages at least may be pointed out as containing prophecies of this kind, two from the writings of St. Paul, and a third from those of St. Peter. The earliest in point of time is the well-known passage in the First Epistle to Timothy (iv. 1) : 'Now the Spirit speaketh expressly, that in the latter times some shall depart from the faith, giving heed to seducing spirits and doctrines of devils;[1] speaking lies in hypocrisy,[2] having their con-

---

[1] διδασκαλίαις δαιμονίων, i.e. doctrines emanating from evil spirits, not *doctrines about devils*. Cf. Pearson *Minor Theol. Works* II. p. 45, and Alford and Ellicott on this passage.

[2] ἐν ὑποκρίσει ψευδολόγων, properly, 'in the hypocrisy of speakers of lies.' The A. V. connects ψευδολόγων with δαιμονίων inaccurately.

science seared with a hot iron; forbidding to marry and commanding to abstain from meats, which God hath created to be received with thanksgiving of them which believe and know the truth.' The expression ἐν ὑστέροις χρόνοις, which our translation renders *in the latter times*, may be more accurately rendered *in after times*, meaning some time subsequent to that at which the Apostle is writing, but by no means necessarily a remote future or a time immediately preceding the end of all things.[1] It seems clear indeed from the context, that the writer is referring to an apostasy the beginning of which was discernible in his own day,[2] though its full development might be reserved for a later period. The false asceticism which we have already pointed out as corrupting the Church at Colossæ, the *judging in meat and drink*, the *Touch not, taste not, handle not*, may here be discerned in the command *to abstain from meats*, though it may be that the prohibition of marriage, which afterwards formed a conspicuous feature in the teaching of Saturninus and Marcion, had not yet extended itself from the Jewish Essenes[3] to any body claiming the name of Christians. That the passage has a prophetic reference to the Gnostics of the second century is expressly maintained by the early Fathers, Clement of Alexandria and Tertullian;[4] and the historical aptitude of the reference perhaps receives further confirmation in this, as in the next prediction to be quoted, by the use of the expression 'them which *know* the truth' (ἐπεγνωκόσιν τὴν ἀλήθειαν).

The other prophecy of St. Paul, from the Second

---

[1] Cf. Alford and Ellicott on this passage.

[2] This may be inferred from the directions given to Timothy personally, vv. 7–11.

[3] On the celibacy of the Essenes, cf. Josephus, *Ant.* xviii. 1. 5, *B.J.* ii. 8. 2; Pliny, *N. H.* v. 17.

[4] Clem. Alex. *Strom.* iii. 12 (p. 550, Potter); Tertullian, *De Præscr. Hær.* c. 33. Cf. Pearson's *Minor Works* II. p. 51.

Epistle to Timothy (iii. 1–7), no doubt has a principal reference to events still future and to be fully accomplished in the times immediately preceding the second coming of the Lord. Yet there is distinct evidence that the Apostle regarded his words as having a partial fulfilment in his own day and in the times immediately to follow his approaching death. Whilst he prophesies that 'in the last days perilous times shall come,' and describes the men of those times in language in which we can only very partially trace a likeness to the false teachers of the Apostolic age, yet his warning to his own son in the faith, 'from such turn away,' and the transition in the next two verses from the future tense to the present, seems to indicate the Apostle's conviction that the features which he prophetically depicted as characterizing the men of the last days were at least partially realised in the age in which he was writing.[1] The words, 'For of this sort are they which creep into houses and lead captive silly women,' might remind us of what the Apostle himself may have seen in Simon Magus and Helena, and in the beginnings, probably already discernible, of the teaching and practice of the Nicolaitans:[2] while the language in which these deluded captives are further described, πάντοτε μανθάνοντα καὶ μηδέποτε εἰς ἐπίγνωσιν ἀληθείας ἐλθεῖν δυνάμενα, seems to imply that one of the chief allurements of this teaching was the promise which it held out of attaining to a superior knowledge.

The third predictive passage, written probably about the same time with the last, is from the Second Epistle of St. Peter, and is one of which the fulfilment appears to have followed very closely upon the prophecy. In this passage, as in the one just cited from St. Paul, the cha-

---

[1] Cf. Bp. Bull, *Sermon* xv, *Works* I. p. 372 (ed. 1827).
[2] Cf. Burton, *B. L.* p. 152.

racteristics of the false teachers who are condemned by the Apostle seem to comprise the two features of immoral living and pretension to a peculiar knowledge. 'There shall be,' he writes, 'false teachers among you, who privily shall bring in damnable heresies, even denying the Lord that bought them, . . . and many shall follow their pernicious ways; by reason of whom the way of truth shall be evil spoken of.'[1] In the continuation of the passage the same persons are spoken of as presumptuous, as despising government, as speaking evil of the things that they understand not;[2] and a little later it is said, 'Spots they are and blemishes, sporting themselves with their own deceivings while they feast with you; having eyes full of adultery and that cannot cease from sin; beguiling unstable souls; an heart they have, exercised with covetous practices; cursed children; which have forsaken the right way, and are gone astray, following the way of Balaam the son of Bosor, who loved the wages of unrighteousness.'[3] . . . And again he continues, 'For when they speak great swelling words of vanity, they allure through the lusts of the flesh, through much wantonness, those that were clean escaped [τοὺς ὄντως ἀποφυγόντας, *al. those that are hardly escaping*, τοὺς ὀλίγως ἀποφεύγοντας] from them who live in error. While they promise them liberty, they themselves are the servants of corruption.'[4]

In these words we have a description of a false teaching and practice partly already present when the Apostle wrote, but to be further developed hereafter, proceeding from persons who bore the name of Christians and took part in the Christian feasts, but whose immoral lives were the occasion of calumnious accusations against the whole

[1] 2 Peter ii. 1, 2. [2] 2 Peter ii. 13, 15.
[3] vv. 10, 12. [4] ii. 18, 19.

body of the Church: persons moreover, who laid claim to a liberty which placed them above the ordinary restraints of morality, and who, under this pretext, seduced many that had once been converts to the Christian faith. How exactly this description applies to some of the Gnostics of the next century will be seen hereafter, but there is evidence also of its partial accomplishment in the Apostolic age itself, as indeed the state of things here described is one of the natural results of teaching extant in that age. The Gnostic tenet of the evil nature of matter, and the consequent worthlessness of the body, might lead and did lead with them, as in other times and countries, to two very opposite moral results. In some, as we have already seen, it manifested itself in a spurious asceticism, which strove in every possible way to mortify the flesh as a means of emancipating the soul from its influence. But in the eyes of others the soul was everything, the body was nothing. Provided the soul were furnished with the true knowledge, it would derive no pollution from a thing so worthless and so foreign to it as a material body; all bodily actions therefore were wholly indifferent, and might be practised at will without affecting the sublime state of the wise soul. Some at a later period even went further than this, and maintained that the moral law, with the whole Jewish economy, having proceeded from an evil being, it was a duty in the enlightened man to transgress the law, in order to free himself from the yoke of the Creator of the material world.[1] The ascetic side of this teaching we have already seen noticed in the Epistle to the Colossians and in the First Epistle to Timothy; the licentious side we have now seen partially described in the Second Epistle to Timothy, and more fully in the contem-

---

[1] Cf. Burton, *B. L.* p. 41.

poraneous Second Epistle of St. Peter, and we shall afterwards see it noticed again in the writings of St. John.

But before proceeding to these last writings, it will be necessary to call your attention to another book of the New Testament, which, as regards the time of its composition, may, I think, be most fitly assigned to some period intermediate between the deaths of St. Peter and St. Paul and the appearance of St. John's writings towards the end of the century. I mean the Epistle of St. Jude. The resemblance between this Epistle and the Second of St. Peter is too close to be accounted for by undesigned coincidences, and we must suppose that one of the writers has availed himself of a similarity of circumstances to repeat in substance the rebukes and warnings of his brother Apostle. Some eminent modern critics have attempted, on the very precarious evidence of style, to assign the priority in time of writing to St. Jude; but there are two circumstances which appear to me to prove most conclusively that St. Jude's Epistle was written after that of St. Peter, and with express reference to it. The first is, that the evils which St. Peter speaks of as partly future, St. Jude describes as now present. The one says, 'There *shall be* false teachers among you;'[1] the other says, 'There *are* certain men crept in unawares, who were before of old ordained to this condemnation.'[2] The other circumstance is still more to the point. St. Peter in his Second Epistle has the remarkable words, τοῦτο πρῶτον γινώσκοντες, ὅτι ἐλεύσονται ἐπ' ἐσχάτου τῶν ἡμερῶν [*al.* ἐπ' ἐσχάτων τῶν ἡμερῶν] ἐμπαῖκται, κατὰ τὰς ἰδίας αὐτῶν πιθυμίας πορευόμενοι.[3] St. Jude has the same passage, repeated almost word for word, but expressly introduced

---

[1] 2 Peter ii. 1. The future tense is continued through the two following verses.

[2] Jude 4.

[3] 2 Peter iii. 3.

as a citation of Apostolic language: ὑμεῖς δὲ, ἀγαπητοί, μνήσθητε τῶν ῥημάτων τῶν προειρημένων ὑπὸ τῶν ἀποστόλων τοῦ Κυρίου ἡμῶν Ἰησοῦ Χριστοῦ, ὅτι ἔλεγον ὑμῖν ὅτι ἐν ἐσχάτῳ χρόνῳ [al. ἐπ' ἐσχάτου τοῦ χρόνου] ἔσονται ἐμπαῖκται, κατὰ τὰς ἑαυτῶν ἐπιθυμίας πορευόμενοι τῶν ἀσεβειῶν.[1] The use of the plural number (τῶν ἀποστόλων) may be explained by supposing that the writer may also have intended to allude to passages similar in import, though differently expressed, in the writings of St. Paul (such as 1 Tim. iv. 1, 2 Tim. iii. 1), but the verbal coincidence can hardly be satisfactorily explained, unless we suppose that St. Jude had principally in his thoughts, and was actually citing the language of St. Peter.[2] On these grounds we are justified in regarding the Epistle of St. Jude as written after the death of St. Peter, and probably some time after, when the evils, which the earlier writer saw only in their commencement, had attained to a fuller development and could be spoken of as actually in being, though not even yet so far advanced as they appear subsequently in the Revelation of St. John.[3]

In the language of St. Jude, as in that of St. Peter, which it closely imitates, we may clearly discern a reference to the Gnostic sect of the Nicolaitans,[4] mentioned by name in the Revelation. The comparison, in all these passages, of the error condemned with that of Balaam

---

[1] Jude 17, 18.

[2] Cf. Wordsworth on both passages, and Hengstenberg on the *Revelation*, I. p. 14 (Eng. Trans.). Alford attempts to explain the coincidence by supposing that St. Peter's words are also a reminiscence of things before said by the Apostles. But St. Peter only mentions in a previous verse, not directly connected with this, 'the words of the holy Prophets and the commandment of us the Apostles,' in general terms. He does not cite the next verse as an Apostolic prediction.

[3] Cf. Hengstenberg on *Revelation*, I. pp. 14, 15, Wordsworth, Introduction to St. Jude, and Schaff, *Hist. of Apost. Church* II. p. 374.

[4] That the Nicolaitans were Gnostics, see Burton, *Bampton Lectures* p. 145.

is decisive as to the identity of the persons intended.[1] The other characteristics noted by St. Peter are also repeated by St. Jude—their denial of the Lord; their profligate lives; their contempt of government, and evil speaking of dignities and of things that they know not; their pollution of the feasts of charity; their great swelling words. The antinomian, no less than the ascetic side of Gnosticism, seems by this time to have fully manifested itself.

Of the writings of St. John we may perhaps, though with considerable hesitation, assign the earliest date to the Apocalypse. The Gospel we may with tolerable confidence regard as prior to the Epistles; and, in the absence of more conclusive evidence, we have at least the authority of tradition for placing the Apocalypse before the Gospel.[2] At all events, it will be convenient to adopt this order in our present examination, on account of the illustration which the Apocalypse affords to the two Epistles which we have just been considering. The general testimony of antiquity assigns the date of the Apocalyptic vision to the close of the reign of Domitian, *i.e.* to the year 95 or 96,[3] nearly thirty years after the death of St. Peter and St. Paul, a date at which we may expect that the heresies which had only begun to manifest themselves to the elder Apostles would have attained to some maturity, and perhaps have divided themselves into various schools.

The Revelation is the only book of Scripture in which

---

[1] See 2 Peter ii. 15; Jude 11; Rev. ii. 14.

[2] Clement of Alexandria, *Quis Dives salvus* § 42 (Potter, p. 959), speaks of St. John as having taken up his abode at Ephesus after his departure from Patmos. Irenæus, iii. 1, says that St. John wrote his Gospel while residing at Ephesus.

[3] So Irenæus, Eusebius, Jerome, and others. The only exception is Epiphanius, in whose statement there is clearly an error. See Alford's Prolegomena.

we find a sect of the Gnostics mentioned by name; for the general testimony of the Fathers warrants us in classifying as a branch of the Gnostics the persons who are there spoken of under the name of Nicolaitans.[1] 'This thou hast,' the Apostle is bidden to write to the angel of the Church of Ephesus, 'that thou hatest the deeds of the Nicolaitans, which I also hate.'[2] And again, to the angel of the Church of Pergamos; 'I have a few things against thee, because thou hast there them that hold the doctrines of Balaam, who taught Balak to cast a stumbling-block before the children of Israel, to eat things sacrificed to idols, and to commit fornication. So hast thou also them that hold the doctrine of the Nicolaitans, which thing I hate.'[3] Two characteristics of the Nicolaitans are here mentioned: first, their eating of things offered to idols; secondly, their immoral living.[4] The former connects them with the γνῶσις reproved by St. Paul in the First Epistle to the Corinthians;[5] while the latter, together with the comparison to Balaam, connects them with the false teachers denounced by St. Peter and St. Jude.

We have the testimony of Irenæus, followed by Hippolytus,[6] as well as of Clement of Alexandria,[7] for deriving the name of these heretics from their reputed founder, Nicolas, the proselyte of Antioch, one of the seven deacons, whose native country, Syria, was one of the homes of early Gnosticism. It is true that the anecdote related of Nicolas by Clement seems to represent his

---

[1] Burton, *B. L.* p. 145. Cf. Neander, *Ch. Hist.* II. p. 119.

[2] Rev. ii. 6.

[3] Rev. ii. 14, 15.

[4] Οὕτως ἔχεις καὶ σὺ κ.τ.λ. Rev. ii. 15; *i.e.* as Balaam taught Balak of old, so do the Nicolaitans teach now. The reference is to Num. xxv. 1, 2, xxxi. 16. Cf. Burton, *B. L.* p. 147; Herzog, X. p. 338.

[5] 1 Cor. viii. 1.

[6] Irenæus, i. 27; Hippolytus, *R.H.* vii. 36. Neander (*Ch. Hist.* II. p. 122) considers the tradition apocryphal.

[7] Clem. Alex. *Strom.* iii. 4 (p. 523 Potter). Cf. Eusebius, *H. E.* iii. 29.

so-called followers as giving a false interpretation to the teaching of their master;[1] but on the other hand both Irenæus and Hippolytus represent Nicolas himself as teaching that all actions are morally indifferent, and the latter expressly speaks of him as an apostate from sound doctrine. Even the anecdote related by Clement, while it appears to deny the charge of personal licentiousness, betrays at least a want of reverence for the sanctity of marriage.[2] The ingenious conjecture of some modern critics, that the name *Nicolaitans* was not derived from a person, but is a Greek equivalent for the name of Balaam, which means *destroyer* or *corrupter of the people*,[3] is probably more ingenious than true. It is opposed to the earliest tradition, and is not without etymological difficulty, *destroyer* or *corrupter* being by no means the same as *conqueror*.[4]

Another passage in the same chapter of the Apocalypse, which has probably a reference to Gnosticism, occurs in the message to the angel of the Church of Thyatira; 'Unto you I say, and unto the rest in Thyatira, as many as have not this doctrine, and which have not known the depths of Satan, as they speak.'[5] In the expression, οὐκ ἔγνωσαν τὰ βάθη τοῦ σατανᾶ, some commentators have supposed an ironical allusion to the Gnostic claim to a knowledge of the deep things of God;[6] but it seems more natural to refer it to their favourite inquiry into the nature and origin of evil,[7] or even more especially to the boast of the Ophites.[8]

---

[1] ὅτι παραχρήσασθαι τῇ σαρκὶ δεῖ.

[2] Cf. Harvey's *Irenæus*, Introd. p. lxx.

[3] See Hengstenberg on Rev. ii. 6, and Neander, *Ch. Hist.* II. p. 120; בלע עם, (absorptio populi).

[4] Cf. Schaff, *Hist. of the Apost. Church* II. p. 377.

[5] Rev. ii. 24.

[6] Schaff, II. p. 378.

[7] Cf. Herzog, *Encykl.*, Art. 'Nikolaiten,' vol. X. p. 338.

[8] Hippol. v. 6. See below, Lecture VII. on the Ophites, p. 105.

As regards the Gospel of St. John, we have the express testimony of Irenæus, that it was written to oppose that form of the Gnostic heresy which was taught by Cerinthus, and, before him, by the Nicolaitans.[1] The nature of that heresy, so far as it concerns our present inquiry, may be stated in the words of the same Father: 'A certain Cerinthus,' he says, 'in Asia, taught that the world was not made by the Supreme God, but by some power altogether separate and distant from that Sovereign Power which is over the universe, and one ignorant of the God who is over all things. He taught moreover, that Jesus was not born of a virgin (for this seemed to him to be impossible), but was the son of Joseph and Mary, born after the manner of other men; though pre-eminent above other men in justice and prudence and wisdom: and that after his baptism the Christ, in the form of a dove, descended upon him from that Sovereign Power which is over all things: and that he then announced the unknown Father, and wrought miracles; but that at the end the Christ departed again from Jesus, and that Jesus suffered and was raised from the dead, while the Christ continued impassible as a spiritual being.'[2]

That the first chapter of St. John's Gospel contains passages directly opposed to this heresy is evident on the most casual inspection. The words, 'All things were made by Him, and without Him was not anything made that was made,'[3] strike directly at the root of that false principle common to all the Gnostic schools, which regarded the Creator of the world as a being distinct and remote from the Redeemer and from the Supreme God; while the declaration that 'the Word was made flesh and

---

[1] Irenæus iii. 11.

[2] Irenæus i. 26, closely followed by Hippolytus vii. 33. The latter is restored by Harvey as the original text of Irenæus.

[3] John i. 3.

dwelt among us,'[1] is equally opposed to that other error of Cerinthus, which taught that the man Jesus and the spiritual being Christ were wholly separate beings, only temporarily united by the indwelling of the one in the other.

We have also other notices, which fix Cerinthus as having been a contemporary of St. John,[2] and it is quite possible that his doctrines may have been directly before the mind of the Apostle when he wrote the above passages. But though Cerinthus may have been one of the first who exhibited the doctrines of the Jewish Alexandrian philosophy in the form of a heresy concerning the Person of Christ, we must look to an earlier writer for the source of the error and for an explanation of the language in which the Apostle's protest is couched.[3] Cerinthus, as we are expressly told, though he taught in Asia, learnt the principles of his heresy in Egypt; and the two great errors of Gnosticism—the separation of the Creator from the Supreme God, and the abhorrence of matter as the source of all evil—may be found before Cerinthus, in that Alexandrian Judaism which has its representative in Philo. The choice of the term ὁ Λόγος as a designation of Christ, the assertion of the eternity and proper Deity and Incarnation of the Logos, have a direct relation and antagonism to the Jewish Gnosticism of Philo, as well as to the Christian Gnosticism of Cerinthus. There was in fact an earlier Gnosticism founded on the perversion of the Law, as there was a later Gnosticism founded on the perversion of the Gospel; and it is possible that when St. John wrote, the influence of both had begun to be felt in the Christian Church, and had modified to some extent

---

[1] John i. 14.
[2] Cf. Irenæus, iii. 3; cited by Eusebius, *H. E.* iii. 28, iv. 21.
[3] Cf. Dorner, *Person of Christ* I. p. 17 (Eng. Tr.), and Burton, *Bampton Lectures* p. 223.

the language of its theology.[1] The aim of the Apostle, in adopting this language as a vehicle of Christian teaching, seems to have been both to correct the errors which had actually crept into the Church, and also to counteract the influence of the source from which they sprang.

As the Gospel of St. John was in some portions of its language directed against the teaching of Cerinthus, who, in common with the Ebionites, denied the Deity of our Lord, so the language of his Epistles seems partly to be directed against another form of the Gnostic error—that of the Docetæ, who denied His proper humanity. The opening words of the First Epistle, 'That which was from the beginning, which we have heard, which we have seen with our eyes, which we have looked upon, and our hands have handled, of the word of life—that which we have seen and heard declare we unto you,'[2] announce the direct sensible evidence of an eyewitness and personal friend to the reality of that human body in which his Master lived on the earth; while the subsequent language of the same Epistle is yet more explicit and more distinctly controversial in its tone:[3] 'Beloved, believe not every spirit, but try the spirits whether they are of God, because many false prophets are gone out into the world. Hereby know ye the Spirit of God; every spirit that confesseth that Jesus Christ is come in the flesh is of God, and every spirit that confesseth not that Jesus Christ is come in the flesh is not of God; and this is that spirit of antichrist, whereof ye have heard that it should come,

---

[1] See Burton, *Bampton Lectures* p. 218.

[2] 1 John i. 1–3.

[3] It seems impossible to refer this language to the mere Jewish expectation of a future Messiah. Jews would never pretend to be inspired by a Christian spirit. The Apostle is clearly warning his reader against a false form of Christianity. The assumption of some critics (*e.g.* Ritschl, *Altkatholische Kirche* pp. 342, 454) of the late origin of Docetism is perfectly arbitrary.

and even now already is it in the world.'[1] The same language is repeated in the Second Epistle: 'For many deceivers are entered into the world, who confess not that Jesus Christ is come in the flesh. This is a deceiver and an antichrist.'[2] It is also possible, as a learned writer on this subject has remarked, that St. John may have had the same heresy in view, when in his Gospel he bears witness in such significant and emphatic language to the actual issue of blood and water from the side of Him whom they pierced: 'And he that saw it bare record, and his record is true; and he knoweth that he saith true, that ye might believe.'[3]

Other passages in St. John's First Epistle seem, from the terms in which they are expressed, to have a more direct reference to the heresy of Cerinthus, which we have already noticed in connection with the Gospel. The vehement language in the second chapter of this Epistle, 'Who is a liar, but he that denieth that Jesus is the Christ?' and the corresponding expression in the fourth chapter, 'Whosoever shall confess that Jesus is the Son of God, God dwelleth in him, and he in God,' though capable of being referred to other forms of error, yet acquire an especial significance when we remember the existence at this very time of heretical teachers who maintained that Jesus and the Christ were two separate beings, and distinguished between Christ who descended from the Supreme God, and Jesus the man upon whom he descended.[4]

---

[1] 1 John iv. 1–3.
[2] 2 John 7.
[3] John xix. 35. Cf. Burton, B. L. p. 170.
[4] Cf. Burton, *Bampton Lectures* p. 185. Dr. Burton also sees a reference to Gnosticism (Cerinthianism) in 1 John v. 6, 'not by water only, but by water and blood' (*B. L.* p. 188). This is very possible, though it seems more natural to understand the *blood* as referring to Christ's death, than to His birth into the world. We might perhaps paraphrase the text, 'Christ was not merely joined to Jesus at His baptism, to leave Him before His

It is not without profit for us in these latter days to examine this record of the Apostolic treatment of early and, it might be thought, obsolete heresies. There are not wanting teachers at the present time who tell us, in the spirit of the Gnostics of old, that dogmas and historical facts are no part of the Christian religion; that there is a spiritual sense in which these things may be understood which is superior to the letter; that we may be Christian in spirit without troubling ourselves about the facts of Christ's earthly life, or the supernatural doctrines connected with His Person. How far this teaching is entitled to call itself by the name of Christian may be tested by the evidence of him who of all the first teachers of Christianity can least be accused of a harsh or narrow view of the terms of Christian communion; who loved to dwell, not on opinions about Christ, but on the hope and spirit of Christ Himself; who is never weary of enforcing the precept of love to our brethren; whose last breath passed away in the constant repetition of the one summary of his teaching, 'Little children, love one another.' Of all men he would surely be the last to deny the claim of Christian brotherhood to any that could truly urge it. Yet it was a dogma—the Incarnation of the Divine Son—a historical fact—the birth of Jesus Christ and His life as a man—which called forth from his lips the strong words of indignation and abhorrence against all gainsayers: 'Who is a liar, but he that denieth that Jesus is the Christ? . . . . Every spirit that confesseth not that Jesus Christ is come in the flesh is not of God: and this is that spirit of antichrist.'[1]

crucifixion. It is one and the same Jesus Christ, who manifested Himself by water in baptism and by blood on the cross.'

[1] 1 John ii. 22, iv. 3.

LECTURE VI.

PRECURSORS OF GNOSTICISM—SIMON MAGUS AND MENANDER.

WHEN, from the incidental notices of Gnostic doctrines existing during the lifetime of the Apostles, we proceed to inquire concerning the history of these doctrines and the persons by whom they were taught, we find the early Fathers almost unanimously agreed in referring the origin of the Gnostic heresies to a man of whom a brief and passing mention is made in the New Testament, and who thus serves as the connecting link between Scripture and ecclesiastical tradition as regards the history of false doctrine.[1] Simon Magus, the person in question, appears sufficiently early in the Apostolic history to allow of the spread of his doctrines almost *pari passu* with the preaching of Christianity, and to account for the notices of those doctrines which we have already pointed out as existing in the Apostolic writings. Within seven years (to take the longest probable interval) after the Lord's Ascension,[2] we read that when the Church was scattered abroad after the martyrdom of St. Stephen, Philip went down to a city (not *the* city, as in the A.V.) of Samaria,[3] and preached Christ unto them. . . . 'But there was a certain man

---

[1] For the authorities who regard Simon as the parent of Gnosticism, see Burton, *Bampton Lectures* p. 87.

[2] For the chronology, see Alford's Prolegomena to the Acts, p. 22. Others shorten the interval to one year, and even less.

[3] The name of the city is not mentioned. Possibly Sychar or Sichem, which is mentioned in the same manner, John iv. 5.

called Simon, which beforetime in the same city used sorcery, and bewitched the people of Samaria, giving out that himself was some great one; to whom they all gave heed, from the least to the greatest, saying, This man is the great Power of God.'[1] If we adopt the reading which has the best claim to be considered as the true text, Οὗτός ἐστιν ἡ δύναμις τοῦ Θεοῦ ἡ καλουμένη μεγάλη, 'This man is that power of God which is called great,' *i.e.* which is known as *the* great one, we obtain a clearer insight into Simon's pretensions than is afforded by the reading from which our version is made. The language of the Samaritans may be most naturally understood as an acknowledgment of the truth of Simon's claims in his own behalf;[2] and it would thus appear that Simon maintained the existence of various powers or emanations from God, and gave himself out to be the chief of all.

We are at once reminded of the δυνάμεις or 'divine powers' of Philo, and of the supreme power, the Λόγος, and we may conclude that Simon had at least borrowed from the Jewish Alexandrian philosophy so much of this hypothesis as was convenient for his own purpose,[3] though in representing this supreme power as assuming a human body in his own person, he seems at first sight to place himself in distinct opposition to the spirit of that philosophy—an opposition which can only be avoided by attributing to him a Docetic doctrine, which, as we shall see hereafter, there is some ground for ascribing to him. Simon indeed seems to have borrowed indiscriminately from Alexandrianism and Christianity, in order to exalt himself and his teaching as the rival of both. In the Jewish philosophy of Alexandria the Logos, or revealed

---

[1] Acts viii. 5, 9, 10.

[2] This obviates De Wette's objection that the Samaritan people were not likely to be familiar with the language of the Alexandrian philosohy. See Alford here.

[3] Cf. Gfroerer's *Philo*, vol. II. p. 372.

God, is identified with the Creator of the world and with the God of the Jewish people. But Simon, a Samaritan by birth,[1] and a teacher among the Samaritan people, represents the spirit of national hatred, hostile alike to the philosophy of the Jewish Platonists and to the Christian revelation which acknowledged a Messiah of Jewish birth.[2] In announcing himself as the supreme Power of God, he probably intended to avail himself of the current language of the Alexandrian philosophy to support his own pretensions to a mission which that philosophy would have been the last to recognise, and at the same time to pervert the Christian doctrine of God manifest in the flesh by setting up himself as a rival Messiah, in the strictest sense of the term an Antichrist. It is true that, awed for a time by the superior powers of the preachers of the Gospel, Simon professed himself a Christian and submitted to be baptized, but his subsequent conduct says little for the sincerity of his profession; and it is probable that he merely regarded the Apostles as magicians of higher powers than himself, and wished to purchase their gifts for his own purposes.[3] At all events the momentary impression in favour of Christianity seems ultimately to have had no other effect than to stimulate his rivalry; and it is not improbable that his continued assumption of the title of the *Logos* in furtherance of an antichristian

---

[1] Justin Martyr, himself a Samaritan, calls Simon a native of Gitton or Gitta in Samaria, *Apol.* i. c. 26; cf. *Apol.* ii. c. 15. Justin's own birthplace makes him in this respect a better authority than Josephus (*Ant.* xx. 7. 2), even supposing that the Jew of Cyprus there mentioned is the same person with Simon Magus. But the name of Simon was so common that we may reasonably suppose them to have been different persons. Cf. Möller, Art. 'Simon Magus,' in Herzog, vol. XIV. p. 392.

[2] From John iv. 25 it is clear that the Samaritans expected a Messiah, but it is probable that they expected one of *Israelitish* (*i.e.* Samaritan, as they opposed the term to *Jewish*) birth. At least this is the view of the later Samaritans; cf. Petermann in Herzog, vol. XIII. p. 373.

[3] Möller in Herzog, XIV. p. 391. Cf. Milman, *Hist. of Christianity* II. p. 45.

teaching may have had some share in prompting the employment of the same term by St. John as a designation of the true Messiah. That Simon actually adopted this name, as well as the cognate term δύναμις, from the Alexandrian philosophy, may be gathered from the language attributed to him by St. Jerome, who professes to be citing from his writings: 'Ego sum Sermo Dei, ego sum speciosus, ego paracletus, ego omnipotens, ego omnia Dei.'[1] According to another account given by St. Irenæus, Simon is said to have spoken of himself as having appeared to the Jews as the Son, to the Samaritans as the Father, and to the Gentiles as the Holy Spirit[2]—language in which we may probably trace the distortion of Christian terms in an heretical sense,[3] to express the superiority of that Divine manifestation which he boasted of as residing in himself to those which had been made of the same Deity to other nations through other representatives. Another account, which, however differing in details, implies the same theoretical doctrine, is alluded to by Justin Martyr, and detailed at length by Irenæus. 'Simon,' says the latter author, 'having purchased a certain woman named Helena, who had been a prostitute in the city of Tyre, carried her about with him, and said that she was the first Conception[4] of his mind, the mother of all things, by whom in the beginning he conceived the thought of making the angels and archangels; for that this Conception (*hanc En-*

---

[1] S. Hieron. *in Matt.* xxiv. 5 (*Opera*, Vallarsii VII. p. 193).

[2] Irenæus, *c. Hær.* i. 23. Cf. Hippolytus *Ref. Hær.* vi. 19 ; Theodoret, *Hær. Fab.* i. 1. In the subsequent language of Irenæus, 'Esse autem se sublimissimam virtutem, hoc est eum qui sit super omnia Pater,' the latter words may perhaps, as Burton supposes (*B. L.* p. 388), be a gloss of Irenæus himself in explanation of the former.

[3] In a Sabellian sense, to denote not three Persons but only three manifestations of the same being. Cf. Massuet, *Diss. Præv. in Irenæum.* i. § 100. Massuet gives a different interpretation of Simon's purpose in assuming these three relations.

[4] Ἔννοιαν, Justin, *Apol.* i. 26 ; and the translator of Irenæus himself uses the Greek word just below.

noian) proceeded forth from him, and knowing her father's wishes, descended to the lower world, and produced the angels and powers; by whom also he said that this world was made. But after she had produced them, she was detained by them through envy, since they were unwilling to be considered the offspring of any other being; for he himself was entirely unknown by them; but his Conception was detained by those powers and angels which were put forth from her, and suffered every insult from them that she might not return upward to her father; and this went so far that she was even confined in a human body, and for ages passed into other female bodies, as if from one vessel into another. He said also that she was that Helen on whose account the Trojan war was fought; . . . . and that after passing from one body to another, and constantly meeting with insult, at last she became a public prostitute, and that this was the *lost sheep*. On this account he himself came, that he might first of all reclaim her and free her from her chains, and then give salvation to men through the knowledge of himself.[1] For since the angels ruled the world badly, because every one of them desired the chief place, he had come down for the restoration of all things, and had descended, being changed in figure, and made like to principalities and powers and angels,[2] so that he appeared among men as a man, though he was not a man, and was thought to have suffered in Judea, though he did not suffer. . . . Furthermore he said that the prophets uttered their prophecies under the

---

[1] διὰ τῆς ἰδίας ἐπιγνώσεως, Hippol. vi. 19; 'per suam agnitionem,' Transl. Iren. The Greek shows clearly the Gnostic element.

[2] Hippol. vi. 19 ἐξομοιούμενον ταῖς ἀρχαῖς καὶ ταῖς ἐξουσίαις καὶ τοῖς ἀγγέλοις;' Transl. Iren. 'assimilatum virtutibus et potentibus et angelis.' Bunsen (*Hippolytus*, vol. I. p. 48) supposes quite arbitrarily, that Simon, or the person writing in his name, is here giving an account, not of himself, but of Jesus. Bunsen's view is rejected by his admirer Milman, *Hist. of Christianity* II. p. 51.

inspiration of those angels who framed the world; for which reason they who rest their hope on him and his Helena no longer cared for them, but as free men could act as they pleased, for that men are saved by his (*i.e.* Simon's) grace, and not according to their own just works, for that no acts were just by nature, but by accident, according to the rules established by the angels who made the world,[1] and who attempt by these precepts to bring men into bondage. For this reason he promised that the world should be released and those who are his set at liberty from the government of those who made the world.'[2] In another passage of Irenæus the doctrine of Simon is summed up more briefly. 'Simon Magus,' he says, ' was the first to declare that he himself was the God who is over all things, and that the world was made by his angels.'[3]

From this strange medley of Christian, Jewish, and heathen ideas, we may without much difficulty disengage the leading principles of Simon's teaching. In common with the Alexandrian Platonists and with all the subsequent Gnostics, he distinguished between the Supreme God and the Creator of the world, and adopting with some modifications a hint furnished by the figurative language of Plato's Timæus, he considered the material world to be the work of subordinate beings who were in rebellion against the higher powers emanating from the Supreme God. Combining with this philosophy a strange perversion of the Christian doctrine of redemption, he seems to have represented himself as the subsequent receptacle of the same Divine power which had

---

[1] οὐ γάρ ἐστι φύσει κακὸν ἀλλὰ θέσει. ἔθεντο γάρ, φησίν, οἱ ἄγγελοι κ.τ.λ. Hippol. vi. 19.

[2] Irenæus, i. 23, partly translated by Burton, *B. L.* p. 390. Cf. Hippol. *Ref. Hær.* vi. 19; Tertullian, *De Anima* c. 34; Epiphanius, *Hær.* xxv. 4; Theodoret, *Hær. Fab.* i. 1.

[3] Irenæus, ii. 9.

previously dwelt in Jesus, and in his person had appeared to suffer in Judea.[1] The mention of our Lord's humanity and suffering as apparent but not real seems to point to Simon as the first teacher of the Docetic heresy; but if this interpretation be put upon his language, we must suppose that in consistency he maintained his own body to be unreal also; and there are not wanting other notices which give an incidental support to this supposition.[2] Combined with these philosophical theories we find that hostility to the Jewish law and scriptures which became afterwards characteristic of a large school of Gnostics, and those licentious doctrines concerning moral distinctions which afterwards conferred an evil notoriety on Carpocrates and Epiphanes, and which were too much in accordance with the practices of Simon himself.

In the wild and grotesque theory of Simon concerning the nature and past history of his companion Helena, we may trace an allusion to that division of the Divine emanations into pairs, male and female, which we find in another form in the Jewish Kabbala, and concerning which we find some further details in other notices of the teaching of Simon. In the recently discovered work of Hippolytus against heresies an account is given of the doctrine of Simon as contained in a work called the 'Great Announcement' ('Ἀπόφασις Μεγάλη), which is cited as the production of Simon himself.[3] According to this work the principle of all things is a certain indefinite power (ἀπέραντος δύναμις) which is spoken of under the name of

---

[1] Cf. Burton, *Bampton Lectures* pp. 117, 396.

[2] See the strange story told in the Clementines, *Hom.* ii. 24, of the staff of Dositheus passing through Simon's body.

[3] Milman (*Hist. of Christianity* II. p. 50) says that it were utter absurdity to suppose this work written by the Simon Magus of the Acts. He gives however no reason for this strong assertion, and allows that it may have been the work of Dositheus or Menander. Hippolytus evidently regarded it as a genuine work of Simon.

Fire, and also under that of *Silence*.[1] Under the name of Fire it is described as having two natures, one secret and one manifest, the secret nature being hidden in the manifest, and the manifest produced by the secret; the one embraces the whole intelligible and the other the whole sensible universe. The world was generated from the ungenerated fire by means of six roots or principles of things, which are produced from the primitive fire in pairs, called νοῦς and ἐπίνοια, φωνὴ and ὄνομα, λογισμὸς and ἐνθύμησις.[2] In these six roots is potentially contained the whole of the primary indefinite power, which power, he says, is manifested as ὁ ἑστώς, στάς, στησόμενος. By this last term seems obscurely to be designated the Gnostic or perfect man represented by Simon himself, who is regarded as the consummation or perfect fruit of this process of manifestation, combining in himself the whole development of the Divine principle and identified with it.[3] The six partial roots or emanations of the same principle have each its material counterpart, νοῦς and ἐπίνοια answering to heaven and earth, φωνὴ and ὄνομα to the sun and moon, λογισμὸς and ἐνθύμησις to air and water.[4] Man, that is to say the perfect man or Gnostic, is the counterpart and complete manifestation of the whole. In a subsequent passage Hippolytus tells us that the roots (ῥίζαι) of Simon's system correspond under a different name with the æons (αἰῶνες) of his successor Valentinus.[5] The whole theory is illustrated by an allegorical interpretation of the Mosaic account of the creation worthy of Philo Judæus himself. Of this theory, which is repeated in an abridged form by Theodoret,[6] the more abstract and

---

[1] Hippol. *Ref. Hær.* vi. 9, 18.
[2] Hippol. vi. 12. The same three pairs are mentioned by Theodoret *Hær. Fab.* i. 1, where however ἔννοια is substituted for ὄνομα.
[3] Cf. Möller in Herzog, vol. XIV. 396, 397.
[4] Hippol. vi. 13.
[5] Hippol. vi. 20.
[6] *Hær. Fab.* i. 1.

metaphysical portion contains much which we have already seen partly represented in the Oriental sources of Gnosticism. The six roots, together with the indefinite power which is their source, remind us of the six Amshaspands of the Persian theosophy, with Ormuzd, their source, as a seventh. The perfect man, the completion of all the Divine powers, corresponds to some extent with the Adam Kadmon of the Kabbala; and the relation of these roots or powers, half of which are represented as female, to the indefinite power which gave rise to them and to the perfect man who is the image of that power, illustrates the position assigned in other notices to Simon as the so-called representative of the Father of all things, and to Helena, under whose form is concealed the first Ennoia or Conception sprung from the Father. But there is another singular feature of this mystic rhapsody which we may doubt whether to refer to an Oriental or to a Greek source, and that is the concrete and physical description of the primitive power under the name of *fire*. Hippolytus notices the analogy in this respect between Simon's philosophy and that of Heraclitus,[1] and it is quite possible that the Samaritan magus may have followed the philosopher of Ephesus in introducing a theory of metaphysical pantheism under the imagery borrowed from the phenomena exhibited by the material element. But we may also remember that the Persian religious philosophy contrasts the good and evil principles under the forms of *light* and *darkness*, and that its disciples, if not literally, as they are commonly called, fire-worshippers, at least regarded fire as an emblem of the Divine power.[2] But whatever may be the origin of the theory, its whole tenor leads to the conclusion that the *fire* of which it speaks is

---

[1] Hippolytus, *Ref. Hær.* vi. 9.
[2] Max Müller, *Chips from a German Workshop* I. p. 169.

not to be understood literally but figuratively, as the emblem of some spiritual force, the several moments of whose development are supposed to explain the real nature of the universe. Thus interpreted, the theory bears a strong resemblance to that scheme of logico-metaphysical pantheism which formed the culminating point of the German spiritual philosophy of the last generation,[1] and which has been strangely enough revived in connection with a materialistic hypothesis by a recent writer in our own country;[2] the scheme which represents the Divine nature in the form of a universal process passing through successive stages of lower development, and finally becoming conscious in man.

One continuous fragment of the Ἀπόφασις Μεγάλη has been preserved by Hippolytus, in which the above theory is exhibited in the author's own language. I will not say that a literal translation will make the above exposition more intelligible; but in this respect Simon Magus (if he be indeed the author of the work) only shares the fate of some of his German followers in recent times. Simon, we are told, speaks expressly in his 'Announcement' as follows: 'Now I say to you that which I say, and write that which I write. The scheme is this: There are two offshoots of the perfect ages,[3] having neither beginning nor end, from one root, which is the invisible, incomprehensible Power, Silence; of which one is manifested from above, the great Power, Intellect (νοῦς) of the universe, that administers all things, the

---

[1] In reading Möller's German exposition of the theory, we might almost fancy, were the Greek citations omitted, that we were reading an extract from Hegel.

[2] Bray, *On Force* p. 75..

[3] τῶν ὅλων αἰώνων, *i.e.* probably *of eternity*. The term αἰῶνες seems to be used in the same sense in which God is called ὁ βασιλεὺς τῶν αἰώνων, 1 Tim. i. 17 (cf. ὁ Θεὸς τῶν αἰώνων, Ecclus. xxxvi. 17), meaning αἰῶνες τῶν αἰώνων, the aggregate of the ages, or *eternity*. Cf. Ellicott and Alford on 1 Tim. i. 17. See also Burton, *B. L.* p. 110.

Male Principle; and the other from beneath, vast Thought (ἐπίνοια), generative of all things, the Female Principle; whence in mutual correspondence (ἀντιστοιχοῦντες) they combine in consort, and exhibit the mean space as an immense atmosphere, having neither beginning nor end. But within it is the Father that upholds and sustains all things that have beginning and end. This is he who standeth, who stood, who will stand (ὁ ἑστώς, στάς, στησόμενος), being a bisexual power (ἀρσενόθηλυς δύναμις), the reflex of the pre-existent indefinite power, still subsisting in solitude, which hath neither beginning nor end; for from him, Thought subsisting in solitude, emanating, made two. Yet he was one, for having her within himself, he was alone, not in truth first, howbeit pre-existent, but himself, manifested from himself, became second. But neither was he called Father, before his Thought so named him. As therefore evolving himself from himself he revealed to himself his own Thought, so also the revealed Thought acted not [otherwise],[1] but seeing him, she hid within herself the Father, which is the power; and thus Thought also is a bisexual power; so that in this way they mutually correspond (for Power differs in no respect from Thought), being one. Power is found to be from above, Thought from beneath. It is thus that the manifestation also emanating from them, being one, is found to be two, a bisexual, having the female within itself. He is Intellect in Thought, and these being separated from each other,[2] being one, are found to be two.'[3]

If we adhere to the distinction pointed out in a pre-

---

[1] οὐκ ἐποίησεν. Harvey conjectures ἐποίησεν ἄλλως.

[2] ἃ χωριστὰ ἀπ' ἀλλήλων, the reading of Duncker and Schneidewin. Miller's text reads ἀχώριστα, rendered by Harvey, 'Being one inseparably from each other.'

[3] Hippol. *Ref. Hær.* vi. 18. The translation is chiefly taken from Harvey, *Irenæus* Introd. p. lxvii.

vious lecture between heresy properly so called and a merely unchristian or antichristian philosophy,[1] it is not easy to assign to the system of Simon (and the same may be said of that of his successor Menander) a definite position in the one class or the other. On the one hand, the conception of a redemption, of a Divine interposition to deliver the world from the dominion of evil, a conception common to Christianity and to the later forms of Gnosticism, and which distinguished both from heathen systems of philosophy, is also present, though in a grossly perverted form, in the teaching of Simon. The material world is the work of, and is under the dominion of, rebellious powers; a divine power descends from above, in a seemingly human form, to effect its deliverance. But on the other hand, this doctrine differs widely even from the most depraved of the later Gnostic systems, in that the heaven-sent deliverer is not Jesus, but Simon himself. There is no recognition of the person and work of Jesus Christ as the Redeemer, save in so far as an inferior and imperfect mission is ascribed to Him, subordinate to that claimed by Simon for himself. Were it not that the office of Christ, however degraded and distorted, is still that of a Redeemer, and not merely of a teacher, we should be disposed to say that the relation of Simon's teaching to that of Christianity more nearly resembles that afterwards assumed by Mahommedanism than that of any sect pretending to the name of Christian. Simon however is a false Christ; not merely a false prophet. If we admit his system to a place among the Gnostic heresies, it is not because it has any pretension to the name even of a heretical Christianity; but partly because it borrows, while it perverts, the Christian idea of Redemption, which the later Gnostics also adopted in a less perverted form, and partly

[1] See above, Lecture I.

because the heathen ideas upon which its metaphysical speculations are based were transmitted by it to the later systems, and constitute an historical as well as a philosophical link of connection between them.[1]

The personal history of Simon Magus, after he disappears from the narrative of the Acts of the Apostles, has assumed various traditional forms, all of these having more or less of a legendary character, though possibly with some fragment of real history imbedded in them. Hegesippus, the earliest ecclesiastical writer by whom his name is mentioned, speaks of him merely as one of the heretics proceeding from the Jewish sects, among whom he reckons the Samaritans.[2] As we proceed to later writers, the notices of Simon become more definite. His countryman, Justin Martyr, tells us that he came to Rome during the reign of Claudius, and obtained such a reputation by his magical powers that he was believed to be a god, and had a statue raised to him on the river Tiber, between the two bridges, with a Latin inscription, *Simoni Deo Sancto*. He adds that Simon is still honoured by nearly all the Samaritans as the first God, and his companion Helena as his first Conception.[3] The story of the statue, which is repeated by Irenæus, Tertullian, and others,[4] has been much discredited in modern times by the

---

[1] Mosheim (*De Rebus Christ. ante Const.* § 65) altogether excludes Simon from the list of Gnostic heretics as being an open enemy of Christianity. He is followed by Neander (*Church History* II. p. 123) and by Dorner (*Person of Christ* vol. I. p. 186, and note v). Bunsen on the other hand (*Hippolytus*, vol. I. p. 54), recognises Simon as a heretical Christian, but on an erroneous interpretation of his doctrine; and Burton (*B. L.* pp. 87–90, and note 38) admits him by taking a wider view of the nature of heresy. The view adopted in the text is intermediate between these opposite judgments.

[2] Hegesippus in Eusebius, *H. E.* iv. 22.

[3] Justin Martyr, *Apol.* i. c. 27 (cf. c. 56), and Euseb. *H. E.* ii. 13.

[4] Cf. Burton, *B. L.* p. 374. He cites Irenæus, i. 23; Tertullian, *Apol.* 13; Theodoret, *Hær. Fab.* i. 1; Cyril. Hieros. *Catechen.* vi. 14; Augustin. *De Hær.* 1, vol. VIII. p. 6.

discovery in the year 1574, on the island in the Tiber, of a fragment of marble bearing an inscription commencing *Semoni Sanco Deo Fidio Sacrum*.[1] Hence the majority of modern critics have supposed that Justin mistook an inscription to the Sabine deity, Semo Sancus, for one to Simon the holy God.[2] Justin's account has nevertheless found many learned defenders, but it is, to say the least, liable to suspicion from the fact that Hippolytus, who lived in the immediate neighbourhood of Rome, who was a suffragan bishop of the Roman Church, who was well acquainted with the treatise of Irenæus, and has copied word for word a considerable portion of his account of Simon, makes no mention of this statue.[3] A still stranger story, and of later origin, is the popular tradition concerning the manner of Simon's death. It is said that while St. Peter and St. Paul were at Rome, Simon, in order to delude the people into a belief in his pretensions, caused himself to be raised into the air by two demons in a chariot of fire, but that the two Apostles having united in prayer against him, the impostor was deserted by his demons, and fell to the ground, breaking both his legs by the fall, after which he destroyed himself through shame and vexation, by throwing himself from the top of a house.[4] The earliest writer in whom we can trace any allusion to this story is Arnobius, in the beginning of the fourth century; and Eusebius, who wrote some years afterwards, evidently knows nothing of it.[5] It was known to Greek writers by the middle of the fourth century, as it

---

[1] Cf. Burton, *B. L.* p. 375. The full inscription is SEMONI SANCO DEO FIDIO SACRUM SEX. POMPEIUS SP. F. COL. MUSSIANUS QUINQUENNALIS DECUR. BIDENTALIS DONUM DEDIT.

[2] For the names of modern writers, who deny or defend the truth of Justin's story, see Burton, *B. L.* pp. 377, 378.

[3] Cf. Bunsen, *Hippolytus* vol. I. p. 52.

[4] Cf. Burton, *B. L.* pp. 94, 371.

[5] Cf. Arnobius, *Adv. Gent.* ii. 12, compared with Euseb. *H. E.* ii. 13; and see Burton, *B. L.* p. 95.

appears with full particulars in the 'Catecheses' of Cyril of Jerusalem, and in the so-called 'Apostolical Constitutions,' which may have been compiled about the same time or a little earlier.[1] Here again the recently recovered treatise of Hippolytus, who wrote nearly a century earlier than Arnobius, refutes the marvellous tradition by giving another and wholly different account of Simon's death. 'He announced,' says Hippolytus, 'that if he were buried alive, he would rise again on the third day. And accordingly, having ordered a trench to be dug by his disciples, he gave directions that he should be buried therein. They then did as they were commanded, but he remained away from them unto this day: for he was not the Christ.'[2]

This story may perhaps agree with the later tradition in attributing the death of Simon to the failure of some trick which he had contrived to support his credit; but in the actual circumstances recorded it is wholly different, and certainly far more probable.[3] Other marvellous narratives of Simon are told in the pseudonymous works known as the Clementine Homilies and Recognitions—works themselves of a Gnostic character, though entirely opposed to the teaching of Simon. Of these we shall give an account in a future lecture.

The doctrine of Menander, the disciple and immediate successor of Simon, was of the same antichristian character, his own name however being substituted for that of his master. Menander, like Simon, was a Samaritan by

[1] Cyril. Hieros. *Catech.* vi. 15; *Const. Apost.* vi. 9. Burton (*B. L.* p. 371) regards the Constitutions as a work of the fourth century. Mansi (*Concil.* I. p. 256) places them between 309 and 325. Some critics place them at the end of the third century, others as (Ussher and Tillemont) as late as the sixth. See Jacobson's Article, 'Apost. Constitutionen' in Herzog, I. p. 449.

[2] Hippol. *Ref. Hær.* vi. 20.

[3] Cf. Harvey, *Irenæus* Introd. p. lxix.

birth,[1] and is said even to have surpassed his master in magical prodigies.[2] He maintained, like Simon, that the world was made by angels, the offspring of the Ennoia or Conception, and that he himself was sent from the unseen supreme power, to deliver men from their dominion by means of the magic which he taught. He is also said to have instituted a form of baptism in his own name, which he called the resurrection, and to have asserted that those who received it would be exempt from old age and death.[3] A promise of this kind, if it was ever made, would admit of being very soon tested by facts, and accordingly the sect of the Menandrians seems to have soon become extinct, while the followers of Simon, though with diminished numbers, lingered on to the sixth century.[4] The antichristian sects founded by Simon and Menander may be regarded as precursors of Gnosticism properly so called. Of some of the early forms of the latter heresy I shall give an account in my next lecture.

---

[1] Irenæus, i. 23; Justin Mart. *Apol.* i. c. 26.

[2] μείζοσιν ἐπιδαψιλεύεται τερατολογίαις, Euseb. iii. 26. Epiphanius, *Hær.* xxii. 1, says that Menander gave himself out as a greater person than Simon.

[3] Irenæus, i. 23. Cf. Justin Mart. *Apol.* i. c. 26.

[4] Herzog's *Encyklopädie*, Art. 'Menander.' Origen (*c. Cels.* i. 57) doubts whether there were in his time as many as thirty Simonians in the world.

LECTURE VII.

THE OPHITE SECTS.

IN regarding Simon Magus as the earliest teacher of Gnostic principles, we follow the almost unanimous testimony of those Fathers who have spoken on the subject, as well as the probable chronology suggested by the early mention of him in the Acts of the Apostles. As the first meeting between him and St. Peter must be placed, at the latest, not more than seven years after our Lord's ascension, it is scarcely possible that any heretical system can have arisen at an earlier date under any Christian influence. Yet though the foundation of Simon's teaching was laid thus early, it is probable that his complete system may have been matured several years later, and that other heretical sects may have come into notice contemporary with, or in some respects earlier than his doctrine in its complete development. This supposition may perhaps serve to explain the circumstance that Hippolytus, who professes to treat of the several heresies in the order of their appearance, commences his account with certain sects which he places before Simon Magus and seems to consider as the earliest Gnostics.[1] It is also probable that some of these sects may have been of Jewish or heathen origin, and may have engrafted some ideas borrowed from

---

[1] Cf. Bunsen, *Hippolytus* I. p. 39. Yet it is quite certain that many of the details of the Ophite teaching, as given by Hippolytus, belong to a later date.

Christianity on tenets existing from an earlier date, and this may perhaps account for the apparently conflicting statements which have been made concerning their chronological position, some writers considering them even earlier than Christianity, while others postpone them to the beginning of the second century.[1]

These sects, to take them in the order in which they are mentioned by Hippolytus, are the Naasseni, the Peratæ, the Sethiani, and the followers of one Justin, who of course must not be confounded with the Christian apologist and martyr of the same name in the second century. The first of these sects, he says, compiled their heresies from principles borrowed from the Greek philosophers and the teachers of the mysteries; the second from astrology; the third from Musæus, Linus, and Orpheus; and the fourth from the marvels narrated by Herodotus.[2] All of these however must be regarded as branches of the Ophite heresy, the serpent being a principal figure with all.

The Naassenes derived their name from the Hebrew word *Naash* (נחש) which signifies *a serpent*; afterwards they assumed the name of Gnostics, professing that they alone had knowledge of the depths.[3] The veneration of the serpent, from which their appellation as well as that of the Ophite generally is derived, was but the logical development of a theory, the germ of which is common to many of the Gnostic sects. Proceeding on the assumption that the Creator of the world is to be regarded as an evil power, acting in hostility to the supreme God, it follows, as a natural consequence, that the fall of man through

---

[1] Cf. Neander, *Church History* II. p. 112; Baur, *Christliche Gnosis* p. 196.

[2] Hippol. v. 2-5.

[3] φάσκοντες μόνοι τὰ βάθη γινώ- σκειν, Hippol. v. 6. May not this conjunction of the *serpent* and the *depths* be referred to by St. John, Rev. ii. 24 οἵτινες οὐκ ἔγνωσαν τὰ βάθεα τοῦ σατανᾶ?

disobedience to the command of his Maker must be regarded, not as a transgression against the will of the Supreme God, but as an emancipation from the authority of an evil being. The serpent therefore, who tempted mankind to sin, is no longer their destroyer but their benefactor; he is the symbol of intellect,[1] by whose means the first human pair were raised to the knowledge of the existence of higher beings than their Creator. This conception, consistently carried out, would have resulted in a direct inversion of the whole teaching of Scripture; in calling evil good, and good evil; in converting Satan into God, and God into Satan. The majority of the Ophite sects however seem to have shrunk from this portentous blasphemy; while acknowledging the fall of man as in some manner a deliverance from evil and an exaltation of human nature, they hesitated to carry out their principle by investing the evil spirit with the attributes of deity. A kind of compromise was made between Scripture and philosophy; the serpent was, notwithstanding his service to mankind, represented as a being of evil nature and an enemy to man, though his work was overruled to man's good, and he himself was, beyond his intention, the instrument of a higher wisdom. But in one sect at least of the Ophites, the more logical and thoroughly blasphemous consequences of their first principles were exhibited, as we shall see, openly and unblushingly.

The assumption, which appears to have been common to all the Ophite sects, was the representation of the highest principle of all things as a Spiritual Man, answering to the Adam Kadmon of the Jewish Kabbala.[2]

---

[1] 'Nun in figura serpentis contortum;' Irenæus, i. 30. 5.

[2] Irenæus, i. 30. 1; Hippol. v. 6. The first principle, according to Hippolytus, is bisexual (ἀρσενόθηλυς), and the second principle may thus have been introduced to form a pair with the third. This seems to have been overlooked by Irenæus.

With him is associated a second principle, called the Son, also known by the name of Ἔννοια, which however does not, as in the teaching of Simon, denote a feminine principle, but a second spiritual man. The feminine principle occupies the third place, and, if we may accept the account of Irenæus, was known as the Spirit; and below and distinct from these principles existed a chaos of material elements. It is impossible to overlook in this representation a profane parody of the Christian doctrine of the Holy Trinity; and, offensive as are some of the details of the theory, it is at least valuable as testifying to the primitive existence of that article of the Catholic faith from which it is borrowed. The theory then proceeds to declare how the union of these spiritual principles gave rise to a fourth spiritual being, whom they called Christ, and indirectly a feminine principle called Sophia or Prunikos,[1] who forms an intermediate link between the spiritual Pleroma of Divine beings and the material world with its Creator. Sophia is represented as sinking down to the material chaos, and giving birth to a son called Ialdabaoth,[2] who in his turn becomes the parent of six successive generations of angels, himself being the seventh, and forming in conjunction with Sophia an ogdoad. Ialdabaoth and his angels are the artificers of the material world and the rulers of the seven planets.

The above account, which is abridged from Irenæus, seems to represent the general principles which, with some slight differences of detail, were common to the various Ophite sects. But at this point, at which the

---

[1] προύνεικος λαγνείας ὑποφαίνει τὸ ἐπώνυμον, Epiphanius, *Hær.* xxv. 4; cf. Petavius on this place. For other explanations cf. Harvey, *Irenæus* I. p. 225.

[2] This name has been variously interpreted by conjecture. Gass, in Herzog, Art. 'Ophiten,' interprets it as יַלְדָּא בְהוּת ('son of Chaos'). Harvey (*Irenæus* I. p. 230) suggests יְהֲ־אֵל־דִּאָבְהוֹת, 'Dominus Deus Patrum.'

serpent, the principal figure in their systems, is introduced, the different theories branch off into the most curious and discordant forms of representation. According to one statement, the serpent is the offspring of Ialdabaoth the Demiurge, in conjunction with the dregs of matter, and is employed by Sophia Prunikos to tempt Adam and Eve to transgress the command of the Demiurge, the latter having designed by means of Eve to deprive Adam of the breath of life, or spiritual intelligence and thought, which he had unwittingly conferred upon him. For thus thwarting his father's designs, the serpent is cast out from heaven, together with Adam and Eve (the Ophite Paradise seems to have been placed in the celestial regions); and from henceforth the serpent and his offspring became the enemies of mankind in revenge for the expulsion which they had suffered on their account.[1] Another version of the legend makes the serpent to be identical with Sophia herself, and to have bestowed knowledge upon man out of hostility to the Demiurge.[2]

Another division of this school seems to have identified the serpent with the Word or Divine Son, and made him, like Philo's Logos, the intermediate link between the Supreme God and matter.[3] They also, perverting our Lord's language to Nicodemus, identified him with the brazen serpent in the wilderness, with the rod of Moses which became a serpent, and with the constellation *Draco* in the heavens. Another sect seems to have identified the serpent, first with the winds, on account of its hissing sound; and then, playing upon the language of Scripture, with the creative spirit moving on the face of the waters;

[1] Irenæus, i. 30. 8.
[2] Irenæus, i. 30. 15. According to Neander (*Ch. Hist.* II. p. 110) this portion of the sect are Ophites proper, the worshippers of the serpent.
[3] These were the Peratæ of Hippolytus, v. 16, 17.

and finally, with the Divine Word, who assumed the form of the Serpent-Creator to deliver the intellectual man from his original bondage.[1] Another sect,[2] apparently representing in a mythical form the Persian doctrine of two principles, placed the serpent among the original ungenerated causes of the universe, as part of a compound being, half woman and half snake, from the human portion of which proceeded certain good angels and mankind, and from the serpentine portion evil angels and the brute creation. One of these evil angels again inherits the serpent nature, and is identified with the tree of knowledge and connected with the introduction of evil into the earth. The boldest and most consistent of the Ophite sects, in the development of their blasphemous principle to its legitimate consequences, were the Cainites. This sect, if we may trust the accounts which have come down to us concerning them, carried out to its minutest details the monstrous assumption that, the God of the Old Testament being an evil being, all that is condemned in that book is to be regarded as good, and all that is approved as evil.[3] Those characters who in Scripture are expressly held up to reprobation as examples of rebellion and disobedience to God—Cain as the leader, the men of Sodom, Esau, Korah— were proclaimed by this sect as their heroes and kindred. Cain and Abel were the offspring of antagonistic spiritual

---

[1] This seems to have been the view of the Sethians, according to Hippolytus, v. 19.

[2] The followers of Justin the Gnostic; see Hippolytus, v. 26. The female monster of this legend is considered by Hippolytus to have been borrowed from the fable told by Herodotus, iv. 9.

[3] Epiphan. *Hær.* xxxviii. 2 διδάσκουσι δὲ ταῦτα καὶ τὰ τοιαῦτα, τοὺς πονηροὺς τιμῶντες καὶ τοὺς ἀγαθοὺς ἀπαγορεύοντες. Cf. Baur, *Die Chr. Gnosis* p. 198 *seq.* Lardner (*Hist. of Heretics*, bk. ii. ch. xiv.) doubts altogether the existence of the Cainites, and supposes the notion of their having existed to have arisen from the Sethites speaking of others metaphorically as children of Cain, as does St. Jude. But Lardner does not see the so-called philosophical principle of which the Cainite heresy is the legitimate development, and therefore sets aside the testimonies on the subject on *à priori* grounds of incredibility.

powers; Cain of the stronger and better, Abel of the weaker and worse. Cain and his successors were the true martyrs, whom the ruler of this world persecuted, but could not finally hurt, for the higher wisdom took them to herself.[1] In consistency with the same teaching, their favourite character in the New Testament was Judas Iscariot. He alone of the Apostles had the knowledge to perceive the true character of Christ's mission to complete by His death the overthrow of the God of the Jews and the victory of the superior power, and therefore he betrayed the Saviour to His death, that this good work might be the more speedily accomplished. They went so far as to compile a sacred book for their own use, which they called the Gospel of Judas—a work which is happily lost, but whose character may be imagined from the tenets of its authors. Their moral practice, unless they are greatly belied, was precisely what might be expected from their theory.[2]

The Sethites, or Sethiani, one of the sects of which I have already spoken as mentioned by Hippolytus, were the antagonists of the Cainites thus far, that they acknowledged the ordinary principles of morality, and selected Seth instead of Cain as their example of the higher human nature. But, as Ophites, they agreed with their antagonists in a common hostility to the Creator of the world. Seth, and the spiritual men of whom he is the leader, were inspired by the *Sophia*, as her instrument, to counteract the work of the Demiurge. The same wisdom sought to destroy the evil race of mankind through the deluge, and to preserve Noah as the father of a spiritual race; but her efforts were thwarted by the powers of the world, who introduced Ham into the ark, and thus continued the evil along with the good.[3] The contest between

---

[1] Irenæus, i. 31; Epiphan. *Hær.* xxxviii. 1.

[2] Irenæus, *l. c.*; Epiphanius, *l. c.*

[3] Epiphan. *Hær.* xxxix. 2, 3.

the powers of good and evil thus continued till the coming of Christ, who, according to these heretics, is no other than Seth himself, sent again upon the earth by Sophia for the completion of her work.

Of the other two Ophite sects mentioned by Hippolytus, the Peratæ have been already alluded to as those who identified the serpent with the Divine Word. They are described as the followers of a certain Euphrates, called ὁ Περατικός, by which is probably meant a Chaldean,[1] and Celbes a Carystian, probably from Carystus in Eubœa. Hippolytus gives many details of their astrological theories, all of which seem to point to Chaldæa, the great seat of astrology, as the source, if not of the original doctrine, at least of many of the subsequent accretions which distinguish this heresy. Justin the Gnostic, of whom nothing was known before the discovery of the work of Hippolytus, seems to have been an early teacher of the Ophite doctrines, who wrote a work called the Book of Baruch for the use of his disciples—Baruch being the name of one of the twelve good angels who form an important feature in his system. From internal evidence we may probably conjecture that this book was written subsequently to the Gospel of St. John,[2] though it is probably an early work of the second century. In it the Ophite principles are mixed up with a wild legend from the Greek mythology, and with a strange allegorical interpretation of the early part of Genesis. In common with Cerinthus, with whom he was probably nearly

---

[1] The most probable derivation seems to be from פְּרָת, the Hebrew name of Euphrates, which makes it doubtful whether the so-called founder Euphrates is not a mythical personage. Cf. Harvey's *Irenæus* I. p. lxxxvii; Matter, *Hist. du Gnosticisme* I. p. 257.

[2] The words which are attributed to Jesus on the cross, Γύναι, ἀπέχεις σου τὸν υἱόν (Hippol. v. 26, p. 228, 41) seem to be a perversion of John xix. 26.

contemporary, he regarded Jesus as the son of Joseph and Mary, called to his Divine mission by the angel Baruch.[1]

The Ophite heresies, shocking as are many of the details of their systems, are, as regards their general principle, so far less antichristian than the schools of Simon Magus and Menander, that they at least recognise Jesus Christ as the central figure in their teachings, and attribute to Him, in however perverted a form, some kind of work which they regard as a redemption. But they differ from the majority of the Gnostic sects in making the work of redemption begin with the creation of man, the work of Christ being only the last act in a series of struggles carried on between the Divine Wisdom and the corrupt Demiurge.[2] The carrying out of the idea involves such a complete inversion of Christian doctrine, that, instead of a Saviour who delivers mankind from the curse of the Fall and bruises the head of the serpent, we have represented one whose saving work consists in perfecting that which the Fall began, who acts in common with the serpent as a minister of the Divine Wisdom, and, according to one form of the teaching, is even identified with the serpent himself. The fundamental principle of the Ophite theory is undoubtedly of Jewish origin. The names of their mythology are clearly Hebrew. The serpent from which they derived their name is the serpent of the Book of Genesis, the tempter of man; and in all the various and discordant phases of their teaching we may trace some kind of perversion of the Mosaic narrative. But upon this Jewish foundation was erected a superstructure, the materials for which were collected promiscuously from every form of

[1] Hippol. v. 26 (p. 226, 26. Duncker).
[2] Cf. Baur, *Die Chr. Gnosis* p. 199 *seq.*

heathen superstition. The Phrygian orgies of Cybele, the Phœnician and Assyrian mysteries of Adonis, the Egyptian rites of Osiris and Isis, the secret doctrines of Eleusis, the dualism of Persia, the astrology of Chaldæa, the fables of Greek mythology, the poetic cosmogony of the Platonic Timæus,[1] all find a place in that comprehensive farrago which marks the Ophites as the most syncretic of heretics.[2] The exact date of these several accretions, and of the consequent development of the different Ophite sects, it is impossible to determine, though the balance of probability seems to incline in favour of the supposition that a certain amount of Judaism and heathenism in combination may have formed the basis of their teaching a short time before the Christian era, and that Christianity, along with fresh accumulations of heathenism, contributed the materials for a superstructure gradually erected on this foundation.[3] The primary conception which underlies all phases of their teaching—that of the antagonism of a good and an evil principle, applied to the Mosaic narrative of the Creation and the Fall—may have been the produce of an apostate Judaism in connection with Parsism; but the great stimulus to the development of their systems must have been given by Christian influences,[4] corrupted, as the Gospel was preached to the dispersed Jews in different lands, by the several mythologies with which they were in contact.

The first appearance of the Ophite heresy in connection with Christian doctrines can hardly be placed later than the latter part of the first century.[5] The Naassenes,

---

[1] Hippolytus, v. 7, 8. Cf. Baur, *Die Chr. Gnosis* p. 196.

[2] Cf. Harvey, *Irenæus* I. p. lxxxvi.

[3] Cf. Neander, *Ch. Hist.* II. p. 112; Baur, *Die Chr. Gnosis* p. 196.

[4] The doctrine of the Trinity appears in a perverted form in all their speculations.

[5] Cf. Baur, *Das Christenthum der drei ersten Jahrh.* 1853, p. 176. He considers that the oldest Gnostic sects are those which do not bear the name of an individual founder, but only one representing Gnostic ideas,

the earliest sect according to the arrangement of Hippolytus, are spoken of by him as the first body who assumed the name of *Gnostics*; and the reason which he assigns for this assumption, μετὰ δὲ ταῦτα ἐπεκάλεσαν ἑαυτοὺς γνωστικούς, φάσκοντες μόνοι τὰ βάθη γινώσκειν,[1] combined as it is with an earlier name derived from the serpent, and their reverence for that being, can hardly fail to remind us of the words of St. John in the Apocalypse; 'But unto you I say, and unto the rest in Thyatira, as many as have not this doctrine and which have not known the depths of Satan as they speak (οἵτινες οὐκ ἔγνωσαν τὰ βάθεα τοῦ σατανᾶ, ὡς λέγουσιν).'[2] From this language we may, I think, infer the existence of an Ophite sect, boasting of its peculiar gnosis before the date of the Apocalypse. On the other hand, the abundant use made by the Naassenes of the Epistles of St. Paul[3] seems to imply that their acquaintance with Christianity was derived from the teaching of that Apostle; and the intermixture of this teaching with legends derived from the Phrygian worship of Cybele seems naturally to refer us to that second Apostolical journey, in which St. Paul went throughout Phrygia and the region of Galatia.[4] The date of St. Paul's first visit to this region may be placed in the year 51 or 52, and that of his second visit in 54;[5] and the rise of the Naassene heresy may therefore probably be placed somewhere between this period and the latter part of the reign of Domitian. The supposition that Ophite doctrines were in existence as a pretended Christian philosophy,

and specifies the Ophites as of this class. It is probable however, that some of the details recorded by Hippolytus represent a later development. Cf. Milman, *Hist. of Christianity* II. p. 83.

[1] Hippol. *Ref. Hær.* v. 6.
[2] Rev. ii. 24.
[3] See the quotations in Hippolytus, v. 7.
[4] Acts xvi. 6. For a second visit, during his third journey, cf. Acts xviii. 23.
[5] Cf. Lightfoot on *Galatians* pp. 22, 24.

and were exercising a corrupting influence on the Church at the date of the Apocalypse, gives an additional significance to a later passage of the same book, in which the Apostle describes the casting out from heaven of the great dragon, 'that old serpent, called the Devil, and Satan, which deceiveth the whole world.'[1]

Notwithstanding the dualism which appears on the surface of the Ophite representation of the struggle between Sophia and Ialdabaoth, we find lurking at the foundation of the theory a conception which, if not identical with pantheism, admits of an easy development into it. The Sophia Prunikos, the great agent in all that goes on in the world, is in fact a mythical representation of the soul of the universe;[2] and, though the relation in which this principle stands to a primitive material chaos prevents us from identifying it with the universe, it nevertheless appears as the one active principle to which all that takes place in the world may ultimately be traced. Ialdabaoth, the antagonistic power, is an emanation from the Sophia, and all the powers deriving their being from him are remotely emanations from the same source. The inert mass of matter plays a merely passive part in the theory; that which forms the central point of it is the doctrine of a mundane soul, the source of all spiritual life, which attracts to itself whatever has emanated from it.[3] The end moreover of the redemption by Christ has a similar pantheistic character. Jesus after his resurrection ascends into heaven and sits on the right hand, not of the Divine Father, but of Ialdabaoth the Demiurge; his office being to draw to himself, unobserved by the latter, all the souls that are purified by the redemption and released from the tabernacle of sense. In proportion as

[1] Rev. xii. 9.
[2] Cf. Neander, *Church History*
II. p. 107.
[3] Neander, *l. c.*

Jesus becomes enriched in his own spirit by this attraction to himself of kindred natures, Ialdabaoth is deprived of his higher virtues, and is finally stripped of all intelligence and power, when the spiritual life confined in nature is fully emancipated, and once more absorbed into the mundane soul from which it originally emanated.[1]

Viewed in this light as an imperfectly developed scheme of pantheism, the Ophite theory acquires a new interest and importance when we see one of its principal features reproduced in the philosophical pantheism of a later age. The πρῶτον ψεῦδος, the fundamental and ineradicable error of pantheism, that of ignoring the difference between good and evil, disguised in Ophism under the image of an evil emanating from good as a transient phenomenon in the action of the mundane soul, appears in a more logical form in the representation which, by making evil a necessary moment in the rhythm of existence, deprives it of all that makes it evil, and even gives it the name of good.

After contemplating the Ophite theory of the fall of man as a stage in the process of his elevation to spiritual life, we are startled to come across the same representation in the writings of a philosopher who stands at the head of German thought in the last generation, and whose genius, doing all that man could do to adorn with Christian embellishment a conception essentially pantheistic, has, consciously or unconsciously, succeeded only in reproducing this wildest of the disordered dreams of heathen Gnosticism. 'The state of innocence,' says Hegel, ' in which there is for man no distinction between good and evil, is the state of the brute, the unconsciousness in which man knows nothing of good nor yet of evil, when

[1] Neander, *Church History* II. p. 111; cf. Irenæus, i, 30. 14.

that which he wills is not determined as the one or the other; for if he knows nothing of evil, he also knows nothing of good.' . . . 'We find,' he continues, 'in the Bible a representation called in an abstract manner the Fall—a representation which in its great depth is not a mere accidental history, but the eternal, necessary history of mankind represented in an external mythical manner.'[1] We are further told that 'it is the eternal history of the freedom of man, that he comes forth from the deadness of his first years, that he advances nearer to the light of consciousness, that good and evil have both an existence for him;' and hence that 'the loss of Paradise must be regarded as a Divine necessity;' and that, as necessitated to come to an end, this representation of Paradise sinks down to a 'moment of the Divine totality which is not the absolutely true.'[2] I do not mean to extend this parallel beyond the point which I have mentioned, or to deny the vast intellectual and moral gulf which separates the profound if misdirected speculations of the German philosopher from the undigested syncretism and immoral ravings of the Ophites. But the parallel, so far as it is admissible, may be pardoned for the sake of the moral lesson which it teaches—a lesson never more needed than at the present time. Every attempt to represent the course of the world, including man as a part of the world, in the form of a necessary evolution, or of a series of phenomena governed by necessary laws, whether it take the pantheistic form which represents human action as part of a Divine process, or the materialistic form which reduces it to an inevitable sequence of consequent upon antecedent, must, as the very condition of its existence, ignore the distinction between good and evil (except as in

---

[1] *Philosophie der Religion* (*Werke* XI. p. 269).
[2] *Ibid.* pp. 271, 272.

their consequences, not in themselves), and must annihilate the idea of sin, which is not a consequence, but a transgression of God's law. Let no philosophy be trusted, however tempting its promises, however great its apparent success, which does not distinctly recognise the two great correlative ideas of a personal God, and a personal, that is, a free-willing, man. With these, its efforts, however feeble, may be true as far as they go; without these, its most brilliant seeming achievements are at the bottom a mockery and an imposture.

LECTURE VIII.

CERINTHUS—CARPOCRATES—THE NAZARENES AND EBIONITES.

THE heresies which we have hitherto been examining exhibit two opposite and equally fatal errors in relation to the Person of Christ: the one the denial of His proper Humanity, the other the denial of His proper Divinity. Simon Magus, as we have seen, though the central figure of his system was not Jesus but himself, yet represented our Lord as in some degree his precursor, and distinctly asserted that He appeared in the form of a man, not being really a man, and seemed to suffer, not having really suffered.[1] The Ophites on the other hand, at least one portion of them, distinctly asserted that Jesus, as regards his original nature, was a mere man, the son of Joseph and Mary; that the Christ was a separate spiritual being who descended upon him at his baptism and left him before his passion: and they are said to have asserted in proof of this theory that no miracles are recorded as having been wrought by him either before his baptism or after his resurrection.[2]

---

[1] Irenæus, i. 23. 3; Hippolytus, vi. 19 (p. 254, Duncker).

[2] Hippolytus, v. 26, says of the followers of Justin the Gnostic (a branch of the Ophites) that they regarded Jesus as the son of Joseph and Mary. Others of the Ophites seem to have acknowledged His supernatural birth of a virgin (Irenæus, i. 30. 12). Still they regarded Jesus as a man distinct from the spiritual power Christ, and alleged the absence of miracles before His baptism and after His resurrection in proof of this (Irenæus, i. 30. 14). The miraculous draught of fishes, John xxi, refutes the latter assertion. Perhaps the miracles of the Gospel of the Infancy were forged to refute the former.

Both these heresies were the natural result of one and the same principle—a principle which before the Christian era had become dominant in the Græco-Jewish philosophy of Alexandria, and which, as that philosophy came in contact with the preaching of the Gospel, found a ready application in relation to the Person of Christ. The principle in question is that which regards matter as eventually evil and the source of all evil, and which consequently found itself at once placed in direct antagonism to the Christian belief in a real Incarnation of the Redeemer. Two possible modes of evasion would naturally suggest themselves, by means of which a kind of nominal Christianity might be professed without the admission of the fundamental doctrine. The bolder and simpler resource was plainly to declare that the body of Christ was a phantom and not a reality, and this gave rise to the heresy of Docetism. A subtler and less violent device was to distinguish between the spiritual Redeemer and the human Person in whom He was manifested; regarding them as two separate and incommunicable personalities, which might for a time be in juxtaposition with each other, yet remaining wholly distinct, as water is distinct from the vessel in which for a time it is contained. This was a doctrine common to many of the Gnostic sects, its coarsest and crudest form being found in the mere humanitarianism of the Ebionites.

I have already pointed out the notices of the existence of the Docetic heresy in the Apostolic age, which may be gathered from the New Testament. The names of its teachers in that age subsequently to Simon Magus are not known (unless indeed Hymenæus and Philetus, whose theory of the resurrection was quite in accordance with Docetic principles, may be reckoned among them); but of the existence of the teaching there is unquestionable evidence in the language of St. John concerning those who deny that Jesus Christ is come in the flesh;[1] and a similar doctrine may, at least with great probability, be attributed to the false teachers condemned by St. Paul in the Epistle to the Colossians and in the Pastoral Epistles.[2]

The other form of heresy, subsequently known as the Ebionite, appears towards the close of the first century in the person of Cerinthus, a man of Jewish descent[3] and educated at Alexandria, the head-quarters of that philosophy from which his corruption of Christianity would mostnaturally emanate. The date of his notoriety as a teacher may be inferred with tolerable certainty from the well-known anecdote recorded by Irenæus on the authority of Polycarp, that St. John, having entered into a bath at Ephesus, and finding Cerinthus within, hastened out of it with the words, 'Let us fly, lest the bath should fall while Cerinthus, the enemy of the truth, is in it.'[4] Other, but less trustworthy, authorities assign to him a yet earlier date. According to Epiphanius, he was one of those Judaising disciples who censured St. Peter after the conversion of Cornelius for having eaten with men uncircumcised, and also one of the multitude who raised a tumult against St. Paul on the charge of having brought Greeks into the temple, and one of the false brethren whom St. Paul mentions in the Epistle to the Galatians.[5] But the narrative of Epiphanius is very confused, and

[1] 1 John iv. 2.
[2] Cf. Dorner, *Person of Christ* I. p. 220 (Eng. Tr.).
[3] His Jewish descent may be inferred from the character of his teachings; cf. Burton, *B. L.* p. 477. His study in Egypt is asserted by Hippolytus, vii. 33, and by Theodoret, *Hær. Fab.* ii. 3. Cf. Burton, *B. L.* p. 175; Milman, *Hist. of Christianity* II. p. 55. Merinthus, who is sometimes supposed to be a contemporary of Cerinthus (Epiphan. *Hær.* xxxi. 2), was probably only a nickname of Cerinthus, from μήρινθος, a *cord*.
[4] Irenæus, iii. 3.
[5] Epiphan. *Hær.* xxviii. Epiphanius seems to have confounded St. Paul's visit to Jerusalem in company with Titus, Gal. ii. 2, Acts xv. 2, with the later one in company with Trophimus, Acts xxi. 28.

LECT. VIII.   *THE NAZARENES AND EBIONITES.*   113

all these supposed early allusions to Cerinthus are at variance with the statement of Irenæus, who speaks of the Cerinthian heresy as much later than that of the Nicolaitans.[1]

The principal features of the teaching of Cerinthus are given in the following brief summary by Irenæus, who is followed almost word for word by Hippolytus. I have already quoted this passage in a former lecture, but it may be as well to repeat it here: 'A certain Cerinthus in Asia taught that the world was not made by the Supreme God, but by a certain power altogether separate and at a distance from that Sovereign Power which is over the universe, and one which is ignorant of the God who is over all things. He represented Jesus as not having been born of a virgin (for this seemed to him to be impossible), but as having been the son of Joseph and Mary, born after the manner of other men, though distinguished above all others by justice and prudence and wisdom. He taught moreover, that after the baptism of Jesus the Christ descended upon Him in the form of a dove from that Sovereign Power which is over all things, and that He then announced the unknown Father and wrought miracles; but that towards the end (of His ministry) the Christ departed again from Jesus, and Jesus suffered and rose from the dead, while the Christ remained impassible as a spiritual being.'[2]

To this brief account a few further particulars may be added from other sources. Epiphanius tells us that Cerinthus adhered in part to Judaism, and taught that the law and the prophets were inspired by angels, the giver of the law being one of the angels who made the

[1] Irenæus, iii. 11. 1. Cf. Massuet, *Diss. Præv. in Iren.* i. § 125.
[2] Irenæus, i. 26. Cf. Hippolytus, vii. 33.

world.[1] Two writers of the third century, Caius the presbyter of Rome, and Dionysius bishop of Alexandria,[2] ascribe to him the doctrine that there would be a temporal reign of Christ upon earth for a thousand years, to be spent in sensual delights; and the former seems to have gone so far as to maintain that Cerinthus forged the Revelation of St. John to give support to his views.[3]

Dismissing this Chiliastic theory, which has nothing in common with Gnosticism, and which, if held by Cerinthus at all, can only have been held by an inconsistent attempt to unite the theories of opposite schools,[4] we may observe in those parts of the teaching of Cerinthus which have a properly Gnostic character one or two peculiarities which indicate, in like manner, a partial and somewhat inconsistent adhesion to the doctrines which he had adopted and developed from his Alexandrian teachers.[5] In common with the majority of the Gnostics he borrowed from the school of Philo the theory which made the Creator of the world a distinct being from the Supreme God, and in common also with the majority of the Gnostics he engrafted a pseudo-Christianity upon this pseudo-Judaism by interposing a series of intermediate powers between the Supreme God and the Creator, so as to make the latter distinct from the former, and to leave room for the work of the Christ as mediating between the two. At the same time Cerinthus must be placed among, and indeed as the earliest known name among, those Gnostics who were on the whole disposed to look favour-

[1] *Hær.* xxviii.
[2] Euseb. *H. E.* iii. 28.
[3] Cf. Routh. *Rel. Sacr.* II. p. 15.
[4] Cf. Dorner, *Person of Christ* I. p. 197. Both Mosheim (*De Rebus Christ. ante Const.* p. 199) and Neander (*Ch. Hist.* II. p. 47) consider the accounts of the sensual Chiliasm of Cerinthus to be misrepresentations.
[5] Neander, *Ch. Hist.* II. p. 43, points out the resemblances between the teaching of Cerinthus and that of Philo.

ably on the Jewish religion, regarding it as imperfect indeed, but not as evil. The Demiurge in his system is represented as ignorant of the Supreme God, but not as hostile to Him; the mission of the Christ is not to oppose and undo the work of the Creator, but to supply its deficiencies by a higher revelation.

The Christology of Cerinthus, though less exaggerated in some of its errors than that of some of the later Gnostics, betrays at the same time its essentially Gnostic character. The mission of the Christ, His purpose in coming into the world, is not to save His people from their sins, but to enlighten their minds by proclaiming the Supreme God. He is not so much a redeemer as a teacher, and a teacher not of righteousness so much as of speculative knowledge. The separation of Christ from Jesus asserted by Cerinthus, and his refusal to allow to the spiritual teacher any share in the sufferings of the human instrument, show how entirely the conception of the supreme excellency of knowledge had removed from his mind all appreciation of Divine love, all apprehension of the nature of sin and the need of atonement.[1] Yet while depriving the death of Jesus of its chief significance, and reducing His birth to the level of that of an ordinary man, Cerinthus seems to have been unable to resist the evidence of a fact which militated against his whole philosophy and overthrew the main pillar on which it rested. He was unable to deny that the crucified Jesus had risen again from the dead. It is scarcely possible that he could have brought this great truth into any coherence with the general principles of his system; but the fact of his accepting it notwithstanding shows the strength of the conviction, produced by the preaching of the Apostles, in

[1] Cf. Dorner, *Person of Christ* I. p. 197 (Eng. Tr.).

this central doctrine to which it was especially their office to bear witness.[1]

According to the testimony of Irenæus in a later part of his work, the Gospel of St. John was written for the purpose of refuting the heretical doctrines maintained by Cerinthus, and before him by the Nicolaitans.[2] The two errors which he specifies are the separation of God the Father from the Creator of the world, and the separation of Christ from Jesus. I have in a former lecture pointed out some passages in the beginning of St. John's Gospel as well as in his First Epistle, which appear to be directed against these errors, and I may now add that a similar purpose may perhaps be discerned in the Apostle's own declaration at the end of the last chapter but one of his Gospel: 'These are written that ye might believe that Jesus is the Christ, the Son of God, and that believing ye might have life through His name.'

A curious circumstance is mentioned by Epiphanius concerning the followers of this heretic, which some modern as well as ancient commentators have applied to explain a difficult passage in the writings of St. Paul. 'A story,' says Epiphanius, 'has come down to us by tradition, that when any of them happened to die without baptism, others were baptized in their name instead of them, that they might not, when they rose again at the resurrection, suffer punishment for not having received baptism, and become subject to the power of the Creator of the world. It was for this reason, as the tradition says

---

[1] Epiphanius (*Hær.* xxviii) speaks of Cerinthus as asserting that Christ had not yet risen, but awaited the final resurrection. But Irenæus, followed by Hippolytus, expressly says that he asserted that Jesus had risen. Dorner (I. p.198) says that to Cerinthus the resurrection of Christ must have been a meaningless fact. If so, how strong must have been the evidence which compelled him to admit it! Burton, *B. L.* note 77, endeavours, not very successfully, to reconcile the contradictory accounts.

[2] Irenæus, iii. 11.

which is come down to us, that the holy Apostle said, *If the dead rise not at all, why are they then baptized for them?* [1] Epiphanius himself does not adopt this interpretation, which however has found favour with one or two of the Fathers and several modern writers.[2] The supposition however, that Cerinthus or his followers are actually alluded to by St. Paul, is hardly reconcilable with chronology; and if we adopt this interpretation, we must suppose the practice to have existed at a somewhat earlier period, either among a party in the Corinthian Church itself, or possibly among some heretics who went beyond the Corinthians in denying the resurrection altogether, and whom St. Paul here refutes by reference to their own practice: 'What will become of those (τί ποιήσουσιν) who are in the habit of being baptized (οἱ βαπτιζόμενοι, not βαπτισθέντες) for the dead?' ... 'Why,' he continues, 'do we (τί καὶ ἡμεῖς) stand in jeopardy every hour?' By this change from the third person to the first, the Apostle seems to separate himself and those to whom he is writing from the persons who observed this custom of vicarious baptism, and thus to imply a condemnation of the practice.[3]

Opinions very similar to those of Cerinthus are attributed to another Gnostic teacher, who probably lived about the same time, Carpocrates.[4] His exact date has been a matter of dispute, and he is said, in conjunction with his son Epiphanes, to have carried his heresy to its height in the reign of Hadrian; but, as Hadrian began his reign in A.D. 117, this statement is perfectly consistent with the supposition that the father may have commenced his teaching in the previous century, and thus far have

---

[1] Epiph. *Hær.* xxviii. 6, translated by Burton, *B. L.* note 78.

[2] See Burton, *B. L.* note 78, and Alford on 1 Cor. xv. 29.

[3] See Alford, *l. c.*, and Burton, *B. L.* p. 180.

[4] Theodoret, *Hær. Fab.* i. 5.

been contemporary with Cerinthus, and with the later years of St. John's life.[1] In favour of assigning this early date, it may be observed that the Fathers in general place Carpocrates before Cerinthus,[2] and that Irenæus seems to speak of his followers as the first who assumed the name of *Gnostics*—a distinction which Hippolytus awards to the Naassenes, a branch of the Ophites.[3] The doctrines of Carpocrates have indeed a considerable affinity to some of the Ophite theories, as well as to those of Cerinthus. His opinion concerning the Person of Christ is stated by Irenæus in language very similar to that which he employs in speaking of Cerinthus. 'Carpocrates,' he says,[4] 'and his followers say that the world and the things that are therein were made by angels far inferior to the unbegotten Father. They also say that Jesus was the son of Joseph and born after the manner of other men,[5] but differed from the rest of mankind in that His soul, being stedfast and pure, remembered those things which it had witnessed in that revolution in which it was carried round with the unbegotten God. On this account they say that a power was sent down to him from God, that by means of it he might be able to escape from the makers of the world; and that this power, having passed through them all, and being made free in all,

---

[1] See Burton, *B. L.* note 75.

[2] Cf. Burton, *B. L.* pp. 175, 480. Pseudo-Tertullian (*De Præscr.* c. 48) and Philastrius (*Hæres.* 36) expressly place Cerinthus after Carpocrates. Eusebius (iv. 7) cites Irenæus as making Carpocrates contemporary with Saturninus and Basilides, which however is not distinctly asserted by Irenæus.

[3] Cf. Irenæus, i. 25. 6, and Hippolytus, v. 6. 'Gnosticos se vocant,' says the translator of Irenæus, which Eusebius, iv. 7, paraphrases by ἑτέρας αἱρέσεως τῆς τῶν Γνωστικῶν ἐπικληθείσης πατέρα.

[4] Irenæus, i. 25; cf. Hippolytus, vii. 32.

[5] 'Et qui similis reliquis hominibus fuerit.' Tr. Iren. The text of Hippolytus probably supplies the original Greek καὶ ὅμοιον τοῖς ἀνθρώποις γεγονότα.

THE NAZARENES AND EBIONITES.

ascended again to God, as the soul which embraces like things will in like manner ascend.'[1]

Closely as the substance of this extract resembles the account given by the same author of the tenets of Cerinthus, there are one or two important differences to be noticed. The maker of the world is not, as in Cerinthus, a power subordinate to, yet ignorant of, the Supreme God, but a power or powers hostile to God, and from whose dominion the highest souls are to be set free. Carpocrates moreover does not merely, like Cerinthus, regard Jesus as a man superior in virtue and wisdom to other men, but he assigns a very remarkable reason for this superiority—that His soul remembered those things which it had witnessed in its revolution (τῇ περιφορᾷ) along with the unbegotten God. We have here an evident allusion to the mythical description in Plato's Phædrus (p. 246 *seq.*), which represents the soul of man as the driver of the chariot with its winged steeds, sometimes permitted to raise his head into the upper sphere, so as to be carried round with the gods in their circuit and to behold the eternal forms of things. Notwithstanding the similarity of their conclusions the two philosophers approach the question from opposite sides. Cerinthus deals with it as a Jew, under the influence of the Platonic philosophy as modified by Philo, and retaining a certain amount of respect for the Jewish religion and Scriptures. Carpocrates

---

[1] I have followed the text of Hippolytus as corrected by Duncker and Schneidewin: ἣν καὶ διὰ πάντων χωρήσασαν ἐν πᾶσί τε ἐλευθερωθεῖσαν ἀνεληλυθέναι πρὸς αὐτόν, [καὶ ὁμοίως τὴν] τὰ ὅμοια αὐτῇ ἀσπαζομένην. The Latin version of Irenæus may perhaps be more exactly rendered: 'On this account they say that a power was sent from God into the soul of Jesus, that it might escape from the makers of the world, and having passed through them all, and being freed in all, might ascend to Him,' etc. *Per omnes*, like the διὰ πάντων of Hippolytus, seems naturally to refer to the makers of the world. In the paraphrase of Epiphanius it seems to be understood of passing through all *actions*.

deals with it as a heathen, under the influence of the Platonic philosophy in its original form, and regarding the Jews and their claims to Divine instruction with feelings partly of contempt, partly of hatred.

These feelings are more plainly manifested in the other portions of the teaching of Carpocrates, as recorded by Irenæus. He maintained that Jesus, though brought up in the customs of the Jews, despised them, and therefore received power to destroy those passions which are given to man as a punishment; and that all those who, like him, could despise the powers which created the world, could become as great and even greater than he and his Apostles. The means which he recommended to those who would show their contempt for the Creator and His laws were of the same flagitious character which we have already seen in the cognate doctrines of the Cainites. He is said to have taught that it was necessary for those who aspired to the higher life to pass through every form of action usually reputed sinful, in order to complete their defiance of the powers which rule the world,[1] and that those who did not complete their allotted task in a single body must migrate after death into another, till the duty was accomplished. Here again we see the conclusion of the poetical mysteries in the Phædrus distorted from its original purpose to serve as a cloak for licentiousness. That transmigration of souls into successive bodies which Plato represents as taking place for their punishment or for their purification [2] is polluted in the hands of

[1] Euseb. *H. E.* iv. 7 τούτοις τε ἀκολούθως πάντα δρᾶν χρῆναι διδάσκειν τὰ αἰσχρουργότατα τοὺς μέλλοντας εἰς τὸ τέλειον τῆς κατ' αὐτοὺς μυσταγωγίας ἢ καὶ μᾶλλον μυσαροποιίας ἐλεύσεσθαι, ὡς μὴ ἂν ἄλλως ἐκφευξομένους τοὺς κοσμικοὺς (ὡς ἂν ἐκεῖνοι φαῖεν) ἄρχοντας, μὴ οὐχὶ πᾶσι τὰ δι' ἀρρητοποιίας ἀπονείμαντας χρέα. Cf. Irenæus i. 25, where this monstrous doctrine is connected with the theory of transmigration. See also Tertullian, *De Anim.* 35, and Hippolytus, vii. 32.

[2] *Phædrus* pp. 248, 249.

Carpocrates so as to become the expected means of wallowing in every variety of vice, and even the mode of representing its practice in the light of a duty.

Epiphanes, the son of Carpocrates by a Cephallenian mother, is said to have been honoured by the inhabitants of Same in Cephallenia as a god, though he died at the early age of seventeen. This precocious philosopher was certainly not overburdened with modesty on account of his youth; indeed his philosophy was of that kind which a forward boy might be very apt at learning and teaching. He wrote a book 'On Justice,' a fragment of which is preserved by Clement of Alexandria; in which, enlarging on a suggestion of Plato, in whose philosophy he had been instructed by his father, he openly advocated the most licentious theories of communism, asserting that the natural life of man was similar to that of the brutes, and that the law, by introducing the distinction of *meum* and *tuum*, was the real author of the sin of theft and adultery. In support of this licentious twaddle he perverted the words of St. Paul, that 'by the law is the knowledge of sin' (Rom. iii. 20), and sneered at the tenth commandment as making the sin which it condemned, by recognising the right of property.[1]

It is difficult to imagine how doctrines like these, so flagrantly opposed to the teaching of the Gospel, can have been coupled with the slightest respect for the person of Jesus or the precepts delivered by Him. In explanation of this difficulty, the disciples of Carpocrates seem to have had recourse to the convenient fiction of an esoteric teaching which they said that Jesus had taught to His Apostles and disciples in private, and had bidden them to teach to those who were worthy of it. The substance of this teaching

[1] Clem. Alex. *Strom.* iii. 2 (p. 514).

seems to have been that faith and love alone were necessary to salvation, all other things being naturally indifferent, and made good or bad by the opinion of men.[1] Here again we find Christianity made the vehicle for teaching a heathen philosophy; not however the philosophy of Plato, but the worst of the paradoxes of his adversaries the Sophists. In the whole teaching of the Carpocratians, not only does the heathen element preponderate over the Christian, but the Christian element is reduced to its least possible dimensions. Going beyond Cerinthus, they not only asserted that Jesus was a mere man, born like other men, but even that the Divine power which was given to him was no more than may be acquired even in a greater degree by other men. In accordance with this teaching they are said to have honoured him among the wise teachers of mankind by placing his image along with those of Pythagoras, Plato, Aristotle, and others, and paying reverence to them after the manner of the Gentiles.[2] Epiphanes is said to have been succeeded by one Prodicus, who founded a sect called the Adamites, professing even more shamelessly than their predecessors the principles of communism and licentiousness of life.[3] Prodicus is said to have rejected prayer, probably as inconsistent with the supposed absolute nature of the Supreme God,[4] and to have held that men ought not to profess their religious belief in times of persecution.[5] Another branch of the same antinomians

---

[1] Irenæus, i. 25.

[2] Irenæus, l. c.; cf. Epiphan. *Hær.* xxvii. 6.

[3] Theodoret, *Hær. Fab.* i. 6; Clem. Alex. *Strom.* iii. 4. The Adamites according to Epiphanius (*Hær.* lii) assembled in their churches, men and women together, naked, in imitation of Adam in Paradise. Lardner (*Hist. of Hær.* bk. ii. ch. 6) doubts the existence of this sect. Yet a similar practice is attributed to the Beghards or Brethren of the Free Spirit in the thirteenth century, and again in the fifteenth. Cf. Mosheim. II. pp. 243, 362 (ed. Stubbs).

[4] Clem. Alex. *Strom.* vii. 7. Cf. Neander, *Ch. Hist.* II. p. 119.

[5] Tertullian, *Scorp.* c. 15.

LECT. VIII.   THE NAZARENES AND EBIONITES.   123

were the *Antitactæ*, or *Adversaries* of the Creator, mentioned by Clement of Alexandria,[1] who held that it was a duty owing to the Supreme God who made all things good, to resist the commands of the Creator, the author of evil.

Cerinthus, with his semi-Judaising tendencies, combined with purely humanitarian views regarding the Person of Jesus, may be considered as the precursor of the sects known in the second century by the names of *Nazarenes* and *Ebionites*. These two sects are not distinguished from each other by the earliest writers on the subject, and the distinction between their doctrines is noticed earlier than their separate names. Irenæus and Hippolytus merely tell us that the Ebionites differed from Cerinthus and Carpocrates in maintaining that the world was created by the Supreme God, but agreed with them in regarding Jesus as a mere man.[2] The former adds that they accepted St. Matthew alone among the Evangelists, rejected St. Paul as an apostate from Judaism, and practised the observances of the Jewish law. Origen, and more fully Eusebius, distinguish between two classes of Ebionites: the one holding, like Cerinthus, that Jesus was a mere man, the son of Joseph and Mary; the other admitting His supernatural birth, but denying His pre-existence.[3]   Finally Epiphanius, who is partly supported by

---

[1] *Strom*. iii. 4. Clement's terse description of these heretics should be read in the original: "Ἄλλοι τινές, οὓς καὶ Ἀντιτάκτας καλοῦμεν, λέγουσιν ὅτι ὁ μὲν Θεὸς ὁ τῶν ὅλων πατὴρ ἡμῶν ἐστι φύσει· καὶ πάνθ' ὅσα πεποίηκεν ἀγαθά ἐστιν. εἷς δέ τις τῶν ὑπ' αὐτοῦ γεγονότων ἐπέσπειρεν τὰ ζιζάνια, τὴν τῶν κακῶν φύσιν γεννήσας, οἷς καὶ δὴ πάντας ἡμᾶς περιέβαλεν, ἀντιτάξας ἡμᾶς τῷ πατρί. διὸ δὴ καὶ αὐτοὶ ἀντιτασσόμεθα τούτῳ εἰς ἐκδικίαν τοῦ πατρός, ἀντιπράσσοντες τῷ βουλήματι τοῦ δευτέρου. ἐπεὶ οὖν οὗτος Οὐ μοιχεύσεις εἴρηκεν, ἡμεῖς φασί, μοιχεύομεν ἐπὶ καταλύσει τῆς ἐντολῆς αὐτοῦ.

[2] Irenæus, i. 26; Hippol. vii. 34. The Greek text of the latter enables us to correct an error in the Latin translation of the former. Instead of 'non similiter ut Cerinthus et Carpocrates opinantur,' we should clearly read 'similiter ut,' etc.

[3] Euseb. *H. E.* iii. 27; cf. Origen, *c. Cels.* v. 61.

Jerome, distinguishes the Nazarenes from the Ebionites, and describes the former in language which seems to identify them with the less heterodox of the two classes of Ebionites mentioned by Origen and Eusebius.[1]

Both names seem to have been transferred in course of time from a general to a special signification. We know from the Acts of the Apostles that the Christians in general were contemptuously called by the Jews of Palestine the sect of the *Nazarenes*;[2] and this appellation probably continued to be applied for some time to all who professed to be believers in Christ, without reference to any difference which may have existed between orthodox and heterodox forms of Christianity. From the testimony of Origen[3] it seems probable that the term *Ebionites* was also originally a name of contempt given by the Jews to the Christians; and this serves to corroborate, if corroboration be needed, the explanation given by the same writer of the meaning of the word as derived from the Hebrew אֶבְיוֹן *poor*.[4] Yet both Origen and Eusebius, who follows him, seem to have mistaken the ground of this appellation, when they suppose it to have been given to the Ebionite heretics on account of the poverty of their conception of Christ. As originally applied by the Jews to the Christians in general, it was probably aimed at the poverty and low estate of the first followers of Christ in the spirit of the language used by the Pharisees of our Lord Himself: 'Have any of the rulers or of the Pharisees believed on Him? but this people who knoweth not the law are cursed.'[5] The heretic Ebion, who is assumed by Tertullian and

[1] See Epiphan. *Hær.* xxix. 7, 8; Hieron. *De Vir. Illustr.* c. 3; *Epist. ad August.* 112, c. 13. Cf. Dorner, *Person of Christ* I. p. 191 *seq.*

[2] Acts xxiv. 5.

[3] Origen, *c. Cels.* ii. 1 Ἐβιωναῖοι χρηματίζουσιν οἱ ἀπὸ Ἰουδαίων τὸν Ἰησοῦν ὡς Χριστὸν παραδεξάμενοι.

[4] Origen, *De Princ.* iv. 22; *In Matt.* T. xvi. c. 12; *c. Cels.* ii. 1; Euseb. *H. E.* iii. 27.

[5] John vii. 48, 49. Cf. Neander, *Ch. Hist.* I. p. 478.

others as the founder of this sect,[1] may be safely dismissed to the region of mythical eponymi. It is interesting however to inquire how two names, originally given to the Christian Church as a body, came afterwards to be employed as the designation of heretical sects. The names, as we have observed, were, one certainly, the other probably, originally given by the Jews of Palestine, and therefore to Christians who were for the most part of Jewish origin and, in their own practice at least, more or less observant of Jewish customs. After the destruction of Jerusalem, this Jewish-Christian Church continued to exist in Pella and the neighbouring region beyond the Jordan, to which it had withdrawn during the siege,[2] and where it appears to have remained until the reign of Hadrian when, after the revolt and destruction of Bar-Cochab and his followers, the Roman city of Ælia Capitolina was founded on the ruins of the ancient Jerusalem.[3] In that city no Jew was permitted to dwell, and the prohibition would naturally extend to those Christians of Jewish origin who had not renounced the customs of their forefathers.[4] This circumstance led to a division in the Church, the Gentile members of it, together with the less rigid Jewish Christians, establishing themselves at Jerusalem under a succession

---

[1] Tertullian, *De Præscr.* c. 33; cf. Epiphan. *Hær.* xxx, and see Neander, *Ch. Hist.* I. p. 477.

[2] Euseb. *H. E.* iii. 5.

[3] Euseb. *H. E.* iv. 6. In chapter 5 Eusebius gives a list of fifteen bishops of Jerusalem of Jewish race, down to the time of the revolt in Hadrian's reign; but these, though nominally bishops of Jerusalem, could hardly have resided in that city, which remained uninhabited except by a Roman garrison in its towers (Josephus, *B. J.* vii. 1), till Bar-Cochab seized it, and attempted to rebuild the temple. Neander (*Ch. Hist.* I. p. 475) says that the Church *is said* to have returned to Jerusalem, but gives no authority for the statement, and seems to doubt its truth (see p. 476). It is possible however, as Milman supposes (*Hist. of Jews* II. p. 431), that some sort of rude town may have grown up on the wreck of the city; and if so, it is possible that the Judaizing Christians may have gone back to Pella after the edict of Hadrian. Cf. Neander, *l. c.* p. 476; Lightfoot, *Galatians* p. 304.

[4] Justin, *Dial c. Tryph.* c. 16. Cf. Neander, *Ch. Hist.* I. p. 475; Ritschl, *Entstehung der Altk. Kirche* p. 257.

of bishops of Gentile birth,[1] while the stricter Judaizers remained at Pella, where after the departure of their brethren they would naturally enforce their own rites with greater strictness than ever. Under these circumstances the Jewish Christian settlement at Pella, retaining its old appellations of Nazarene and Ebionite, which from terms of reproach had probably become among themselves titles of honour, seems to have gradually relapsed still more into Judaism, retaining a certain kind of acknowledgment of Jesus as the Messiah, but ceasing at last to acknowledge His Deity and pre-existence. These heretical views would naturally be developed into more consistency by some than by others, and thus give rise to the two divisions of the Ebionites, of whom the less heterodox, or Nazarenes, were probably the earlier in point of time.[2]

The Ebionites (using the term in its more general sense) made use of a Gospel which is called by Irenæus the Gospel of St. Matthew, and by Eusebius the Gospel according to the Hebrews.[3] This work is supposed by some critics to be the Hebrew original of St. Matthew's Gospel;[4] but, to say nothing of the doubt whether such a Hebrew original ever existed at all,[5] it is certain that the Ebionite gospel differed from the text of St. Matthew in many important particulars,[6] and almost certain that it was an Aramaic translation of the canonical gospel, with alterations and additions from other sources.[7] In the fourth century, if not earlier, there were two different

---

[1] Euseb. *H. E.* iv. 6.

[2] Cf. Dorner, *Person of Christ* I. p. 191 (Eng. Tr.); Neander, *Ch. Hist.* I. p. 476.

[3] Irenæus, i. 26; Euseb. *H. E.* iii. 27.

[4] See Harvey's *Irenæus*, I. p. 213. For a full account of various opinions on this question, see Bleek, *Einl. in das N. T.* pp. 101–103.

[5] See Bleek, *Einleitung* p. 109, who shows the probability that the translation was mistaken for the original.

[6] For some of the variations, see De Wette, *Einleitung in das N. T.* § 65a; Bleek, *Einleitung* p. 107.

[7] See Bleek, *Einleitung* p. 108.

THE NAZARENES AND EBIONITES.

recensions of it, one of which omitted, while the other retained, the first two chapters of St. Matthew. The former was used by the Ebionites proper, who denied the supernatural birth of our Lord. The latter was accepted by the more orthodox Nazarenes.[1]

The most noteworthy feature in the heresies described in this and the two previous lectures, is the testimony which they indirectly bear to the universal belief of the Church in the Divine Nature of her blessed Lord. Had it not been that the Christian consciousness in the Apostolic age was penetrated and pervaded by this belief, it would have been hardly possible that the early heretics, who desired to retain a nominal Christianity as a cloak for their own speculations, should not have thought of the device, so simple and natural to the unbelievers of later times, of regarding the Saviour as a mere man, a wise philosopher, a great teacher of truth, a great moral example, as other wise and good men had been before Him. But this idea, so familiar to us in the present day, is nowhere to be found among the early heresies. It seemed to them more simple and obvious to deny that which was natural and human than that which was supernatural and Divine. The earliest form of Gnosticism, so far as we can trace its development in chronological order, seems to have been pure and simple Docetism.[2] The Divine Being who came down from the Supreme God had no human body, but only the appearance of one. The modification of this belief, which manifested itself in the Cerinthian and Ebionite theories, was probably due to the circulation of the first three Gospels, and to the testimony which they bore to

---

[1] Epiphan. *Hær.* xxix. 9, xxx. 14. Cf. Bleek, *Einl.* p. 105; Mosheim, *De Rebus Chr. ante Const.* p. 328.

[2] The hypothesis of some critics (e.g. Ritschl. *Altk. Kirche*, pp. 342, 454) of the late origin of Docetism is very arbitrary, and by no means established by the authorities adduced.

the real humanity of Him of whom they wrote.[1] Even then a purely humanitarian theory was felt to be impossible. The Divine element must be retained in some form or other; and this was done by distinguishing between Jesus the man and Christ the spiritual being, regarding the former as merely the vessel or abode in which the latter for a short season condescended to dwell.[2] The work of redemption was still Divine, though carried on by means of a human instrument; it was the work of Christ the Spirit, not of Jesus the man. Even Carpocrates, the most heathen of the early Gnostics, and the least conscious of the real nature of Christ's work and kingdom, cannot divest himself of the idea of some supernatural being, some Divine power, dwelling in and inspiring the human teacher. The testimony of the enemies of the faith is thus far at one with that of its Apostles and Evangelists. The whole world was groaning and travailing together, waiting for its redemption, and none but God could satisfy the universal yearning.

[1] Cf. Burton, *Bampton Lectures*, p. 481.
[2] *Ibid.* pp. 244–246.

LECTURE IX.

SYRIAN GNOSTICISM—SATURNINUS—TATIAN—BARDESANES.

'FROM Menander, the successor of Simon,' says Eusebius, 'there went forth a power, as it were of a two-mouthed and two-headed serpent, which established leaders of two different heresies, namely Saturninus, a native of Antioch, and Basilides, an Alexandrian, who founded schools of heresies hateful to God, the one in Syria, the other in Egypt. Saturninus, as we are told by Irenæus, for the most part taught the same false doctrines as Menander, while Basilides, under the pretence of revealing deeper secrets, extended his fancies into the region of immensity, forging for himself monstrous fables of impious heresy.'[1] Thus far Eusebius. Of Basilides, the founder of the Egyptian form of Gnosticism, we shall treat in our next lecture; our present will be devoted to an examination of the Syrian Gnosticism, commencing with its founder Saturninus. The remark quoted by Eusebius from Irenæus, that Saturninus taught the same doctrines as Menander, is not, taken by itself, strictly accurate; nor, when we examine the context of Irenæus, does that Father seem to intend an assertion of the identity of the teaching of the two heresiarchs in all respects, but only in the common points from which both started, namely, that the Supreme God is unknown, and that the world was made by angels.[2] In other respects there is a wide difference between the two systems.

[1] Euseb. *H. E.* iv. 7.   [2] Irenæus, i. 24.

Menander, like his master Simon, announced himself as the being sent down from the invisible powers as the Saviour of the world. No such blasphemy as this can be detected in the teaching of Saturninus, who, however erroneous his views may have been, propounded them in connection with the person and work of Christ, not assuming to himself any higher office than that of teaching them. Hence he is the first person who gave to the doctrines of Simon the distinct character of a Christian heresy, whereas in the hands of Simon himself, and of Menander, they appear as anti-Christian schemes, exalting their own teachers into the place of Christ.

From Menander and Simon, Saturninus appears to have borrowed three of his principal doctrines, namely that of the malignity of matter, which made it impossible for the Supreme God to have any direct relation to the material world, and its two immediate consequences, that the world was created by inferior powers, and that the body of Christ was a phantom only, not a reality. With these however he combined other principles of a different kind, borrowed from the dualism of Persia; the result of the whole being a somewhat incoherent eclecticism, less bold than the teaching of his predecessors, but at the same time less consistent. The angels who made the world are represented in the teaching of Simon as beings who, though emanating remotely from God, are in rebellion against him, and whose power it is the primary object of the Redeemer to destroy. In the scheme of Saturninus, the source of evil is referred, as in the Persian doctrine, to an independent power, antagonistic to the good principle, who does not create the world, but endeavours to usurp a dominion over it. Hence the direct enemy of God is not found in the creative angels, but in Satan, the leader of the powers of darkness; and the creative angels hold an intermediate position between good and evil, fallen away from the good power from whom they emanated, but hostile to Satan and the powers of darkness, with whom they contend for the government of the world. So too the malignity of matter holds a somewhat incongruous position in the teaching of Saturninus. His Docetic views of the person of Christ and the rigid asceticism of his practical teaching imply the inherent and essential evil of matter as their fundamental assumption. But by adding to this assumption the Persian theory of a spiritual kingdom of darkness (according to which theory matter is not in itself evil, but only capable of being employed for evil by spiritual powers), Saturninus encumbered his teaching with a double hypothesis, whose separate results, though held in conjunction, can hardly be said to fit into each other as parts of a system.

The following is the summary of the doctrines of Saturninus as given by Irenæus, the original Greek of whose text in this passage may now be restored from the recently recovered treatise of Hippolytus: 'Saturninus, like Menander, taught that there is one Father unknown to all, who made angels, archangels, powers, and principalities; that the world, and all that therein is, was made by certain angels, seven in number; and that man was made by the angels in the following manner. A shining image was manifested from above from the supreme power, which the angels were not able to detain, because, as he says, it immediately again ascended above; they therefore exhorted each other, saying, *Let us make man according to the image and likeness.* When this was done, he continues, and when the thing made was unable to stand upright, through the inability of the angels, but writhed upon the ground like a worm,[1] the superior power, pitying him, because he was made in his own likeness, sent a spark of life, which raised man upright, and formed his joints, and made him live. This spark of life then, he says, returns after death to those things which are of the same nature with itself, and the remaining portions are resolved into the elements out of which they were made. The Saviour he supposed to have no human birth,[2] and to be without body and without form, and to have been manifested as a man in appearance only. The God of the Jews, he says, was one of the angels, and because the Father wished to depose all the principalities from their sovereignty,[3] Christ came to depose the God of the Jews, and for the salvation of those who trust in him, that is to say, of those who have in them the spark of life. For he said that there were two classes of men formed by the angels, one evil and the other good,[4] and that because the demons were in the habit of assisting the evil, the Saviour came down for the overthrow of the evil men and demons, and for the salvation of the good. He asserted also that marriage and procreation are of Satan. Many of his followers also abstain from animal food, and by this false austerity seduce many. The prophecies, they say, were partly inspired by the angels who made the world, partly by Satan; the latter being held to be himself an

---

[1] A similar fancy to this occurs in the Ophite theory; Irenæus, i. 30. 5.

[2] *Innatum* (ἀγέννητον, Hippol.), which Neander understands to mean *not born of a woman*. Cf. Harvey's *Irenæus*, I. p. 197. A similar view was afterwards held by Marcion.

[3] The Latin translation of Irenæus renders 'propter hoc quod dissolvere voluerint Patrem ejus omnes principes.' But the Greek text, as preserved by Hippolytus, is διὰ τοῦτο (l. τὸ) βούλεσθαι τὸν πατέρα καταλῦσαι πάντας τοὺς ἄρχοντας, which admits of either construction. The one adopted in the text seems more probable in itself and more suitable to the context.

[4] Epiphanius (*Hær.* xxiii. 2) adds, δύο γὰρ πεπλάσθαι ἀπ' ἀρχῆς ἀνθρώπους φάσκει, ἕνα ἀγαθὸν καὶ ἕνα φαῦλον, ἐξ ὧν δύο εἶναι τὰ γένη τῶν ἀνθρώπων ἐν κόσμῳ, ἀγαθόν τε καὶ πονηρόν.

angel, the enemy of the makers of the world, and especially of the God of the Jews.'[1]

In this description it is not difficult to discern the Persian accretions engrafted by Saturninus on the original teaching of Simon and Menander. The seven angels who made the world are obviously borrowed from Ormuzd and his six Amshaspands; only instead of being placed, as in the Zoroastrian system, as the highest rank of the celestial hierarchy, they are degraded to the extreme verge of the kingdom of light,[2] and regarded as alienated from the Supreme Father, though hostile to the powers of darkness. A supposition of this kind was necessary in the scheme of Saturninus in order to make room for the work of the Saviour, just as in the theory of Simon and others, borrowed from the Alexandrian Judaism, the creation of the world is transferred from the Logos to an inferior order of emanated powers. The material world, as in the Persian theory, occupies the intermediate space between the regions of light and darkness; only the conflict for its possession is in the first instance not between Ahriman and Ormuzd directly, but between Satan and the inferior angels by whom it was created. The nature of man, formed as regards his bodily frame by the inferior angels, but quickened by a spark of life from above, seems intended to combine the theory of the evil nature of matter with the belief in a spiritual principle in man and a capability of salvation; though the assumption of two races of men, good and evil, descended from two pairs of parents, good

[1] Irenæus, i. 24.

[2] Matter, vol. I. p. 334, 'Sur le dernier degré du monde pur, Saturnin place sept anges, qui sont ce qu'il y a de moins parfait dans les régions *intellectuelles*.' This position of the angels is not mentioned by Irenæus: it is however quite in accordance with Saturninus's modification of Parsism, and is perhaps a fair expansion of the language of Epiphanius, *Hær.* xxiii. 1. τοὺς δὲ ἀγγέλους διεστάναι ἀπὸ τῆς ἄνω δυνάμεως.

and evil likewise,[1] while quite in accordance with the arrogant pretensions of Gnosticism, substitutes a kind of inherited fatalism and rigid necessity for the free choice between the powers of good and evil which is allowed to man in the Zoroastrian philosophy. The hatred of the Jewish nation and religion, which is conspicuous in the teaching of the Samaritan Simon, appears in a modified form in that of his Syrian successor. Having combined the Persian doctrine of an active power of evil with the Græco-Alexandrian hypothesis of a passive source of evil in matter, Saturninus was unable so fundamentally to contradict both the phenomena of the world and the traditional source of his own teaching, as to identify the maker of the world with the evil spirit. The Creator, the God of the Jews, is permitted so far to partake of an imperfect goodness as to be the antagonist of Satan, while at the same time his nature and his government of the world are so far removed from the goodness of the Supreme Being, that it is a part of the mission of the Redeemer to overthrow his empire, along with that of his enemy Satan.

In his rigid asceticism and condemnation of marriage Saturninus is quite consistent with his assumption of the evil nature of matter and the imperfect, if not evil, character of the Creator, though at variance with the theory and practice of his predecessor Simon, as well as of some of the other Gnostics who held the same assumptions. But it has been well observed that this principle, which supposes an antagonism between the Creator of the world and the Supreme God, may find two ways of expressing

[1] Epiphan. *Hær.* xxiii. 2. Milman (*Hist. of Christianity* II. p. 63) remarks on the difficulty of reconciling the theory of the divine origin of the soul of man with the assumption of two distinct races, good and bad. 'Whether the latter became so from receiving a feebler and less influential portion of the divine spirit, or whether they were a subsequent creation of Satan, who assumes the station of the Ahriman of the Persian system, does not clearly appear.'

LECT. IX. *SATURNINUS, TATIAN, BARDESANES.* 135

itself, both at variance with the spirit of Christianity. 'Among the nobler and more sensible class it took the form of an extreme and rigid asceticism, of an anxious abhorrence of all contact with the world, though to mould and fashion that world constitutes a part of the Christian vocation. In this case, morality could at best be only negative, a mere preparatory purification to contemplation. But the same eccentric hatred of the world, when coupled with pride and arrogance, might also lead to wild fanaticism and a bold contempt of all moral obligations. When the Gnostics had once started upon the principle that the whole of this world is the work of a finite, ungodlike spirit, and is not susceptible of any revelation of the Divine; that the loftier natures, who belong to a far higher world, are held in bondage by it; they easily came to the conclusion that everything external is a matter of perfect indifference to the inner man; nothing of a loftier nature can there be expressed; the outward man may indulge in every lust, provided only that the tranquillity of the inner man is not thereby disturbed in its meditation. The best way to show contempt of, and to bid defiance to this wretched alien world, was not to allow the mind to be affected by it in any situation. Men should mortify sense by indulging in every lust, and still preserving their tranquillity of mind unruffled.[1] . . . Not only in the history of Christian sects of earlier and more recent times, but also among the sects of the Hindoos, and even among the rude islanders of Australia, instances may be found of such tendencies to defy all moral obligations, arising either from speculative or mystical elements, or, it may be, from some subjective caprice opposing itself to all positive law.'[2] The author of these remarks

[1] Neander refers to Clement of Alexandria; *Strom.* ii. 20 (p. 411).

[2] Neander, *Church History* II. p. 26.

concludes with a warning which has lost none of its force since the time when he wrote, now upwards of forty years ago. 'In the general temperament of the present period, the false yearning of the subjective after total emancipation, and the breaking loose from all the bonds, holy or unholy, by which society had been previously kept together, is quite apparent. And this tendency might seem to find a point of sympathy in that unshackling of the spirit, radically different however in its character, which Christianity brought along with it.'

Some of the leading features of the Gnosticism of Saturninus, his separation of the Creator of the world from the Supreme God, and consequently of the Old Testament revelation from the New, his Docetism as regards the person of Christ, and his practical asceticism, appear in the later tenets of Tatian and in those of his followers the Encratites. Tatian was an Assyrian or, as some say, a Syrian by birth,[1] and by profession a sophist or teacher of rhetoric, often travelling in various countries. He came to Rome, where he became acquainted with Justin Martyr and was converted to Christianity. It was probably as a Christian convert that he wrote his extant work, 'Ad Græcos' (Πρὸς "Ελληνας), an exhortation addressed to the Greeks in commendation of Christianity as compared with the Greek philosophy and mythology. Though this work contains some strange and fanciful speculations, it is difficult to discover in it any positive traces of the Gnostic theories which the author subsequently adopted.[2] After the death of Justin, Tatian

---

[1] In the *Oratio ad Græc.* c. 42, Tatian calls himself an Assyrian. Clement Alex. (*Strom.* iii. 12, p. 547 Potter) calls him a Syrian. Tatian may have used the words ἐν τῇ τῶν Ἀσσυρίων γῇ in a wide sense; but the probability is rather in favour of Assyria proper. See Möller in Herzog, vol. XV. p. 420.

[2] For Tatian's views on the Logos see Dorner, *Person of Christ* I. p. 280. His errors approach more to Sabellianism than to Gnosticism. Matter, vol. III. p. 48, finds Gnosticism in the

seems to have returned to the East, where he took up his abode in Syria, and was carried away by the Gnostic speculations prevalent in that country. His opinions as a Gnostic seem to have had some connection with those of Valentinus[1] and Marcion, but were more nearly allied to those of Saturninus.[2] He distinguished between the Creator of the world and the Supreme God, and maintained that the words *Let there be light* were to be interpreted as a prayer from the former to the latter,[3] an interpretation which reminds us of the doctrine of Saturninus, which represents the body of man as formed by the creative angels, while the spark of light which gives life is communicated from above. He also regarded the Old and New Testament as the work of different Gods,[4] and denied the salvation of Adam as being the author of transgression, and as condemned by the words of St. Paul, *In Adam all die*.[5] His most remarkable tenets however, from which his disciples derived their name, were those of practical asceticism. Like Saturninus he condemned marriage and the use of animal food,[6] and even went so far as to use pure water instead of wine at the Eucharist; for which reason his followers were called *Hydroparastatæ*.[7] These ascetic doctrines were probably, like those of Saturninus, the result of an assumption of the evil nature of matter, which appears also to have led him to Docetic

---

Oratio ad Græcos, which on the other hand is defended by Möller in Herzog, Art. 'Tatian,' vol. XV. p. 423. Cf. Bull, *Def. F. N.* iii. c. 6.

[1] From Valentinus he seems to have borrowed the theory of Æons. See Irenæus, i. 28; Euseb. *H. E.* iv. 29.

[2] Möller in Herzog, Art. 'Tatian,' vol. XV. p. 423. Cf. Irenæus, i. 28, who regards his doctrine as derived from Saturninus and Marcion.

[3] Clem. Alex. *Ecl. Prophet.* 38, p. 999 (Potter).

[4] Clem. Alex. *Strom.* iii. 12, p. 548 (Potter).

[5] Hippol. viii. 16; Irenæus, i. 28, iii. 23; Euseb. *H. E.* iv. 29.

[6] Irenæus, i. 28; Euseb. *H. E.* iv. 29; Theodoret, *Hær. Fab.* i. 20.

[7] Theodoret, *Hær. Fab.* i. 20. Cf. Clem. Alex. *Pædag.* ii. 2 (p. 186, Potter); Epiphan, *Hær.* xlvi. 2.

views concerning the body of Christ.¹ In accordance with these views Tatian is said to have compiled a Diatessaron or harmony of the four Gospels, omitting the genealogies of our Lord and all allusion to His human descent from David.²

If we regard the Syrian Gnosis solely with reference to the country of its teachers, we must add to the names previously mentioned that of Bardesanes, who lived in the latter part of the second century. Bardesanes (or more correctly Bar-Daisan, so called from the river Daisan³ which ran by his native city) was born at Edessa in Mesopotamia, close to the borders of Syria, formerly the capital of King Agbarus, whose correspondence with our Saviour is one of the fabulous embellishments of ecclesiastical history.⁴ The dynasty of the Abgars appears to have continued down to the middle of the third century; and one of these is mentioned as having been the friend and patron of Bardesanes. According to the brief account given of this heresiarch by Eusebius, who however is not supported by other authorities, he was at first a disciple of Valentinus, but afterwards rejected his master and refuted many of his mythical fictions; but though thus seeming to return more nearly to orthodoxy, he did not entirely wipe off the stain of his early heresy.⁵ Epiphanius, on the other hand, represents him as having been originally sound in the faith, but as having been afterwards infected by the heretical doctrines of the

---

¹ Hieron. *in Epist. ad Gal.* vi. 8 'Tatianus .... putativam Christi carnem inducens,' where however Vallarsi reads 'Cassianus.' Yet the doctrine is quite in keeping with Tatian's opinion. Cf. Möller in Herzog, Art. 'Tatian,' vol. XV. p. 423.

² Theodoret, *Hær. Fab.* i. 20.

³ Also called *Scirtus*. Both names have the same meaning, 'leaping.'

⁴ Euseb. *H. E.* i. 13. Bardesanes is called a Syrian by Eusebius, *Præp. Evang.* vi. 9.

⁵ Euseb. *H. E.* iv. 30. Epiphanius and Theodoret say nothing of his return to orthodoxy, and the account of the former seems to place the orthodox writings of Bardesanes earlier than the heretical ones.

Valentinians.[1] As a Christian, he wrote in defence of the faith and against the errors of Marcion,[2] and showed his constancy by refusing to abjure his belief when threatened with death by Apollonius the Stoic in the name of the Emperor Verus.[3] As a Gnostic, his opinions for the most part closely resembled those of Valentinus, of which we shall give an account in a subsequent lecture, but there are one or two features of his teaching which more nearly connect him with the Gnostics of Syria, among whom, on account of his birthplace, he is classed by some distinguished authorities.[4] Like Saturninus, he is said to have combined the doctrine of the malignity of matter with that of an active principle of evil; and he connected together these two usually antagonistic theories by maintaining that the inert matter was co-eternal with God, while Satan as the active principle of evil was produced from matter (or, according to another statement, co-eternal with it), and acted in conjunction with it.[5]

He also agreed with Saturninus in holding Docetic views concerning the person of Christ; though this error was not peculiar to the Gnosis of Syria, but was shared by some of the followers of Basilides as well as by Valentinus and others of the Egyptian school, and also in another form by the antagonist of Bardesanes, Marcion. Bardesanes, in common with some other of these heretics, asserted that our Lord, though born of the Virgin Mary, took nothing of her substance, and merely assumed the appearance of a man, as he had appeared in human form

---

[1] Epiphan. *Hær.* lvi. 2. This account is accepted by Mosheim (*De Rebus Chr. ante Const.* p. 396) and by Matter (I. p. 363) as the more probable.

[2] Euseb. *H. E.* iv. 30; Theodoret, *Hær. Fab.* i. 22.

[3] Epiphan. *Hær.* lvi. 1.

[4] e.g. Gieseler and Matter.

[5] Cf. Eph. Syr. *Adv. Hær.* Serm. xiv, *Opera* V. p. 468; Pseudo-Origen, *De Recta Fide* sect. iii. Matter (vol. I. p. 365) considers Marcion in the latter dialogue to have misrepresented the doctrine of Bardesanes, but this is not clear.

to Abraham and others of the older patriarchs,[1] and that his suffering likewise was a suffering in appearance only. In consistency with these opinions he also denied the resurrection of the body.[2]

Yet Bardesanes must be considered as only partially a Gnostic. At least, the one cardinal error which may be considered as characteristic of Gnosticism, the separation between the Supreme God and the Creator of the world, finds no place in his teaching. God the Father in conjunction with the Divine Word or, according to another representation of his view, the Divine Word in conjunction with Wisdom or the Holy Spirit, is the maker of the world and of man.[3] Bardesanes also accepted all the Scriptures of the Old and New Testament, as well as some apocryphal books[4] — in this again showing himself the antagonist of Marcion; and probably, notwithstanding his many aberrations in the direction of Gnosticism, there was no time in his life in which he did not consider himself a Christian.[5]

Bardesanes was the author of a work in Syriac on Fate, of which a remarkable fragment in a Greek translation has been preserved by Eusebius,[6] and of which the whole has recently been published in the original Syriac text with an English translation by the late Dr. Cureton.[7] In

---

[1] Theodoret, *Epist.* 145 Βαλεντῖνος δέ, καὶ Βασιλείδης, καὶ Βαρδεσάνης, καὶ Ἁρμόνιος, καὶ οἱ τῆς τούτων συμμορίας, δέχονται μὲν τῆς παρθένου τὴν κύησιν καὶ τὸν τόκον, οὐδὲν δὲ τὸν Θεὸν Λόγον ἐκ τῆς παρθένου προσειληφέναι φασίν, ἀλλὰ πάροδόν τινα δι' αὐτῆς ὥσπερ διὰ σωλῆνος ποιήσασθαι, ἐπιφανῆναι δὲ τοῖς ἀνθρώποις φαντασίᾳ χρησάμενος καὶ δόξας εἶναι ἄνθρωπος, ὃν τρόπον ὤφθη τῷ Ἁβραὰμ καί τισιν ἄλλοις τῶν παλαιῶν. Cf. Pseudo-Origen, *De Recta Fide*, sect. iv.

[2] Pseudo-Origen, *De Recta Fide*, iii, v; Epiphan. *Hær.* lvi.

[3] *De Recta Fide* iii, iv. Cf. Eph. Syr. *Adv. Hær.* Serm. 55 (*Opera* V. p. 557), Serm. 3 (p. 444). Cf. Burton, *Lectures on Eccl. Hist.* II. p. 184; Matter, I. p. 367 *seq.*

[4] Epiphan. *Hær.* lvi. 2.

[5] Cf. Burton, *Lectures on Eccl. Hist.* II. p. 184.

[6] *Præp. Evang.* vi. 10; cf. *H. E.* iv. 30.

[7] *Spicilegium Syriacum*, London 1855.

this work, which Eusebius calls περὶ εἱμαρμένης διάλογος,[1] but which in the Syriac is entitled 'The Book of the Laws of Countries,' Bardesanes reasons with much acuteness and good sense against the assumption that the actions of men are caused either by nature, or by fortune or destiny. From both these he carefully distinguishes free will, and maintains that while the body of man and its animal functions are governed, like those of other animals, by natural laws, the soul is free to choose its own course of action, and is responsible for the choice it makes. In support of this position he adduces among other arguments one which is well known to most of us from its employment in Aristotle's Ethics, namely, that men are not blamed for their bodily deformities, which come by nature, but are blamed for their vicious actions, as being in their own power to avoid.[2] Against the astrological fatalism of the Chaldeans he very sensibly argues that the customs and actions of men vary in different countries, though some of the natives of these several countries are born under the same conjunction of the planets.

Though sharing the opinions of Saturninus concerning matter, and connecting it even more closely with the evil principle, Bardesanes did not carry out his doctrines in practice to the ascetic conclusions of his predecessor. He was the father of a son named Harmonius, who inherited his father's philosophical opinions.[3] Both father and son were poets as well as philosophers. Bardesanes is said to have written 150 hymns, according to the number of the Psalms of David;[4] and his hymns with those of his son

[1] *H. E.* iv. 30.
[2] *Spicil. Syr.* p. 19. Cf. Arist. *Eth. Nic.* iii. 5, 15.
[3] Sozomen, *H. E.* iii. 16; cf. Theodoret, *Hær. Fab.* i. 22.
[4] Ephr. Syr. *Adv. Hæret.* Serm. 53 (*Opera* V. p. 554); cf. Matter, *Hist. du Gnost.* I. pp. 359–361; Milman, *Hist. of Christianity* II. p. 74.

Harmonius, notwithstanding their heterodox character, continued to be used by the Syrian Christians for two centuries, till they were superseded by those of St. Ephraim.[1]

The above teachers have been classed together as Syrian Gnostics, because, taking the term in a somewhat wide sense, they may all be considered as natives of that country, and because a general affinity may be observed between the features of their several systems. Yet it would be difficult to select any one positive doctrine which can be regarded as specially characteristic of the Syrian Gnosis as distinguished from that of other countries. The Docetism which is common to all the above systems is shared by others of different local origin; and the morbid asceticism which is characteristic of Saturninus and Tatian does not appear in Bardesanes. The feature which is usually selected as characteristic of the Syrian Gnosis is the doctrine of dualism; that is to say, the assumption of the existence of two active and independent principles, the one of good, the other of evil.[2] This assumption, as we have seen, was distinctly held by Saturninus and Bardesanes; and if it is not so directly traceable in Tatian, we have the authority of Epiphanius for attributing it to his followers the Encratites, who probably borrowed it from their master, with the remainder of whose teaching it is perfectly in accordance.[3] We are therefore perhaps justified in selecting this tenet as the characteristic feature of the Syrian Gnosis, in contradistinction to the

---

[1] Sozomen, *H. E.* iii. 16.

[2] Gieseler, *Eccl. Hist.* vol. I. p. 143 (Eng. Tr.).

[3] Epiphan. *Hær.* xlvii. 1 ('De Encratitis') φάσκουσι δὲ καὶ οὗτοι ἀρχάς τινας εἶναι τήν τε τοῦ διαβόλου ἀντικειμένην πρὸς τὰ τοῦ Θεοῦ ποιήματα καὶ μὴ ὑποτασσομένην Θεῷ, ἀλλὰ ἰσχύοντα καὶ πράττοντα ὡς κατ' ἰδίαν ἐξουσίαν, καὶ οὐχ ὡς ἐν παρεκτροπῇ γενόμενον. Cf. J. C. Wolf. *Manichæismus ante Manichæos* p. 211.

Platonic theory of an inert semi-existent matter, which was adopted by the Gnosis of Egypt. The former principle found its logical development in the next century in Manicheism; the latter, as we shall see hereafter, leads with almost equal certainty, if not with the same logical necessity, to Pantheism.

LECTURE X.

EGYPTIAN GNOSTICISM—BASILIDES.

In proceeding from the Syrian to the Egyptian form of Gnosticism, our first attention is directed towards a man who, if we could accept the various and conflicting notices concerning his teaching which have descended to us from different quarters, might be regarded as being the connecting link between the two systems, and as having occupied that position by virtue of uniting in his own teaching the heterogeneous ingredients of the one and the other. And as if at first sight to justify this conclusion, we find the same man described as belonging in his own person to both countries: Syrian by birth,[1] Egyptian by residence,[2] the disciple of the Samaritan Menander and fellow pupil with the Syrian Saturninus,[3] the preacher, according to one account, in Persia,[4] the resident at Alexandria, and the student of the Greek philosophy.[5] Basilides, the teacher concerning whom these several statements have been made, has been the object of dispute as regards the time in which he lived, no less than as regards the doctrines which he taught. The language of Clement of Alexandria, who was likely to be well informed on this

---

[1] Epiphanius (*Hær.* xxiii. 1, 7), cited by Neander, *Ch. Hist.* II. p. 47: cf. Matter, I. p. 402. In the *Disp. Archelai et Manetis* (Routh, *Rel. Sacr.* V. 196) he is called a Persian, possibly to account for the dualism there ascribed to him.

[2] Irenæus, i. 24; Euseb. *H. E.* iv. 7.

[3] Euseb. *H. E.* iv. 7.

[4] *Disp. Archelai, l. c.*

[5] Hippolytus, vii. 14.

point, would lead us to fix the close of his life at the beginning of the reign of the elder Antoninus, who ascended the throne A.D. 138.[1] St. Jerome however enumerates him among the heretics of the Apostolic age, from which statement some critics suppose that he must have promulgated his opinions at least before the death of St. John.[2] Though the statement of Clement is quite compatible with the supposition that the youth of Basilides was contemporary with the latter days of the Apostle, the preponderance of testimony seems to place his principal activity in the reign of Hadrian, i.e. from A.D. 117 to 138.[3]

Among the various and not easily reconcilable accounts which have come down to us concerning the doctrines of Basilides, the most trustworthy are probably the occasional notices furnished by Clement of Alexandria and the detailed account of the system given in the recently discovered work of Hippolytus against heresies. The former of these Fathers, from his residence in the city where Basilides had taught, had peculiar opportunities of becoming acquainted with the particulars of his teaching, while the latter was in possession of a work written by Basilides himself, from which he quotes several passages *verbatim*. Irenæus on the other hand, though earlier in point of time than both the above-named Fathers, seems to have obtained his information from less direct sources, and possibly in some degree confounded the teaching of Basilides himself with that of some of his professed followers.[4] In the account which I shall attempt to give

[1] Clem. Alex. *Strom.* vii. 17, p. 898, οἳ ... καὶ μέχρι γε τῆς Ἀντωνίνου τοῦ πρεσβυτέρου διέτειναν ἡλικίας, καθάπερ ὁ Βασιλείδης.

[2] Massuet, *Diss. Præv. in Irenæum* i. § 112.

[3] Euseb. *H. E.* iv. 7; *Chron.* ii. p. 168, ed. *Schöne;* Theodoret, *Hær. Fab.* i. 2.

[4] Neander, *Church Hist.* vol. II. p. 113. Cf. Matter, vol. II. p. 20. So also Baur, *Chr. Gnosis* p. 210, and in his later works referred to by Ueberweg, *Gesch. der Philosophie* II.

of their doctrine, I propose to take as a groundwork the exposition of Hippolytus, as the most complete and systematic, illustrating it as far as possible from the notices of Clement, leaving the other accounts to be compared subsequently with the results derived from these sources.

Basilides, according to Hippolytus, who is supported by Clement,[1] professed to derive his doctrines from a secret teaching communicated by the Saviour to St. Matthias.[2] He also claimed as his teacher a certain Glaucias, said to have been the companion and interpreter of St. Peter,[3] of whom nothing further is known. According to this teaching, the first principle of all things, the supreme Being, is one whose nature cannot be expressed by any language, for he is above every name that is named. He cannot properly be even said to exist; for he cannot be identified with any one thing that exists: he is rather to be called absolute non-existence. This nonexistent Deity Hippolytus compares, not very happily, with the νόησις νοήσεως of Aristotle, and illustrates the theory by an imaginary resemblance to the Aristotelian doctrine of genera and species, which are not identical with any of the individuals comprehended under them. It is tolerably evident however, both historically and philosophically, that the source of this teaching is to be found in another quarter, and that Plato, whose authority was predominant in Alexandria, was the philosopher to whose influence the theory is mainly due. The language in which the ideal good is described in the Republic, οὐκ οὐσίας ὄντος τοῦ ἀγαθοῦ, ἀλλ᾽ ἔτι ἐπέκεινα τῆς οὐσίας πρεσβείᾳ καὶ δυνάμει

---

p. 31. Hilgenfeld on the other hand (see Ueberweg *l. c.* p. 33) holds that the exposition of Irenæus represents the earlier doctrine. Jacobi, *Basilidis Philosophi Gnostici Sententiæ*, Berolini 1852, Uhlhorn, *Das Basilidianische System*, Gött. 1855, Baur, *Das Christenthum der drei ersten Jahrh.* 1853 and 1860, and in *Theol. Jahrb.* 1856, p. 121 *seq.*, all regard Hippolytus as the most reliable authority.

[1] Hippol. vii. 20. Cf. Clem. Alex. *Strom.* vii. 17, p. 900.

[2] Clem. Alex. *Strom.* vii. 17, p. 898.

[3] Hippol. vii. 20.

ὑπερέχοντος,[1] with the further development of the same doctrine by Philo, in which God is represented as without qualities and not to be expressed in speech,[2] contains in substance the very same thing which Basilides has expressed with some little rhetorical exaggeration, but without any substantial change. In the next century the same theory reappears in the Neoplatonism of Plotinus, who speaks of the supreme unity as above existence,[3] and again, two centuries later, in the expiring Neoplatonism of Proclus, who speaks of God as above substance and life and intelligence;[4] and it has reappeared with all the advantages of modern philosophical genius and learning in the resuscitated Neoplatonism of Germany, in Schelling, who speaks of the Absolute as neither ideal nor real, neither thought nor being,[5] and in Hegel, who identifies pure existence with pure nothing.

The continuation of the exposition of Basilides, strange as it may sound, is nothing but the same theory expressed as before in somewhat rhetorical terms. 'Since therefore,' he continues,[6] 'there was nothing, neither matter, nor substance, nor unsubstantial, nor simple, nor compound, nor inconceivable, nor imperceptible, nor man, nor angel, nor God, nor in short any of the things that are named or perceived by the senses or conceived by the intellect, but all things being thus, and more minutely than thus, simply obliterated, the non-existent God (whom Aristotle calls thought of thought, but these men, non-existent), without thought, without sense, without counsel, without choice,

---

[1] Plato, *Resp.* vi. p. 509.

[2] Philo, *De Mundi Opif.* c. 2 (p. 2); *Legis Alleg.* i. c. 13 (p. 50), c. 15 (p. 53); *De Somn.* i. 39 (p. 655).

[3] *Enn.* v. 1. 10 τὸ ἐπέκεινα ὄντος τὸ ἕν.

[4] *Inst. Theol.* c. 115.

[5] *Bruno,* p. 58.

[6] Hippol. vii. 21. The text seems incomplete. We should perhaps read οὐχ ὕλη, οὐκ ἄνυλον, and (with Uhlhorn, approved by Duncker and Schneidewin) οὐ νοητόν, οὐκ ἀνόητον, οὐκ αἰσθητόν, οὐκ ἀναίσθητον.

without passion, without desire, willed to make a world. When I say *willed*, I mean to signify without will and without thought and without sense; and by *the world* I mean not that which was afterwards made and separated by size and division, but the seed of the world. For the seed of the world had everything in itself, as a grain of mustard seed in the smallest compass comprehends all things together, the roots, the stem, the branches, the leaves, and the innumerable seeds of other and yet other plants mingled with the grains of the plant. Thus the non-existent God made a non-existent world from things non-existent, having cast down and deposited a single seed, having in itself the universal seed of the world.'[1] We are further told that Basilides rejected the hypothesis of creation by emanation (προβολή) or out of pre-existent matter; 'for what emanation,' he asked, 'or what matter need be assumed, that God may make a world, as if He were a spider spinning its threads, or a mortal man who takes for his work brass or wood or some other material? But, he said, God spake and it was done, and this, as they say, is what Moses expresses in the words *Let there be light and there was light*. Whence, says Basilides, came the light? from nothing. For it is not written whence, but only that it came from the voice of him that spake. And the speaker, he continues, was not, and that which was produced was not. The seed of the world was produced from things that were not, and this seed is the Word which was spoken, *Let there be light;* and this, he adds, is that which is spoken in the Gospels, *That is the true light which lighteth every man coming into the world.*'[2]

In this description, in which it is hard to say whether sublimity or extravagance predominates, one or two things are expressly worthy of notice. First, it will be seen that

[1] τὴν τοῦ κόσμου πανσπερμίαν.   [2] vii. 22.

Basilides altogether rejects the attempt, so common among the Gnostics, to account for the origin of evil by the hypothesis either of an eternal inert matter, or of a self-existing, active, malignant principle. The unity of his first principle is maintained in terms whose intenseness borders on absurdity. He plunges at once into the most abstract representation of the absolute, and seems to admit evil in no other form than as a phase in the world's development. His theory, if not distinctly pantheistic, needs but one step to make it so.[1] The name of God has but to be transferred from the non-existent to the only recognised existence, the process of the evolution of the world, and evil at once ceases to be evil and becomes a part of the Divine manifestation. Secondly, it is easy to trace in this exposition the influence of Greek philosophy modified by Alexandrian Judaism. The non-existent God, as I have already observed, is the Platonic absolute good, above all definite existence; the seed of the world, with its development into definite existences, bears a close resemblance to the ὁμοῦ πάντα or primitive chaos of Anaxagoras; and the word πανσπερμία, which Basilides borrows, is employed by Aristotle to denote the relation of the ὁμοιομερῆ of Anaxagoras to the four elements.[2] The λόγος σπερματικός again holds an important position in the Stoical philosophy as denoting the productive power of nature, by which the world is developed according to a fixed and rational

---

[1] Cf. Uhlhorn, *Das Basilidianische System*. Gött. 1855, p. 34; Hilgenfeld in *Theol. Jahrb.* 1856, pp. 88, 115; Baur, *ibid.* p. 138. Yet this pantheism is not incompatible with a certain kind of dualism, as in Spinoza: the One presents the opposite side of thought and extension. See Baur, *l. c.*

[2] Arist. *De Gen. et Corr.* i. 1, 5. Cf. Zeller, *Phil. der Gr.* I. p. 670. The word is also used by Aristotle, *De An.* i. 2, 3, with reference to the philosophy of Democritus. It had previously been employed by Plato, *Timæus* p. 73 c. On the resemblance between Basilides and Anaxagoras, see Baur in *Theol. Jahrb.* 1856, p. 146.

law;[1] and this philosophy, with its pantheistic conception of the world and its phenomena, presents many analogies to the theory of Basilides.[2] But these heathen materials are here combined with a higher teaching borrowed from the book of Genesis interpreted somewhat after the manner of Philo. But, thirdly and especially, we should observe that Basilides attempts to reinforce his heathen and Jewish cosmogony by a Christian element borrowed from the Gospel of St. John; and this newly recovered quotation, coming in a work written at latest during the reign of Hadrian, is fatal to the favourite hypothesis of the Tübingen critics, who would persuade us that the Gospel was not written till the middle of the second century.[3]

The conception of matter as part of the divine creation, and therefore not necessarily evil, is further carried out in the sequel of the theory. In the seed of the world, says Basilides, there is a threefold sonship, of one substance[4] with the non-existent God, produced from things that are not. Of this sonship, divided into three parts, one part was fine, another gross, and a third needing purification.[5] The first of these immediately sprang up to the non-existent God; the second strove to ascend, but was only enabled to do so by the assistance of wings, such as those described in Plato's Phædrus, and which Basilides calls, not wings, but the Holy Spirit. By the aid of this wing or spirit the second sonship ascended, not to the non-existent

---

[1] See Zeller, *Phil. der Griechen* III. 1, p. 146.

[2] Cf. Uhlhorn, *Das Basil. Syst.* p. 12, and Baur in *Theol. Jahrb.* 1856, p. 145, who refers especially to the doctrine of Cleanthes in Stobæus, *Ecl.* i. 372. Baur denies that there is any trace of Platonism in Basilides. Yet he admits that the representation of the Deity as οὐκ ὤν is not to be found in the Stoical philosophy; and it is exactly here that the Platonic influence may be traced.

[3] Bunsen, *Hippolytus* I. p. 87.

[4] ὁμοούσιος.

[5] The words ταχυμερές, τὸ δὲ must clearly be supplied from the summary (x. 14). So Duncker and Schneidewin read.

Deity, but to the next inferior place, while the spirit became separated from the sonship and occupied the intermediate place between the world and the supermundane region, being placed as a firmament between the one and the other.[1] The third sonship, which needed purification, remained in the mass which constituted the seed of the universe.

In this strange allegory it seems natural to recognise a very embellished form of the Mosaic account of the creation. The first sonship seems to indicate that portion of finite existence which is purely spiritual, and which, like the ideas of Plato, is in immediate connection with and subordination to the ideal good which is above all definite existence. In the second or grosser sonship, we seem to recognise the finer portion of the material creation, the 'waters which are above the firmament,' borne up by the spirit, which is here identified with the firmament and the atmosphere pervading the sphere below the firmament. The third sonship, that which needs purification, seems to represent that portion of the spiritual creation which remains on earth united to material bodies, from which however it is to be separated hereafter. Having thus described the generation of the supermundane region and the firmament by which it is separated from the world, Basilides next proceeds to the formation of the world below the firmament. 'After the firmament was formed, there sprang forth from the seed of the world the great Ruler, the head of the world, of indestructible beauty and magnitude and power. He sprang up and ascended as high as the firmament, but being unable to

---

[1] This πνεῦμα μεθόριον (Hipp. vii. 23) seems to answer to the διάκονος or *ministering spirit*, cited from the teaching of Basilides by Clem. Alex. *Excerpt. Theod.* 16, p. 972. Cf. Baur in *Theol. Jahrb.* 1856, p. 154. The expression in the latter case seems to be taken from Heb. i. 14, εἰς διακονίαν ἀποστελλόμενα: and here also the reference is in the first instance to the wind, as seems to be also the interpretation of the theory as stated by Hippolytus. Cf. Alford on Heb. i. 14.

ascend higher, and being ignorant of the existence of the region beyond, he became the wisest and most powerful and brightest of mundane existences, superior to all beneath except that portion of the divine sonship which still remained in the world. Believing himself to be the highest of all beings, he undertook the formation of a world of definite existences. First he begat a son wiser and more powerful than himself, whom he seated at his right hand, thus forming what in the language of these philosophers is called the Ogdoad; the whole celestial or ethereal creation being formed by the great Ruler with the aid and counsel of his greater son. In thus acting, the Ruler of the world did but accomplish unwittingly the counsel of the non-existent God, which he had predetermined when he created the seed of the universe.' The relation between the ruler of the visible world and his son is explained by Hippolytus as identical with Aristotle's distinction between the body and the soul, the latter being the ἐντελέχεια or completeness of the former, by which it is governed and acts.[1]

The great Ruler and his son govern the whole ethereal region down to the sphere of the moon, where the finer ether is succeeded by the grosser air. Within the lower sphere is generated in like manner a second ruler inferior to the first, whose region is called the Hebdomad, and who is the creator and governor of all below him, commencing his creation like the first ruler with the generation of a son greater than himself. He too acts unwittingly in subordination to the non-existent Deity, and the things that are produced come into existence according to the laws first ordained in the seed of the world. The great Archon, the ruler of the Ogdoad, we are further told, bears the mystical name of *Abrasax*, or, as other authors

[1] Cf. Baur in *Theol. Jahrb.* 1856, p. 148, who identifies the son of the Archon with the world-soul.

give it, *Abraxas*, and rules over 365 heavens,[1] his name containing the number 365, according to the numerical powers of the Greek letters of which it is composed. Many and various attempts have been made to discover a hidden meaning in this name and in the parts of which it is composed,[2] but probably no other explanation is needed than that supplied by the numerical force of its letters.[3] The number 365 has an obvious connection with the solar year, and it is not impossible that the so-called 365 heavens may have been a mistaken interpretation of some theory connected with the 365 days of the year,[4] or they may merely represent the apparent diurnal revolution of the sun. But be this as it may, there can be no doubt that the personified Abraxas was meant as a symbol of the sun. The name is to be met with on numbers of stones which still exist, and which are known generally by the name of Abraxas gems, though the name is often incorrectly given to other remains besides those to which it properly belongs. These gems confirm the explanation which identifies Abraxas with the sun-god.[5]

---

[1] That it is improbable that the doctrine of 365 heavens was literally held by Basilides, see Lardner, *Hist. of Heretics* b. ii. c. 2. sec. 4. Hence the probability, as suggested below, that it was the misrepresentation of some theory concerning the year.

[2] For some of these explanations, see Matter, *Hist. du Gnosticisme* vol. I. p. 412 *seq.*

[3] See Harvey's *Irenæus*, I. p. 202, where a similar explanation is cited from St. Augustine, *De Hæres.* 4. The sum is as follows:—

$$\begin{aligned} a &= 1 \\ \beta &= 2 \\ \rho &= 100 \\ a &= 1 \\ \xi &= 60 \\ a &= 1 \\ s &= 200 \\ \hline &365 \end{aligned}$$

[4] Something of this sort might naturally arise from the Egyptian doctrine of a guardian genius for every day in the year. Abraxas would then be the head of all these. Cf. Matter, II. p. 4. Massuet (Irenæus, *Diss. Præv.* i. § 116) supposes the 365 apparent revolutions of the sun to be meant.

[5] Cf. King, *The Gnostics and their Remains* p. 35, 78 *seq.* Pseudo-Tertullian, *De Præscr.* c. 46, and Jerome, *Comm. in Amos* iii. 9 *seq.*, say that *Abraxas* in Basilides is the name of the Supreme God. This is by no means so clear in the representation of Irenæus, nor in Epiphanius and Theodoret, who follow him. Hilgenfeld in *Theol. Jahrb.* 1856, p. 118, and Baur, *ibid.* p. 157, state the difference between Hippolytus and the other authorities too generally. For an

The second ruler, the Lord of the Hebdomad, is expressly identified with the God of the Jews who appeared to Moses in the burning bush. As the number 365 is connected with the solar year, we are naturally tempted to suppose a connection between the number seven and the four phases of the moon, within whose sphere the Hebdomad is placed, as well as with the seven days of creation and the consequent institution of the week of seven days. It is also probable that the Hebdomad and the Ogdoad contain an allusion to the seven spheres of the planets, and the eighth of the fixed stars;[1] but without attempting to fix minutely the details of these allusions, we may at least conclude in general that this portion of the cosmogony of Basilides contains an allegorical application of the scriptural account of the creation as symbolical of theories of astronomy. Such is a brief outline of the creation of the world according to the theory of Basilides.

We have next to consider his account of its redemption. This consists in the lifting up to God of that third class of sonship which was described in the beginning as needing purification. In this third sonship it is easy to recognise the Gnostic distinction of the πνευματικοί or spiritual persons, that portion of mankind who are capable of attaining to knowledge, but who are compelled for a time to reside in the material world imprisoned in material bodies, and having their spiritual part clogged and hindered by bodily senses and passions. The means of their deliverance is the Gospel, which is characteristically defined as ἡ τῶν ὑπερκοσμίων γνῶσις,[2] the knowledge of those

---

account of the so-called Abraxas gems, many of which are heathen, see Lardner, *Hist. of Heretics* b. ii. c. 2, sect. 22.

[1] The Hebdomad may perhaps represent the sublunar sphere, while the Ogdoad represents the sum of all the spheres, corresponding in number to those of Plato, *Resp.* x. p. 616. Cf. Baur in *Theol. Jahrb.* 1856, p. 158.

[2] Hippol. vii. 27 (p. 376, Duncker).

Divine things which are above the world, in the region of the non-existent God and of the spiritual offspring who have already ascended to him. It is the need of this deliverance which is expressed in the language of St. Paul, 'The whole creation groaneth and travaileth in pain together, waiting for the manifestation of the sons of God;'[1] and by the sons of God, says Basilides, are meant the spiritual men who are left here to arrange and mould and rectify and complete those souls which are constituted by nature to remain below in this region. The former state of the world may be divided into two periods. In the first, as it is written, 'Sin reigned from Adam to Moses;'[2] that is to say, the great Archon, the ruler of the Ogdoad, whose name is unspeakable, had his dominion, and believed himself to be the only God, for all above him was hidden. After this came the government of the second Archon, the ruler of the Hebdomad, who is the God who revealed himself to Moses as being the God of Abraham and of Isaac and of Jacob, but as not having revealed to them the unspeakable name of the first Ruler. From the inspiration of this Archon spoke the prophets who lived before the time of the Saviour. Then came the third period, when the sons of God should be revealed, when the Gospel came into the world, passing through every principality and power and dominion and every

---

[1] Hippol. vii. 25. It will be seen that this quotation is a combination of two verses of Romans viii, the first part from ver. 22, the second from ver. 19. The πνευματικός of Basilides, as described in the extract cited by Hippolytus, is the same as the person described by Clement, *Strom.* v. 1 (p. 645 Potter) φύσει πιστοῦ καὶ ἐκλεκτοῦ ὄντος, ὡς Βασιλείδης νομίζει, and *Strom.* ii. 3 (p. 433) ἐνταῦθα φυσικὴν ἡγοῦνται τὴν πίστιν οἱ ἀμφὶ τὸν Βασιλείδην καθὸ καὶ ἐπὶ τῆς ἐκλογῆς τάττουσιν αὐτήν, τὰ μαθήματα ἀναποδείκτως εὑρίσκουσαν καταλήψει νοητικῇ. Here again the ἐκλεκτὸς is from Rom. viii. 33, the whole chapter being pressed to the support of the theory. Cf. Baur in *Theol. Jahrb.* 1856, p. 152 *seq.*

[2] Rom. v. 14. St. Paul however says ἐβασίλευσεν ὁ θάνατος, not ἡ ἁμαρτία.

name that is named.[1] It did not indeed come down, for nothing which is in the region above can quit the presence of God and descend, but it kindled the intellects which rose to it from below, as the Indian naphtha attracts fire from a distance. First, the great Archon of the Ogdoad was illuminated by means of his son, and learned that he was not the Supreme God, and he feared and confessed his sin in having magnified himself, as it is written, 'The fear of the Lord is the beginning of wisdom.'[2] From the first Archon and his kingdom the light of the Gospel was communicated to the second Archon with similar results; and after the whole of his dominion had been illuminated, the light came down from the Hebdomad to the earth and enlightened Jesus the son of Mary. From that time the constitution of the world is to continue till the remaining sons of God have been formed after the likeness of Jesus, and have been purified and enabled to ascend on high. When this ascension is completed, God shall bring upon the whole world the great ignorance, that all things may remain in the place assigned to them by nature, and desire nothing beyond. All souls which are designed by nature for the world, and not for the region above the world, from the Archon of the Ogdoad downwards, shall be involved in utter ignorance of all that is above them, that thus they may have no sense of deficiency or pain of desire; and thus will be brought about the restoration of all things which in the beginning were established in the seed of the universe, and shall be restored in their own season.

---

[1] An adaptation of Ephes. i. 21.

[2] Cf. Clem. Alex. *Strom.* ii. 8 (p. 448). Clement uses the expression ἀρχὴν γενόμενον σοφίας φυλοκρινητικῆς τε καὶ διακριτικῆς καὶ τελεωτικῆς καὶ ἀποκαταστατικῆς, which quite agrees with the representation of Hippolytus, according to which Basilides regarded redemption as a separation of the spiritual element. Indeed Hippolytus uses the same language, vii. 27 ἵνα ἀπαρχὴ τῆς φυλοκρινήσεως γένηται τῶν συγκεχυμένων ὁ Ἰησοῦς κ.τ.λ. Cf. Uhlhorn, *Das Bas. Syst.* p. 49; Baur in *Theol. Jahrb.* 1856, p. 151.

In addition to this theory of the generation and restoration of the universe, Hippolytus tells us that the disciples of Basilides accepted the Gospel narrative of the life of Jesus, and admitted the reality of his sufferings, which however, they said, were endured for no other purpose than the separation of the spiritual element in the universe from the inferior things which were mingled with it. Of that separation Jesus himself was the first-fruits. His bodily nature suffered and was resolved into formlessness. The several constituents of his higher nature ascended each to its cognate region; the psychical to the domain of the great Archon; the spiritual to the intermediate region of the spirit; the divine to the supermundane abode of the Supreme God and his true sons. From this statement of Hippolytus, which is indirectly confirmed by Clement of Alexandria,[1] it appears that Basilides did not adopt the Docetic views of the person of Jesus which were attributed to him (or perhaps rather to his followers) by Irenæus and others.[2] Especially that strange and profane fancy, that Simon of Cyrene was changed into the likeness of Jesus and suffered in his stead, while Jesus, in the form of Simon, stood by and laughed at his enemies, could have had no place in the original teaching of Basilides, though it may have been engrafted on his system by some of its later exponents.

A comparison of the notices of Hippolytus with those of Clement will also enable us to correct another erroneous impression which has generally prevailed concerning the teaching of Basilides, namely, that he was one of those

---

[1] *Strom.* iv. 12 (p. 600), where Basilides is represented as speaking of the sufferings of Jesus, and likens them to those of the infant, who has committed no actual sin, yet suffers, ἔχων ἐν ἑαυτῷ τὸ ἁμαρτητικόν. Cf. Uhlhorn, *Das Bas. Syst.* p. 43.

[2] Irenæus, i. 24. 4. Cf. Epiphan. *Hær.* xxiv. 3; Theodoret, *Hær. Fab.* i. 4. So also Tertullian, *De Res. Carn.* c. 2; and Pseudo-Tertull. *De Præscr.* c. 46. Cf. Uhlhorn, p. 50; Matter, II. p. 22.

who accounted for the existence of evil by the Persian hypothesis of two independent principles.[1] A passage in Clement, which was once supposed to give some support to this view, receives quite a different interpretation when examined by the light of the new information furnished by Hippolytus. Basilides and his followers, according to Clement, called the passions of man *προσαρτήματα*, or *appendages*, and regarded them as spirits appended to the rational soul in consequence of a certain *disturbance and confusion of principles* (*κατά τινα τάραχον καὶ σύγχυσιν ἀρχικήν*);[2] with these were connected other spurious spirits of different natures, such as those of the wolf, the ape, the lion, or the goat, or even of plants and minerals, which form desires in the soul of a similar kind.[3] We are reminded of Plato's figurative representation of the appetitive portion of the soul as a many-headed monster, and of the shells and seaweed clinging round the divine form of the sea-god Glaucus;[4] but there is nothing in the passage to suggest a dualistic origin of evil, unless it be in the words *κατὰ σύγχυσιν ἀρχικήν*, which have often been explained as implying a conflict between the good and evil principle, but which the exposition of Hippolytus, who uses the same term, clearly shows to be employed in their more natural sense as denoting a mixture of elements, spiritual and material. The only

[1] This has been maintained by Neander, Ritter, Baur (in his *Chr. Gnosis*, subsequently dropped in his later exposition), and recently by Hilgenfeld in *Theol. Jahrb.* 1856.

[2] Clem. Alex. *Strom.* ii. 20 (p. 488, Potter). On this passage, see Baur in *Theol. Jahrb.* 1856, p. 152.

[3] Plato, *Resp.* ix. p. 588, x. p. 611. The argument of Isidore recorded by Clement against the plea of necessity based on the doctrine is also Platonic. The rational soul must contend with and overcome the material accretions.

[4] Hippol. vii. 27 (p. 244 Miller, 378 Duncker) ὅλη γὰρ αὐτῶν ἡ ὑπόθεσις σύγχυσις οἱονεὶ πανσπερμίας καὶ φυλοκρίνησις καὶ ἀποκατάστασις τῶν συγκεχυμένων εἰς τὰ οἰκεῖα. Cf. Uhlhorn, *Das Basilidianische System* p. 44; Baur in *Theol. Jahrb.* 1856, p. 152.

evidence which exists, for distinctly charging Basilides with dualism, is found in a work, the authority of which has been much disputed,[1] the extant Latin translation of a lost original,[2] purporting to be the account of a discussion between the Persian Manes and Archelaus, Bishop of Caschar in Mesopotamia. In that work Basilides is named as a precursor of the Manichean doctrine, and a fragment is quoted from a writing of his, in which he maintains the doctrine of certain barbarians concerning two eternal principles. But the fragment as quoted does not show whether Basilides accepted this doctrine; and the assertion that he does so rests only on the very doubtful authority of the writer by whom he is quoted, and is too much at variance with what we know of his philosophy from other sources to have any claim to acceptance.[3]

In fact, the philosophy of Basilides, as described in our previous notice, is of all Gnostic systems the one which least requires or admits of such a hypothesis. In its external character it seems to be an allegorical representation of the religious progress of the world, from Sabaism to Judaism, and from Judaism to Christianity; the first stage being represented by the reign of Abraxas, the Sun-God, from Adam to Moses; the second by the revelation of the Archon of the Hebdomad to the Hebrew lawgiver; the third by the period of purification introduced by the Gospel. In its internal or philosophical character, it is a pantheistic representation of the evolutions of the world in a series of necessary developments, in which, as in all systems conceived in a pantheistic spirit, free-will and

[1] As by Beausobre, *Histoire de Manichée* I. c. 12, 13, and by Milman, *Hist. of Christianity* II. p. 272. Cf. Routh, *Rel. Sacr.* V. p. 23.

[2] It was originally written in Syriac; thence translated and epitomised in Greek, and thence into Latin.

[3] Cf. Uhlhorn, *Das Bas. Syst.* p. 53.

moral guilt have no place,¹ and the only form of evil admitted is that of a mere temporary disturbance of the natural position of things; the spiritual being mingled with the material instead of being exalted above it.²

With the views which Basilides entertained of the nature o fevil and of the relation of the world to God, there could be no need of the hypothesis adopted in other Gnostic systems of a series of emanations or intermediate beings between God and the world, so disposed as to make the creation of the material universe the work of an inferior and imperfect agent; and accordingly, in the extract above cited, we find Basilides expressly repudiating the theory of creation by emanations, as well as that of an eternally pre-existent matter. Nevertheless, in the commonly-received account of his doctrine as given by Irenæus and those who have followed his statements, we find this doctrine expressly ascribed to Basilides. 'He sets forth,' says Irenæus, 'that from the unborn Father sprang Νοῦς, and from this again Λόγος, from Λόγος, Φρόνησις, from Φρόνησις, Σοφία and Δύναμις, and from Δύναμις and Σοφία, powers and principalities and angels, whom he calls the first, and by whom the first heaven was made. From these by emanation were derived others who made a second heaven, similar to the first; and in like manner, by emanation from these, others were made, the counterparts of those above them, and these formed a third heaven; and from the third again in downward succession a fourth; and in succession after this manner they say that other principalities and angels were made, and heavens to the number of 365. Wherefore the year

---

¹ Clement expressly charges Basilides with excluding free-will, *Strom.* ii. 3, p. 434. Cf. Uhlhorn, *Das Bas. Syst.* p. 38.

² Cf. Uhlhorn, *Das Bas. Syst.* p. 35; Baur in *Theol. Jahrb.* 1856, p. 142.

contains so many days, according to the number of the heavens.[1]

The theory as here exhibited is probably a later modification of the original teaching of Basilides, under the influence of the school of Valentinus.[2] But though it is scarcely possible that Basilides himself could have held the theory in the form in which it is here attributed to him, it is by no means improbable that he may have prepared the way for it, by recognising something like the personification of spiritual attributes which head the above list, though not in the form of successive emanations. The resemblance which has been already noticed between the non-existent Deity of Basilides and the ideal Good of Plato renders it probable that Basilides, like Plato, may have connected his absolute first principle with a subordinate intelligible world of ideas, though these would form but minor details in his system, and could not be interposed as successive links in the world of creation.[3] This supposition receives some support from a brief notice in Clement of Alexandria, who speaks of Basilides as recognising an Ogdoad of which two of the members were Justice and her daughter Peace.[4] If we add these to the five intellectual qualities personified in the list of Irenæus, and omit the creative powers and angels which seem to belong to a later form of the theory, we shall have, with the addition of the absolute first prin-

---

[1] Irenæus, i. 24. 3. Cf. Epiphan. *Hær.* xxiv. 1; Theodoret, *Hær. Fab.* i. 4.

[2] Cf. Uhlhorn, *Das Bas. Syst.* p. 58, 60. The change probably was made by cutting off the οὐκ ὢν θεός, an abstraction which few could follow, and with it all the ὑπερκόσμια. The first Archon will then take the place of the Supreme God (which explains the statement of those who refer the name *Abraxas* to the latter). The πανσπερμία being cut off with the first part of the system, a theory of emanation became necessary, and the dualistic assumption of a primitive matter can come in. Cf. Baur in *Theol. Jahrb.* 1856, p. 158.

[3] Cf. Uhlhorn, *Das Bas. Syst.* p. 48.

[4] *Strom.* iv. 25 (p. 637).

ciple, a spiritual Ogdoad bearing considerable resemblance to the ideas of Plato.[1]

It was natural, according to the distinction drawn by Basilides between the spiritual and the material and his theory of redemption as a separation of the former from the latter, that he should deny the resurrection of the body.[2] But he is also said to have maintained the doctrine of a transmigration of souls from one body to another,[3] which, though not a natural consequence of his chief doctrine, is not inconsistent with it, if we suppose the several transmigrations to be admitted, as in Plato,[4] as steps in the purification of the soul. Besides this Pythagorean doctrine, Basilides is also said to have required of his followers a probation of five years of silence,[5] a rule which might probably have been adopted also from the Pythagorean philosophy, which at this time was being resuscitated in Alexandria.[6] Another of the minor details of the teaching of Basilides as recorded by Irenæus has received a fuller explanation from the discovery of the work of his disciple Hippolytus. According to Irenæus and Theodoret, the disciples of Basilides gave to the Saviour of the world the strange title of *Caulacau*.[7] The meaning of this term, which had been partly explained by Epiphanius,[8] is more fully illustrated by

---

[1] This class of spiritual ideas will correspond to what Hippolytus describes as the first $viότης$, which ascended immediately to the Father. Cf. Jakobi in Herzog, Art. 'Basilides,' I. p. 709.

[2] Irenæus, i. 24. 5.

[3] Origen *in Rom*. lib. v. (*Opera* VI. p. 336, Lommatzsch). Cf. Clem. Alex. *Strom*. iv. 12 (p. 601), and Matter, *Hist. du Gnosticisme* II. p. 2.

[4] *Phædrus* pp. 248, 249.

[5] Agrippa Castor in Euseb. *H. E*. iv. 7.

[6] Cf. Matter II. p. 18.

[7] Irenæus, i. 24. 5; Theodoret, *Hær. Fab*. i. 4. The text of the former, which is obviously corrupt, may be corrected by the latter. Epiphan. *Hær*. xxv. 3 attributes a similar doctrine to the Nicolaitans.

[8] *Hær*. xxv. 4, where the three words $καυλακαῦ$, $σαυλασαῦ$, and $ζηρσάμ$, are traced to their origin, though their significance in the Gnostic teaching is not explained.

Hippolytus, who however attributes it, not to the Basilideans, but to the Ophites. He refers to these heretics the use of these mystical words, καυλακαῦ, σαυλασαῦ, and ζεησάρ;[1] the first as meaning the heavenly, spiritual man; the second, the mortal man upon earth; the third, the spirit raised by the Gnostic doctrine from earth to heaven.[2] The words as thus given represent in a complete form the original Hebrew of Isaiah xxviii. 10, *precept upon precept, line upon line, here a little*.[3] The celestial man was called *line upon line*, or perhaps rather, as in the LXX version, *hope upon hope*; the earthly man was *precept upon precept*; while the illuminated Gnostics, the chosen few, were *here a little*.[4] This classification, though quite in accordance with the general spirit of Gnosticism, has little connection with the peculiar theory of Basilides, and may have been one of the later features of the school, introduced by his followers.

Irenæus charges the disciples of Basilides with gross immorality of life;[5] but the testimony of Clement of Alexandria seems to show that the teaching of Basilides himself, as well as of his son Isidorus, was of a very different character.[6] Yet as Clement expressly says that he cites their teaching to refute those Basilideans who assumed a licence not permitted by their first teachers, we may conclude that there was some foundation for the charge as regards the later members of the sect. It is not improbable that the distinction, on which so much of the teach-

---

[1] Hippol. *Ref. Hær.* v. 8.

[2] The last word is explained to mean τοῦ ἐπὶ τὰ ἄνω ῥεύσαντος Ἰορδάνου. But in v. 7 the backward flow of the Jordan is interpreted as signifying the πνευματικὴ γένεσις of the Gnostic. Cf. Harvey's *Irenæus* I. p. 201.

[3] צַו לָצָו קַו לָקָו זְעֵיר שָׁם.

[4] Cf. Harvey's *Irenæus* I. p. 201.

[5] Irenæus, i. 24. 5.

[6] Clem. Alex. *Strom.* iii. 1. Epiphanius, *Hær.* xxxii. 4, cites the same passage from Isidorus with a very immoral interpretation; but the context of Clement shows that this is not the true meaning. See also Clem. Alex. *Strom.* iv. 12 (p. 600).

ing of Basilides was based, between his own followers as *the elect*, and the rest of mankind as *carnal*, might foster the delusion that these privileged persons were not bound by the same laws as other men;[1] though it was far from the intention of the teacher to inculcate this licentious doctrine. In one respect however the practice of Basilides himself gave just offence to Christian writers, in that he taught that it was lawful to partake of sacrifices to idols and to deny the faith in time of persecution.[2]

We cannot trace in Basilides any of that hostility to the Jewish religion and the God of the Jews which distinguished some of the Gnostic sects. On the contrary, he seems to have regarded Judaism as a necessary stage in the development and education of the world; and he appears to have received and made use of the Jewish Scriptures, at least in part, as well as the New Testament, though he added to these sacred books certain apocryphal writings by pretended prophets of his own, called Barcabbas and Barcoph or Parchor, of which it is difficult to say whether they were real books of Eastern theosophy or forgeries of his own composition.

The system of Basilides is of all the Gnostic systems the one which least recognises any break or distinction between the Christian revelation and the other religions of the world, heathen or Jewish. His leading thought is the continuity of the world's development, the gradual purification and enlightenment, we might almost say in modern language, the education of the world, by means of a progressive series of movements, succeeding to one another by a fixed law of evolution. But while the system thus gains in philosophical unity, it loses in moral

---

[1] ὡς ἤτοι ἐχόντων ἐξουσίαν καὶ τοῦ ἁμαρτεῖν διὰ τὴν τελειότητα, Clem. Alex. *Strom.* iii. 1.

[2] Agrippa Castor in Euseb. *H. E.* iv. 7. Cf. Irenæus, i. 24.

and religious significance. No place is left for the special providence of God, nor for the freewill of man. The scheme almost approaches to a Stoical pantheism, and quite to a Stoical fatalism. The Supreme God is an impersonal being, capable of no religious relation to man, and introduced for no other purpose than to give the first impulse to the mechanical movement of the world's self-development; even this amount of activity being introduced as it were *per saltum*, by a gratuitous and inconsistent assumption. As a mere system of metaphysics the theory of Basilides contains the nearest approach to the conception of a logical philosophy of the absolute which the history of ancient thought can furnish, almost rivalling that of Hegel in modern times; but in the same degree in which it elevates God to the position of an absolute first principle, it strips Him of those attributes which alone can make Him the object of moral obedience or religious worship.

LECTURE XI.

EGYPTIAN GNOSTICISM—VALENTINUS AND THE VALENTINIANS.

THE Egyptian Gnosticism attained to its fullest development and its greatest popularity in the system of Valentinus, who, while building on the same foundations, and for the most part with the same materials, as his predecessor Basilides, obtained for his philosophy a more general reception by exhibiting it in the form of poetical personifications instead of metaphysical abstractions. Valentinus is reported, though not upon very certain testimony, to have been a native of Egypt, and to have been educated at Alexandria, where he received instruction in Greek literature.[1] From Egypt he came to Rome during the pontificate of Hyginus, and remained there during that of Pius, and until the succession of Anicetus;[2] a period which may be roughly stated as extending from A.D. 140 to 157 or later.[3] Subsequently he is said to have retired to Cyprus, and there to have openly proclaimed his secession from the Church, having previously been in at least a nominal communion.[4] According to

---

[1] Epiphan. *Hær.* xxxi. Epiphanius confesses that the earlier writers give no account of the birthplace of Valentinus, and that he merely follows tradition. His Greek training however is manifest from the character of his system.

[2] Irenæus, iii. 4; Euseb. *H. E.* iv. 11.

[3] Hyginus became Pope A.D. 139; Pius A.D. 142; Anicetus A.D. 157.

[4] Epiph. *Hær.* xxxi. 7.

Tertullian, his open secession was occasioned by disappointment in the hope of succeeding to a bishopric.[1]

The heresy of Valentinus has an especial interest for us, as having, through one of its branches, given occasion to the great work of Irenæus in opposition to Gnosticism, 'The Refutation and Overthrow of Knowledge falsely so called.'[2] The branch of the Valentinians which had attained to the greatest celebrity at this time, and whose tenets are directly described by Irenæus in the first nine chapters of his work, seems to have been that founded by Ptolemæus, a disciple of Valentinus,[3] whose variations from the teaching of his master we shall have to consider hereafter; but the doctrines of Valentinus himself, as well as of other schools of Gnosticism, are also noticed in detail in the course of the work. The main principles of the system remain in the subsequent schools as they were invented by the master, varying only in some subordinate details.

The system of Valentinus is an eclecticism derived from various sources, but we may trace in it the influence especially of three leading ideas. The first, which is derived from the Platonic philosophy, is that which considers the higher existences of the terrestrial world[4] as having their superior and more real counterparts in the celestial world, the ideal substances being but imperfectly reflected in their earthly shadows.[5] The second, which is derived in a modified form from the pantheistic

---

[1] Tertull. *Adv. Valent.* c. 4.

[2] 'Ελέγχου καὶ ἀνατροπῆς τῆς ψευδωνύμου γνώσεως, Euseb. *H. E.* v. 7. That this was the title adopted by Irenæus himself, see Harvey's *Irenæus* I. p. clxiii.

[3] See Massuet, *Diss. Præv. in Iren.* i. § 83. The Ptolemæans described subsequently by Irenæus, i. 12, seem to have been a later perversion of the sect.

[4] According to the original conception of Plato himself, as represented by the youthful Socrates in the *Parmenides*, p. 130, where the higher class of existences only are regarded as having ideal counterparts.

[5] Cf. Baur, *Die Chr. Gnosis* p. 124.

philosophy of India, is that which regards the origin of material existence as due to an error, or fall, or degradation of some higher mode of being; material existence, if not relative existence in general, being regarded as a transient blot on the perfection of the absolute.[1] The third, derived from the Judaism of Alexandria, is that which attributes the creation of the world, notwithstanding its deterioration from a higher excellence, as due to the *Wisdom* of God, an attribute which appears in a representation approaching to a separate personality, such as is figuratively given to it occasionally even in the canonical books of the Old Testament (as in Job, chap. xxviii, and Proverbs, chap. viii), and still more in the apocryphal books of Ecclesiasticus and the Wisdom of Solomon.[2] The influence of the Persian religious philosophy may perhaps be seen in some of the minor details of the system, but only as regards external form and arrangement applied to a very different philosophical conception. To the first of these ideas is due the addition which Valentinus made to the system of Basilides, by filling the supermundane region beyond the firmament with a succession of *Æons* or celestial beings, the ideal prototypes of things imperfectly realised on earth.[3] The vague conception which appears in the earlier Gnostic of the *Sonship* of God finding its appropriate place in the celestial region, assumes in the hands of his successor the form of a definite multitude of personified ideas. The

---

[1] Baur, *l. c.*, derives this idea also from Platonism. But first, Plato recognises an eternal unformed matter, which is not to be found in the system of Valentinus, and which precludes the pantheistic hypothesis of the origin of matter; and secondly, Plato does not regard the creation as a fall, but distinctly attributes it to the goodness of God; and refers even the material world to the Supreme God as its creator. It is only the mortal bodies of men which are the work of inferior beings, and even this is done by the command of God. Cf. *Timæus* pp. 29–34, 41 *seq.*

[2] Cf. Eccles. i. 1–10, xxiv. 1–18; Wisd. vii. 22–30, viii. 1–9, ix. 9–11.

[3] Cf. Harvey's *Irenæus* I. p. cxi. *seq.*

half-material, half-spiritual conception of the firmament, or air, or spirit, which in the theory of Basilides forms the boundary between the supermundane and the mundane region, is replaced in the system of Valentinus by the Æon Horus (ὅρος), not the Egyptian deity of that name, but a personification of the Greek term signifying limit or boundary.[1] To the combination of the second and third ideas is due the strange fancy of the passion and sorrow of the lower or mundane *Sophia*, whose distinctive name, *Achamoth*, borrowed from the word designating creative wisdom in the Book of Proverbs,[2] together with the whole description of her fall and sufferings, is intended to intimate that divine wisdom cannot stoop to the work of material creation without being first degraded from her divine nature, and expelled, as it were, from her heavenly habitation.

The system of Valentinus commences with an assumption which, though cognate to that of Basilides, differs from it as a poetical personification differs from a merely metaphysical abstraction. In the place of the non-existent God, who is simply described by negatives, who has no name in language and no attributes, not even that of definite existence, Valentinus substitutes the conception of a primary being who is named Βυθὸς or *Depth*; a term which, while it is not much more definite than the οὐκ ὢν θεὸς of Basilides, yet serves to exhibit the absolute first principle in a positive rather than a negative aspect, as potentially containing all existence rather than as actually determined by none.[3] The negative or meta-

---

[1] Cf. Baur, *Die Chr. Gnosis* p. 128.

[2] Achamoth is the Hebrew חָכְמוֹת. The exact word, in its plural form, though with a singular sense, occurs Prov. ix. 1, '*Wisdom* hath builded her house;' while the singular חָכְמָה is used of creative wisdom in viii. 1, 12. Cf. Harvey's *Irenæus* I. p. cxxiii.

[3] Cf. Neander, *Church Hist.* II. p. 72 (Bohn). Irenæus gives the name of Βυθὸς to the first principle of those Valentinians whom he is de-

physical side of the same conception appears however in the other name said to be given by Valentinus to the same principle, that of Ἄρρητος or the *Unspeakable*. After this first assumption, we are told that the disciples of Valentinus differed from each other, some regarding the first principle as a solitary monad, developing all derived existence from itself alone, while others, following the analogy of natural generation, by the union of male and female, assigned to the first principle a consort called Σιγή or *Silence*.[1] If we may venture to conjecture, both from the natural development or rather corruption which such a system was likely to undergo, as well as from the relation which probably existed between Valentinus and Basilides, we should be disposed to consider the former as the original theory; the two epithets bestowed upon the primary Being, Βυθός and Ἄρρητος, having been subsequently, in order to give a supposed symmetry to the system, developed into two separate beings, Βυθός and Σιγή.[2] The rest of the system proceeds according to a regular co-ordination of pairs, a masculine and a feminine principle. From Βυθός, or from Βυθός and Σιγή, sprang Νοῦς and Ἀλήθεια; from these Λόγος and Ζωή; and from these again Ἄνθρωπος and Ἐκκλησία.[3] According to one, and

scribing in i. c. 1, who are probably the Ptolemæans. But in c. 11, when describing the theory of Valentinus himself, he seems to speak of the terms Βυθός and Ἄρρητος as applied by him to the same being, the former being cut off from the rest of the Pleroma by the first Ὅρος. Here Βυθός perhaps comprehends Ἄρρητος and Σιγή, and may thus have designated at the same time the unity and generative power of the first principle. Hippolytus, who professes to give a system common to Valentinus and his followers, substitutes the name Πατήρ, which Irenæus, under the equivalent Προπάτωρ, seems to assign especially to the Ptolemæans, while he gives the name of πατήρ to the second male principle, i. 11.

[1] Hippol. *Ref. Hær.* vi. 29. Bunsen (*Hippolytus* I. p. 63) supposes the extracts cited by Hippolytus to be from Valentinus himself, and thus confirms the supposition that the monadic assumption was the original.

[2] Cf. Matter, *Hist. du Gnosticisme* II. p. 55.

[3] Irenæus, i. 1; cf. i. 11, where Πατήρ is substituted for Νοῦς; Hippolytus, vi. 29.

LECT. XI. *VALENTINUS AND THE VALENTINIANS.* 171

probably the earlier, representation, these three pairs, omitting the first principle, formed the beginning of an Ogdoad, which had yet to be completed by a fourth pair; according to another representation, they formed in conjunction with the first pair, Βυθὸς and Σιγή, an Ogdoad complete.[1]

The number of the Ogdoad may perhaps have been suggested by the eight primary gods of the Egyptian mythology,[2] but it had also a further mystical signification connected with the Pythagorean theory of numbers. For the eight were in a manner reduced to four, by regarding the four feminine elements as mere negative complements of the masculine, the latter being represented as bisexual, and as giving names to the four members of the series.[3] The first series of Æons thus answers to the celebrated Pythagorean Tetrad, i.e. the first four numbers, which added together form the perfect number ten. The Ogdoad, including the feminine elements, was also subdivided into two Tetrads.[4]

It was probably this arithmetical and philosophical relation between the numbers four and ten which suggested the next step in the generation of the Valentinian Æons, in which Λόγος and Ζωή, or, according to another view, Νοῦς and Ἀλήθεια—these being in different statements the completing numbers of the first Tetrad—gave birth to a second order of Æons, ten in number.[5] These

---

[1] The former view is given by Hippolytus, vi. 29, 31; the latter by Irenæus, i. 1. 11.

[2] Herodotus, i. 46, 145.

[3] Irenæus, i. 1. 1. Cf. Harvey, p. cxv; Matter, *Hist. du Gnost.* II. p. 56.

[4] Cf. Irenæus, i. 1. 1 and i. 8. 5. For the Pythagorean theory, see Sext. Empir. *Adv. Math.* vii. 94 *seq.* Cf. Hippolytus, vi. 23.

[5] Irenæus, i. 11. 1; Hippolytus, vi. 29. The former view seems to accord with the theory of those who excluded Βυθὸς from the Ogdoad and left it for a time incomplete; and this view is attributed by Irenæus to Valentinus himself. The second view belongs more naturally to those who framed the first Tetrad by Βυθὸς and Σιγή, Νοῦς and Ἀλήθεια.

ten Æons of the second order are arranged, like the former, in pairs, male and female, and are named Βύθιος and Μίξις, Ἀγήρατος and Ἕνωσις, Αὐτοφυὴς and Ἡδονή, Ἀκίνητος and Σύγκρασις, Μονογενὴς and Μακαρία.[1] After this, Ἄνθρωπος and Ἐκκλησία (or, according to another account, Λόγος and Ζωή) produce a third order of Æons, comprised in the imperfect number twelve (a number perhaps suggested by the twelve secondary gods of the Egyptian mythology). These twelve are, like their predecessors, arranged in pairs, male and female, and are called Παράκλητος and Πίστις, Πατρικὸς and Ἐλπις, Μητρικὸς and Ἀγαπή, Ἀείνους [perhaps read Αἰώνιος] and Σύνεσις, Ἐκκλησιαστικὸς and Μακαριότης, Θελητὸς and Σοφία.[2] The entire sum of the Æons of the three orders, the Ogdoad, the Decad, and the Dodecad, amounts to thirty, or, with the imperfect Ogdoad, to twenty-eight; and the circumstance that these numbers correspond also, according to different modes of reckoning, with those of the *Izeds* of the Persian mythology (with or without Ormuzd and Mithra), the six *Amshaspands* also corresponding in number with the imperfect Ogdoad,[3] has led some writers to suppose a Persian origin for this portion of the Valentinian system.[4] But when we consider that the principle of the Valentinian doctrine is wholly incompatible with the Persian dualism, that the elements of the calculation can be obtained from other and more cognate sources, and that both Irenæus and Hippolytus expressly refer this portion of the Valentinian theory to a Pythagorean source,[5] we may perhaps doubt whether the affinity

[1] Irenæus, i. 1. 2. Cf. Hippolytus, vi. 30.
[2] Irenæus, *l. c.*; Hippolytus, *l. c.*
[3] See above, Lecture II. p. 26.
[4] See Matter, *Hist. du Gnosticisme*,
I. p. 118; Harvey's *Irenæus* I. p. cxi; Massuet, *Diss. Præv. in Iren.* i. § 45.
[5] Irenæus, i. 1. 1; Hippolytus, vi. 21–23, 29.

with the Zoroastrian numbers is more than an accidental coincidence.

Amid much that is fanciful and arbitrary in this wild play of the imagination, it is yet possible to trace a philosophical principle and method disguised under a luxuriance of poetical imagery. The first order of Æons, the Ogdoad, is obviously intended to represent the Supreme Being in two aspects: first, in his absolute nature, as inscrutable and unspeakable; secondly, in his relative nature, as manifesting himself in operation.[1] We have, first, Βυθὸς and Σιγή, the impenetrable depth, the unutterable silence. Then the first manifestation, Thought, preparatory to action, a purely intellectual process indicated by Νοῦς, whose counterpart is 'Αλήθεια, that perfect truth which belongs to Divine thought, the companion, as in Plato,[2] of real existence. Then comes Λόγος, or Speech, representing the manifestation of the Divine thought, with Ζωή, indicating the life-giving power of the creative word, and finally "Ανθρωπος, the ideal man, the most perfect expression of the Divine thought, regarded, like the *Adam Kadmon* of the Kabbala, as the sum of all the Divine attributes, to whom is assigned as a companion 'Εκκλησία, indicating the Gnostic theory of a perfect separation between the higher and the lower orders of men; the ideal man being the type only of the Gnostic or spiritual man, who is separated from the rest of mankind, as the Church is separated from the world.[3] All these however it must be remembered, have thus far

---

[1] This explanation is perhaps confirmed by the appellation διαθέσεις given to the Æons by Ptolemæus (Irenæus, i. 12. 1); cf. Matter, II. p. 49, See also Matter, II. p. 59, for the germ of a similar explanation of the Æons.

[2] *Resp.* vi. p. 508.

[3] Cf. Harvey's *Irenæus* I. p. cxxi.

Matter (vol. II. p. 57) traces "Ανθρωπος and 'Εκκλησία to the Christian doctrine of Christ being the Head of the Church, and 'Αλήθεια and Ζωή to our Lord's words, John xiv. 6. The language may perhaps have been partly suggested by these expressions, but the Christ proper in the system of Valentinus is a later emanation.

no relation to the actual creation of a material world. The spiritual man is not, as in the system of Basilides, regarded as first existing in combination with matter, and afterwards purified from material accretions and exalted to the celestial region. The ideal man of Valentinus is a being who not only has not as yet any reflected counterpart in the material world, but who ought not to have any. He exists only as a Divine conception; the subsequent imperfect realisation of that conception in connection with matter, and indeed the existence of matter and the material world altogether, being no part of the Divine plan, but only taking place in consequence, as we shall see hereafter, of a fall from the original perfection of the ideal world. The only existence recognised at present is that of the Divine Being, evolving and contemplating his own perfections. The philosopher has sprung *per saltum*, apparently without being conscious of the difficulty, over the first problem of ontology, how the absolute can give existence to the relative; but he has not yet approached the second and yet more difficult problem, how perfection can give rise to imperfection, good to evil.

If now we examine the second and third orders of Æons, the Decad and the Dodecad, we shall see that the masculine terms in nearly every instance represent some epithet which may be applied directly or indirectly to the Deity, while the feminine terms represent some operation or gift by which he is manifested in nature, or in grace. In the Decad the terms Βύθιος, Ἀγήρατος, Ἀκίνητος, with their feminine counterparts, Μίξις, Ἕνωσις, Σύγκρασις, speak for themselves; they are clearly meant to represent that combination of unity with variety, of the infinite with the finite, of identity with difference, which is implied in the notion of derived and definite existence. These then are intended to represent the action of the Deity, through his attributes, in the formation of a world, not however of a material world, but only of a primary ideal world—a conception which may perhaps have been suggested by Philo's commentary on the first chapter of Genesis.[1] Of the two remaining pairs of the Decad, the masculine elements, Αὐτοφυὴς and Μονογενής, are of the same character with the others. The feminine elements, Ἡδονὴ and Μακαρία, do not so readily lend themselves to this interpretation: but perhaps when we remember that Plato in the Timæus describes the Creator as rejoicing in his work,[2] and that in the Book of Genesis God is described as seeing 'everything that He had made, and behold it was very good;' and when we consider the mixture of Platonism and Judaism in the Alexandrian philosophy, in which Valentinus was brought up, we shall perhaps be able to comprehend the original introduction of these terms into the system, though they may have been afterwards perverted to a less innocent meaning.[3] Finally, the conception which represents the Decad as having sprung, not from the absolute Βυθός, but from Λόγος and Ζωή, or from Νοῦς and Ἀλήθεια, seems intended to indicate that God, in the aspect of Creator, is viewed, not in his absolute and secret nature, but in his relative character, as manifested by his attributes.

In the Dodecad in like manner, the masculine terms παράκλητος, πατρικός, κ.τ.λ., represent God, especially in His

---

[1] *De Mundi Opif.*

[2] Εὐφρανθεὶς, *Timæus* p. 37.

[3] For the perversion of ἡδονή, see Harvey's *Irenæus*, I. pp. lxxxi, lxxxii. Μακαριότης in the Dodecad (the explanation might perhaps more naturally apply to the μακαρία of the Decad) is supposed by Harvey (p. cxxiii) to refer to Astarte, the Syrian *Fortuna*, incorporated to attract converts from the Syrian heathen. But the doctrine of Valentinus belongs to Egypt, not to Syria, and a much simpler explanation can be found for both μακαρία and μακαριότης. The former is given in the text; the latter simply denotes blessing or happiness, as the result of religious grace.

religious relation towards man; while the feminine terms πίστις, ἐλπίς, κ.τ.λ., represent the gifts of grace which that relation conveys and implies. Here also it must be remembered that we are considering not the terrestrial and mortal man, but his ideal archetype. The Platonic conception is carried out to the end, and every operation in nature or in grace is considered as first existing in idea, and as only realised in a lower stage through imperfection. The especially religious relation indicated by the Dodecad gives a fitness to its production from the quasi-human terms of the Ogdoad, Ἄνθρωπος and Ἐκκλησία, though the same relation is also indicated less immediately by the other derivation from Λόγος and Ζωή.[1]

In support of their theory, the Valentinians adopted some wild allegorical interpretations of various passages in the New Testament, in which they asserted their views to be figuratively intimated.[2] But they also professed to find a more direct assertion of them in the opening words of the Gospel of St. John,[3] and if the use of this last

---

[1] The explanations above given are based on the Greek names assigned to the Æons, which both Irenæus and Hippolytus give as if they were original to the system. It is true that Epiphanius (*Hær.* xxxi. 2, 6) gives the names in a different language (probably Aramaic), and this list is considered by Matter, II. p. 64, as the original. But the text as given in Epiphanius is too corrupt for any certain explanation without the aid of the Greek; and it is more than probable that the latter was the original form. Valentinus, educated at Alexandria, and a devoted Platonist, would be most likely to use the Greek language. The names, which Epiphanius gives three times, are obviously taken from the work which he quotes in §§ 5, 6; and this work, which some have erroneously thought to be by Valentinus himself, is expressly cited by Epiphanius as the work of one of his disciples (cf. Massuet, *Diss. in Irenæum* i. § 10). It would be quite in the spirit of a Palestinian impostor like Marcus to render his master's terms into an Oriental language, to terrify his dupes by mysterious sounds in an unknown tongue. For the Aramaic names of the Æons, with an attempted explanation, see Matter, vol. II. pp. 65, 66.

[2] See the various passages in Irenæus, i. 8. 1-4.

[3] Since the recovery of the work of Hippolytus, who (vi. 35) refers to St. John x. 8, apparently as cited by Valentinus himself. Even this is hardly needed, for the same work (vii. 22, 27) shows that this Gospel was also used by the earlier Basilides.

authority can be traced, as it now almost certainly can, to Valentinus himself, it will furnish an additional proof of the untenable character of the Tübingen hypothesis, which maintains this Gospel to have been written as late as the middle of the second century.[1] The fourth verse of this Gospel, ἐν αὐτῷ [sc. τῷ Λόγῳ] ζωὴ ἦν, καὶ ἡ ζωὴ ἦν τὸ φῶς τῶν ἀνθρώπων, was interpreted by these heretics as speaking of the second portion of the Ogdoad, Λόγος and Ζωή, Ἄνθρωπος and (by implication) Ἐκκλησία, while the latter part of the fourteenth verse, καὶ ὁ Λόγος σὰρξ ἐγένετο, καὶ ἐσκήνωσεν ἐν ἡμῖν (καὶ ἐθεασάμεθα τὴν δόξαν αὐτοῦ, δόξαν ὡς μονογενοῦς παρὰ Πατρὸς) πλήρης χάριτος καὶ ἀληθείας, was interpreted in like manner with reference to the first Tetrad, the unseen Father, the Σιγή (identified with χάρις), the only-begotten Νοῦς, and his feminine counterpart Ἀλήθεια.[2] This exposition, as cited by Irenæus, appears to be taken from a work of Ptolemæus, the disciple of Valentinus, the date of which, though it cannot be determined exactly, can hardly be placed later than A.D. 170.[3] The evidence which we now possess of the use of St. John's Gospel by Valentinus himself would lead to the conclusion that the nomenclature of the heresiarch himself, as well as that of his disciple, was partly borrowed from this source; and even were that testimony not in existence, it is utterly inconceivable that a forgery of the middle of the second

---

[1] Baur, *Kanon. Evang.* p. 357, deals very unfairly with the testimony of Irenæus, i. 8. He builds on the fact that St. John is not cited in the first four sections, to show that the early Valentinians were unacquainted with this Gospel, but omits the fifth section in which it is expressly quoted. But either the whole testimony of this chapter is earlier than the date assigned by Baur to the Gospel, in which case § 5 overthrows the hypothesis; or the whole is later, in which case §§ 1-4 prove nothing.

[2] Irenæus, i. 8. 5.

[3] Matter, II. p. 102, places the *floruit* of Ptolemæus about A.D. 166. The composition of the work of Irenæus can hardly be placed later than A.D. 188, or, according to another computation, 190 (cf. Harvey, p. clviii; Beaven, *Account of Irenæus* p. 34), and twenty years is not too long to allow for the spread of Ptolemæan doctrines to the point at which they appear in Irenæus.

century should have been generally received as a canonical book, and the work of an Apostle, within twenty years after its composition.

The use of the term Æons (αἰῶνες) to denote these personifications of the Divine attributes appears to have originated with Valentinus.[1] The term, as we have seen, had previously been used by Simon Magus (if the 'Great Announcement' is his work) in its more ordinary sense of *ages*, to denote *eternity*, and also in the same sense by St. Paul (1 Tim. i. 17), and previously in the Book of Ecclesiasticus (xxxvi. 17).[2] All these may be traced back to the use of the same term in the singular number by Plato[3] to signify the ever-present form of the Divine existence prior to the creation of time, i.e. *eternity*. The transition from this sense to that of the different modes or attributes by which this eternal existence was supposed to be manifested is not very violent.

As regards the other Valentinian term πλήρωμα, employed to designate the entire system of thirty Æons regarded as a collective whole,[4] there are no positive data to determine the time when it was first used in connection with Gnostic doctrines. There is no reason why it may not have been used to denote the ῥίζαι of Simon Magus, as well as the αἰῶνες of Valentinus; and its employment by St. Paul, as we have pointed out in a former lecture, may possibly in some passages have been suggested by some such application of the term by the early Gnostics; but the word itself is a common one, and may naturally have been employed independently of any such suggestion,

---

[1] Hippol. vi. 20 (p. 258, Duncker). See above Lect. IV, p. 62. See also Matter, vol. II. p. 53, and on the Æons, as manifestations of God, *ibid.* p. 59.

[2] See above, Lect. VI, p. 88.

[3] *Timæus* 37 D.

[4] Irenæus, i. 1. 3 τοῦτο τὸ ἀόρατον καὶ πνευματικὸν κατ' αὐτοὺς πλήρωμα, τριχῆ διεσταμένον εἰς ὀγδοάδα καὶ δεκάδα καὶ δωδεκάδα.

and though there is probably some connection between its use as applied to God in the New Testament and its similar use by the Gnostic teachers, it is impossible to decide whether the former suggested it to the latter or the latter to the former.[1]

The remainder of the Valentinian theory carries out with the utmost exactness the same Platonic conception which is predominant in the portion already exhibited. As there is an ideal archetype of the Divine manifestation in nature and in religion, so there must be an ideal archetype of the fall and the redemption of the world, and even the Christ who comes into the world for the redemption of mankind must find his ideal pattern in another Christ who has a redeeming office in heaven. And in strict accordance with the Gnostic doctrine the work of redemption consists in the communication of knowledge. In the application of this theory the different Valentinian schools differed from each other; and those details which are expressly ascribed to Valentinus himself are unfortunately the most meagre and incomplete of all. Much however of what is recorded by Irenæus as the doctrine of his disciple Ptolemæus must have been common to both teachers, the differences probably extending only to some unimportant particulars, on which it is not necessary to dwell.[2] The several Æons according to this exposition

---

[1] See Olshausen on Eph. i. 23. The word is often used in the Septuagint in relation to material objects, as in Ps. xxiii. (xxiv.) 1, τοῦ Κυρίου ἡ γῆ καὶ τὸ πλήρωμα αὐτῆς. Philo, De Præm. et Pæn. 21 (p. 418), uses it with reference to the soul of man, γενομένη δὲ πλήρωμα ἀρετῶν ἡ ψυχή. As applied to God in the N. T., it means in like manner God as filled with all divine excellencies; and the Gnostic error consisted merely in the mode in which they viewed these excellencies as separate existences. See Olshausen, l. c.

[2] Valentinus himself is said to have imagined first a dyad without name, comprising Ἄρρητος and Σιγή, probably, as observed above, a bisexual monad, the two names being identical in sense; then a second dyad, called Πατήρ and Ἀλήθεια (Πατήρ being thus applied to the second masculine Æon Νοῦς: this more nearly approaches to Basilides, Father being thought too definite a concep-

were not originally equal in knowledge. Νοῦς alone was cognisant of the nature of the supreme Father,[1] which he wished to communicate to the others, but was withheld according to the Father's will by Σιγή. This created in them a desire of the forbidden knowledge, which was moderate in elder Æons, but became a violent passion in the youngest, Σοφία. In her the desire to comprehend the Father became an agony and a struggle which would have ended in her entire absorption into the Divine essence, had she not come into contact with Ὅρος, the limiting power, which keeps all things apart from the ineffable magnitude.[2] By this power she was finally restrained and convinced that the Father is incomprehensible, and thus laid aside her former design (τὴν προτέραν ἐνθύμησιν) with the passion that had accompanied it. This abandoned design, which is itself personified, plays an important part in the subsequent portion of the theory, being separated by Ὅρος from Σοφία and banished to the region outside the Pleroma, while Σοφία herself was restored to her place within it.

---

tion for an absolute first principle); then the other Æons as enumerated in the account given in the text. He also assumed two Ὅροι, one between Βυθὸς and the rest of the Pleroma, the other separating the whole Pleroma from all beyond it. He also regarded Christ, the second Christ, as generated, not from all the Æons, but from the mother (Achamoth) without the Pleroma. See Irenæus, i. 11. 1. That this is not Valentinus's original view, see Baur, *Chr. Gnosis* p. 133.

[1] Perhaps an application of Matt. xi. 27, though the Valentinian Νοῦς is distinguished from Christ. Cf. Matter, II. p. 68.

[2] Ὅρος is also called Σταυρός (perhaps with a play upon the two meanings, *a cross* and *a stake-fence*, the latter however being principally intended), Λυτρωτής, Καρπιστής (perhaps, as Neander interprets it, the reaper, or rather winnower, as separating the grain from the chaff or the wheat from the tares), Ὁροθέτης, and Μεταγωγεύς (as restoring Σοφία to her place in the Pleroma): cf. Irenæus, i. 2. 4. Also Μετοχεύς (Hippol. vi. 31), as the boundary of the Pleroma, and therefore common to that within and that without. According to one form of the theory (Irenæus, i. 2. 4; Hippol. vi. 31) this Horus was at this time first put forth by the Father to restrain the *purpose* of Sophia. The other account (Irenæus, i. 2. 2) seems to regard him as already existing.

LECT. XI. *VALENTINUS AND THE VALENTINIANS.* 181

We are next told that to prevent the recurrence of a similar disturbance in the Pleroma, the forethought of the Father caused Μονογενὴς (Νοῦς) to put forth by emanation another pair of Æons, who are called Christ and the Holy Spirit [the latter being, as in some other Gnostic systems, represented as feminine].[1] Christ prevented any future longing of the Æons for unattainable knowledge by teaching them that the supreme Being is incomprehensible in himself and can only be known through the Only-begotten (Νοῦς), and that their existence and continuance depended upon this truth. After this the Holy Spirit rendered all the Æons equal to each other, so that the same names became applicable to all; and having thus given them perfect rest, taught them to unite in giving gifts as a thank-offering in honour of the Father. Each Æon contributed that which was most excellent in himself, and from these contributions emanated a Being, 'the most perfect beauty and constellation of the Pleroma,' called Jesus and Saviour and Christ and Logos, and also τὰ πάντα, as produced from all. With him were also produced the Angels, who acted as his body-guard.[2] In support of this hypothesis of the generation of the Saviour, the Valentinians perverted the words of St. Paul, ἐξ αὐτοῦ καὶ δι᾽ αὐτοῦ καὶ εἰς αὐτὸν τὰ πάντα (Rom. xi. 36), and ἐν αὐτῷ κατοικεῖ πᾶν τὸ πλήρωμα τῆς θεότητος (Col. ii. 9), and ἀνακεφαλαιώσασθαι τὰ πάντα ἐν τῷ Χριστῷ (Eph. i. 10). It will be observed

---

[1] Cf. Harvey's *Irenæus*, I. p. cxxxvii; Matter, *Hist. du Gnost.* II. p. 70. The accounts given by Irenæus, i. 2. 5, and by Hippolytus, vi. 31, slightly differ in detail. According, to the former "Ορος is emitted first, to separate the ἐνθύμησις from Σοφία and to restore the latter to the Pleroma; then Christ and the Holy Spirit are emitted to teach the Æons and restore harmony. According to the latter, Christ and the Holy Spirit are emitted first from Νοῦς and 'Αλήθεια, to separate the ἔκτρωμα (ἐνθύμησις) and to console the mourning Σοφία, and then "Ορος is emitted by the Father to keep the ἔκτρωμα for ever apart from the perfect Æons.

[2] Irenæus, i. 2. 6. Cf. Hippolytus, vi. 31, who describes the second Christ under the names of Jesus and ὁ κοινὸς τοῦ πληρώματος καρπός.

that this theory recognises two Christs, one emanating, together with the Holy Spirit, from the first Æon Noûs, the other subsequently emanating from the contributions of all the Æons.

Thus far we have given only the first portion of the Valentinian theory, relating to the divine economy within the Pleroma prior to the existence of the material world. Stripped of its allegorical imagery, the general meaning of this part of the theory seems to be the exposition of a doctrine in itself far from heretical, and indeed expressly admitted by some of the most orthodox of the Fathers, namely, that the representation of the divine nature by a plurality of attributes, each attribute being distinct from and therefore limited by others, is but an inadequate and imperfect manifestation of the Unlimited, and that these attributes, though manifested to the finite intellect as different, are, in their own nature, one with each other, and with the divine Essence. The futile desire of Σοφία to comprehend the absolute nature of the supreme God, the assertion that this desire could not be gratified save by her entire absorption into the Divine essence, intimates the doctrine that each attribute of the Deity, so long as it is a separate attribute, contains but a partial and relative manifestation, and that in His absolute nature this distinction of attributes does not exist. In conformity with this view, the emanation of the relative from the absolute, of the many from the one, though it be but the manifestation of God Himself under various attributes, is regarded in some sort as a Fall, typical of the lower Fall which gave existence to the material world; and the recognition of the real unity and indifference of these apparently diverse manifestations is in some sort a redemption, typical of the redemption of the lower world. That this recognition is due to revelation made by a Christ, is in accordance with the Platonic character of the whole system, which requires a first Christ for the redemption of the celestial world, to be followed by a second Christ, whose office will afterwards appear in the redemption of the terrestrial world. That this representation of redemption by knowledge involved a grave misconception of the office and work of Christ, cannot, even on the most favourable view of the theory, be denied; and many of its details, literally taken, might undoubtedly lead to heretical views of the Saviour's person and nature. Yet every error is but a truth abused, and under the veil of the wild fancies and the poetical allegory of Valentinus we may perhaps find hidden the doctrine distinctly expressed in the philosophical theology of St. Augustine: 'Deus multipliciter quidem dicitur magnus, bonus, sapiens, beatus, verus, et quidquid aliud non indigne dici videtur; sed eadem magnitudo ejus est quæ sapientia; non enim mole magnus est, sed virtute; et eadem bonitas quæ sapientia et magnitudo, et eadem veritas quæ illa omnia; et non est ibi aliud beatum esse, et aliud magnum, aut sapientem, aut verum, aut bonum esse, aut omnino ipsum esse.'[1]

The remainder of the system of Valentinus, containing his theory of the creation and redemption of the lower world, must be reserved for our next lecture.

[1] *De Trin.* vi. 7. Cf. *De Trin.* xv. 5. See Aquinas, *Summa,* P. I. Qu. iii. Art. 5, 6, 7; Qu. xl. Art. i.

LECTURE XII.

VALENTINUS AND THE VALENTINIANS.

THE philosophical romance of Valentinus consists of three parts. The first, which has been described in our last lecture, contains an account of the nature and system of the Pleroma itself, that is, of the fulness of the Divine attributes and operations: the second relates to the condition of things beyond the Pleroma, before the formation of the visible world, constituting the stage of transition from the celestial to the terrestrial; the third describes the origin and constitution of the sensible world itself.[1] In the second portion, to which we have now to direct our attention, the principal interest is created by the description of the sorrows and sufferings of a lady who figures under the name of the younger Sophia or Achamoth, the latter name (חָכְמוֹת), as I have already stated, being taken from the Hebrew word signifying 'wisdom' in the Book of Proverbs.[2] This interesting heroine is a personification of the design ($ἐνθύμησις$) of the elder Sophia, the last of the Æons, to comprehend the absolute nature of the Deity. We have seen that Sophia, when finally restrained by

---

[1] Massuet, *Diss. Præv. in Iren.* i. § 12.

[2] Especially Prov. ix. 1 חָכְמוֹת בָּנְתָה בֵיתָהּ, 'Wisdom hath builded her house,' where the word is singular in sense, though plural in form. This text is cited by the author of the *Didasc. Orient.* with reference to the second Sophia, as through the Demiurge forming the material world (Clem. Alex. *Excerpta ex Theodoto* 47, p. 980).

VALENTINUS AND THE VALENTINIANS.

Horus, and convinced that the Deity is incomprehensible, is described as having laid aside her former design, with the passion which accompanied it, and that this abandoned design was taken away by Horus and banished to a region outside the Pleroma. The adventures of the Design, thus personified as a child deserted by its parent, form the second portion of our romance. At first, we are told, she lay as it were stranded (ἐκβεβράσθαι) in the region of shadow and emptiness outside of the Pleroma, being herself without shape or form, as a defective birth.[1] In this state she remained till the higher Christ, the emanation from Νοῦς,[2] took compassion on her, and extending her power beyond the limit of the Ὅρος and Σταυρός,[3] conferred upon her form, though without knowledge.[4] Having done this, he withdrew his influence, leaving her however with a certain odour of immortality,[5] and desire after higher things. Under the influence of this desire, Achamoth attempts to follow after the light which had been withdrawn, but was restrained by Horus, and unable to enter the Pleroma.[6] Upon this she became afflicted with every kind of passion: grief, fear, and perplexity,

---

[1] ὥσπερ ἔκτρωμα, διὰ τὸ μηδὲν κατειληφέναι, Iren. i. 4. 1. The theory was, that form is given by the male parent, substance by the female. Hence Achamoth, as the offspring of Sophia alone, was formless, having *received nothing* from a father.

[2] τὸν [ἄνω] Χριστόν, *superiorem Christum* (Iren. i. 4. 1: the Greek text as preserved by Epiphanius, must be completed from the Latin), *i.e.* the elder or first Christ, the emanation of Νοῦς (ὁ Χριστὸς ἐπιπροβληθεὶς ἀπὸ τοῦ Νοῦ καὶ τῆς Ἀληθείας, Hippol. vi. 31).

[3] ἐπεκτανθῆναι διὰ τοῦ Ὅρου καὶ Σταυροῦ καλουμένου, Theodoret, *Hær. Fab.* i. 7, explaining the language of Irenæus, διὰ τοῦ Σταυροῦ ἐπεκτανθέντα.

There is a play on the double meaning of Σταυρός.

[4] μορφῶσαι μόρφωσιν τὴν κατ' οὐσίαν μόνον, ἀλλ' οὐ τὴν κατὰ γνῶσιν. Achamoth was not enlightened like the Æons, in order that she might strive after higher knowledge.

[5] This resembles the theory of Basilides concerning the Holy Spirit when left by the second υἱότης; ἀλλὰ γὰρ ὥσπερ εἰς ἄγγος ἐμβληθὲν μύρον εὐωδέστατον, εἰ καὶ ὅτι μάλιστα ἐπιμελῶς ἐκκενωθείη, ὅμως ὀσμή τις ἔτι μένει τοῦ μύρου καὶ καταλείπεται κ.τ.λ., Hippol. vii. 22.

[6] καὶ ἐνταῦθα τὸν Ὅρον κωλύοντα αὐτὴν τῆς εἰς τοὔμπροσθεν ὁρμῆς εἰπεῖν Ἰαώ· ὅθεν τὸ Ἰαὼ ὄνομα γεγενῆσθαι φάσκουσι, Iren. i. 4. 1.

together with ignorance, and finally an earnest desire of returning to the source of her life (i.e. Christ). From these different affections the lower world came into existence; the soul of the world, and that of the Demiurge, sprang from her desire of returning to God; the material portions from her several passions, all liquid substance, having sprung from her tears, all that is bright from her laughter; and the corporeal elements from her grief and consternation.[1] The principal agent in these transmutations was, according to the Valentinian theory, the second Christ, the Saviour sprung from all the Æons, who being sent down from the Pleroma, together with his attendant angels, at the prayer of the suffering Achamoth, imparted to her knowledge and healed her passions, separating them from her and consolidating them, so as to change them from incorporeal passions to unorganised matter, out of which subsequently the world was formed. This matter (using the term in a wide sense) was of two kinds: the first (brute matter), which was evil, sprang from the passions of Achamoth; the second (the animal soul) sprang from her desire after higher things, not in itself evil, but liable to passions.[2] After this, Achamoth is said to have brought forth a spiritual progeny after the likeness of the attendant angels, by gazing on their light. Thus then came into existence three kinds of substance, all in different ways the offspring of Achamoth; the material (ὕλη) sprung from her passions; the animal (ψυχικόν) from her conversion or repentance; and the spiritual (πνευματικόν) from her joy at the angelic light.

---

[1] Hippolytus gives the particulars differently; *R. H.* vi. 32. See the next note.

[2] Cf. Hippol. vi. 32 ἐποίησεν οὖν ἐκστῆναι τὰ πάθη ἀπ' αὐτῆς, καὶ ἐποίησεν αὐτὰ ὑποστατικὰς οὐσίας, καὶ τὸν μὲν φόβον ψυχικὴν ἐποίησεν οὐσίαν, τὴν δὲ λύπην ὑλικήν, τὴν δὲ ἀπορίαν δαιμόνων, τὴν δὲ ἐπιστροφὴν καὶ δέησιν καὶ ἱκετείαν ἄνοδον καὶ μετάνοιαν καὶ δύναμιν ψυχικῆς οὐσίας, ἥτις καλεῖται δεξιά.

The last of these, being of the same nature as herself, was not susceptible of any further formation by her; but to the second, the animal, she gave a form; and thus produced the Demiurge, by whom the material world was afterwards created out of the remaining substance. The formation of the Demiurge concludes the second portion of the romance, which relates to things intermediate between the Pleroma and the visible world.

In this marvellous narrative, we seem at first sight to have fallen on a poetical metamorphosis as fanciful as any in Ovid, and far more difficult to reduce to any definite meaning. A spiritual attribute, an impersonation of Wisdom shedding tears (even 'tears such as angels weep'), and these tears, immaterial tears, afterwards becoming condensed into matter, is a representation in which it is difficult at first sight to see anything but an utter confusion between both kinds of existence. But in truth Valentinus had a difficult, indeed an impossible, task before him, and we must not be surprised if he betrays an inclination to evade rather than to accomplish it. Hitherto he had exhibited the Absolute and the Relative as merely different aspects of one and the same spiritual being. He has now to take the next step, or rather leap, and explain the manner in which this spiritual being gives existence to matter. He does not content himself, like Plato, whom in other respects he so closely follows, with assuming as the germ of the natural world an unformed matter existing from all eternity;[1] this is to assume two independent principles, the Deity and matter existing in contrast to each other, and therefore neither of them the one absolute existence. He has commenced with one sole absolute spiritual existence; and the material must, in some way

[1] That Valentinus does not recognise an eternal matter, see Baur, *Die Chr. Gnosis* p. 165.

or other, be evolved from it. In this difficulty he adopts, in a disguised form, a hypothesis which is virtually that of pantheism: the material world has no real existence; it is, as it were, but the shadow or reflection of the spiritual. In proportion as consciousness becomes definite and limited, and therefore unable to apprehend the absolute in its fulness, in the same proportion it becomes conscious of an inability, a limitation, a something hindering complete knowledge. As spiritual knowledge becomes fainter and less complete, this indefinite negation of knowledge becomes stronger and more intense, till at last the substance and the shadow, as it were, change places, and the mere limit to the consciousness of the spiritual assumes a definite existence as the material. The second Sophia, the Achamoth, banished from the Pleroma to the region of emptiness and shadow, represents the development of the absolute existence to that degree of self-limitation in which the positive consciousness of the absolute is on the point of being superseded by the negative consciousness of limitation. She is the abortion, the mere negative side of the higher wisdom, at first wholly formless, then wrought to a form in substance, but not in knowledge, assuming a definite, but unreal consciousness; the negative sense of limitation, indicated by the suffering or passion, having a distinct and definite presence, the positive side assuming the form only of an indefinite longing after the unknown; this last, the only germ remaining of true knowledge, being derived from the same Christ to whose revelation is ascribed the higher enlightenment of the Æons. This last representation seems intended to exhibit, in the form of an ideal archetype, that which was historically realised in the state of the world before the Christian revelation—a fallen world, with the material and the sensual predominant, yet with a dim consciousness of a relation to God, and a partial illumination by the Divine Word. The mission of the second Christ, the Saviour, to impart knowledge to Achamoth and separate her from her passions, is the counterpart of the mission of the first Christ (or, according to another version, of the "Ορος), to separate the first Σοφία from her ἐνθύμησις. The whole theory may be described in general terms as a development, in allegorical language, of the pantheistic hypothesis which in its outline had been previously adopted by Basilides. All finite existence, first spiritual and then material, though seeming to have separate and substantial being, is but a mode of the existence of the absolute; becoming gradually more definite and concrete as it becomes more limited and further removed from the primitive absolute. Real existence, according to this hypothesis, has no distinctive attributes, not even self-consciousness. With the first development of consciousness begins the unreal, a seeming relation of subject to object, becoming more unreal as the development increases in definiteness, and finally culminating in the grossness of an apparent matter, opposed to thought in nature as well as in relation.[1] This representation, like most others of the kind, is, I fear, not transparently intelligible; but it is at least as clear and as satisfactory as any other of the attempted solutions of the insoluble problem, How can the absolute give birth to the relative, unity to plurality, good to evil?

The third portion of the romance treats of the formation and redemption of the visible world, which, in conformity to the author's general plan, presents an imperfect counterpart of the previous sketch of the celestial world.

[1] Cf. Baur, *Die Chr. Gnosis* p. 167.

Achamoth, the second Sophia, as the highest being outside the Pleroma, takes the place of Bythus, the supreme Father; and her offspring, the Demiurge, corresponds to Nous, the first and only begotten Æon;[1] his nature however, as we have already noticed, being not spiritual, but only animal. This animal Demiurge is the framer of the visible world out of the unorganised matter whose origin has been already described; he also brings into existence two classes of men, the animal, similar to himself, of whom he is called the Father, and the purely material, of whom he is called the Maker (δημιουργός). He also framed the seven heavens (i. e., as in Basilides, the spheres of the seven planets), which are regarded as angels, forming the Hebdomad, and, with the addition of his mother Achamoth, the Ogdoad, after the likeness of the celestial Ogdoad of the Æons.[2] In this work of formation, the Demiurge wrought blindly, as the instrument of his mother Achamoth, ignorant of her existence and ignorant of the celestial forms which he imitated, believing himself to be the source of all things, the one and only God. But, though ignorant of the higher spiritual world, the Demiurge is nevertheless the maker of a lower world of spiritual existences, namely, evil spirits; the Devil, the prince of this world,[3] and his angels, who are formed from the grief of Achamoth, and, as being spiritual, surpass their maker in knowledge, being cognisant of the higher spiritual system of which he, as being merely animal, is ignorant. The Devil, as the prince of this world, has his

---

[1] καὶ αὐτὴν μὲν ἐν εἰκόνι τοῦ ἀοράτου πατρὸς τετηρηκέναι, μὴ γινωσκομένην ὑπὸ τοῦ δημιουργοῦ, τοῦτον δὲ τοῦ μονογένους υἱοῦ, τῶν δὲ λοιπῶν Αἰώνων τοὺς ὑπὸ τούτων [τούτου] γεγονότας ἀρχαγγέλους τε καὶ ἀγγέλους, Iren. i. 5. 1.

[2] From this account it would seem that the Demiurge himself presided over one of the planetary spheres; probably, like the Abraxas of Basilides, he represents the sungod. The whole of this part of the theory is borrowed from Basilides.

[3] Κοσμοκράτωρ, Iren. i. 5. 4.

residence in the lower world; the Demiurge in the heavens; and the mother Achamoth in the region above the heavens, between them and the Pleroma.[1]

In the formation of man, the Demiurge is described as having first given him a body, formed of an invisible and transcendental matter, and as having breathed into this body the breath of life, i.e. the animal soul. Afterwards, the gross sensible body of flesh was added, which is figuratively signified by the coats of skins in which God is said to have clothed Adam and Eve. Thus framed however, man had but two natures, the animal and the material: the spiritual principle was infused into a select few from a higher source, through the mother Achamoth, who infused into the Demiurge, without his knowledge, the spiritual offspring which she had brought forth from the vision of the angelic glory, and which he unwittingly communicated to the souls of those whom he created.[2]

The Valentinian theory thus recognises three distinct classes of men, the material, the animal, and the spiritual, typified by the three sons of Adam, Cain, Abel, and Seth, each of whom represents separately one of the three natures which in Adam were united in one person.[3] The work of redemption in Valentinus as in Basilides consisted in the separation of the spiritual from the inferior portions of man's nature; but Valentinus allowed a second and inferior kind of redemption to the second class of men, the psychical or animal, whose nature was incapable of being exalted to the purely spiritual life of the Pleroma, but who might be capable of dwelling with the Demiurge in the region without. For the material or carnal portion of mankind there was no redemption; and hence they maintained that Christ when he came into the world took

[1] Iren. i. 5. 4.
[2] Irenæus, i. 5. 6.
[3] Cf. Harvey, on Irenæus, i. 7. 5, Mass. (vol. I. p. 65).

not on Him a body of flesh,[1] but assumed those portions of humanity only which were capable of redemption, namely, a seeming body given by the Demiurge, composed of the same substance as the animal soul, prepared in a marvellous manner so as to be, like the material body, visible and tangible and capable of suffering, and a spiritual nature bestowed by Achamoth. At the end of all things, when the redemption of the spiritual seed shall be complete, Achamoth, the mother of the spiritual seed on earth, shall be received within the Pleroma and united to the Saviour (a perversion of the Scriptural figure of the marriage of Christ with the Church); the spiritual seed, by whom are meant the initiated Gnostics, shall also enter into the Pleroma and be united to the angels attendant on the Saviour. Without the Pleroma, in the region previously occupied by Achamoth, there shall be a second kingdom, that of the Demiurge or father of the animal race of men, who shall give rest to the souls of his own children, the men of animal nature, i.e. the ordinary Christians of the Church, including probably also religious Jews and all who worshipped the Creator of the world as their God.[2] The material race of men, and all else that is material, being incapable of salvation, shall be consumed with fire, and utterly cease to exist.[3]

The exact views of the Valentinians concerning the nature of Christ by whom this redemption was accomplished, are not very clearly expressed; but if we may judge from some incidental notions, as well as from the

---

[1] In order to separate Christ entirely from connection with the flesh, the Valentinians, or at least some of them, maintained of the psychical Christ, εἶναι τοῦτον τὸν διὰ Μαρίας διοδεύσαντα, καθάπερ ὕδωρ διὰ σωλῆνος; Iren. i. 7. 2.

[2] Cf. Möller in Herzog, Art. 'Valentinus,' XVII. p. 37. The ὑλικοί would in like manner be generally represented by the heathens, though these also would include some few of the higher classes. Cf. Heracleon in Origen, *In Ioann.* t. xiii. c. 16; Neander, *Ch. Hist.* II. p. 85 (Bohn).

[3] Irenæus, i. cc. 6, 7.

whole analogy of the system, we may conclude that they regarded him as the son of the Demiurge (thus answering to the Æon Christ of the Pleroma, who is an emanation from Νοῦς), and as having derived from his Father a psychical nature consubstantial[1] with that of the Demiurge himself, but having also a spiritual nature whereby He is superior to his Father. The source of this spiritual nature seems to have been variously stated by different disciples of the school. According to some, it was imparted by Sophia Achamoth, the mother of the spiritual seed on earth; according to others, it was given by the Saviour, the combined production of all the Æons, who descended upon the psychical Jesus at his baptism, and left him before his passion.[2] Some seem to have combined these two theories, attributing to the Redeemer a threefold nature: the psychical, derived from the Demiurge; the spiritual from Achamoth; and the celestial nature of the Saviour, who descended from above, to which they added a fourth element, the marvellous constitution of his psychical body, so as to have the attributes without the reality of matter; and by this addition they succeeded in finding, in the compound nature of Christ, a fanciful resemblance to the Tetrad, the first and mystical member

[1] Cf. Irenæus, i. 5. 4, speaking of the invisible body and psychical life supposed to have been given by the Demiurge to the first man, καὶ εἰκόνα μὲν τὸν ὑλικὸν ὑπάρχειν παραπλήσιον μέν, ἀλλ' οὐχ ὁμοούσιον τῷ Θεῷ, καθ' ὁμοίωσιν δὲ τὸν ψυχικόν κ.τ.λ. From this we may infer that the psychical nature was regarded by Valentinus as ὁμοούσιον with the Demiurge. The same word is used, i. 5. 1, of the spiritual nature, as cognate to that of Sophia Achamoth. This may be noted as an early use of the word afterwards so important in the Arian controversy. Cf. Harvey's *Irenæus* I. p. 49.

[2] That these two views were sometimes held separately, may be inferred from Hippolytus, vi. 35, who gives the first alone. That the two in combination were held by some of the Valentinians, is stated by Irenæus, i. 7. 2. According to those who held this latter view, the Soter was supposed to have left Jesus when he was brought before Pilate (Irenæus, *l. c.*), while the pneumatic element departed with the words Πάτερ, εἰς χεῖράς σου παρατίθεμαι τὸ πνεῦμά μου, Luke xxiii. 46. Cf. Orig. *in Ioann.* x. 19; Neander, *Ch. Hist.* II. p. 91.

of the Pleroma. In this complex form, the Christology of the Valentinians exhibits a curious combination of the Docetic and Ebionite hypotheses; the psychical immaterial body attributed to our Lord being characteristic of the former of these heresies, while the separation of the person of Jesus from that of the Saviour is identical with the alternative assumption of the latter. The general philosophical theory which gave rise to these assumptions —that of the incompatibility between the Divine Nature and the material body—might have been satisfied by the adoption of either separately; but the union of the two is in accordance with the spirit of the philosophy of Valentinus, whose exaggerated Platonism, carrying out the relation of idea and imitation in every successive stage of existence, acknowledged no less than three Christs, a first for the redemption (i.e. the enlightenment) of the celestial Æons; a second for the redemption of Achamoth, the Wisdom without the Pleroma; and a third, born into the world for the redemption of mankind.[1]

The philosophical teaching which is embodied in this last portion of the Valentinian allegory is of the same tendency with that of the former portions, though the tendency is in some degree checked by other considerations, and does not attain to its full development. As the thought which underlies his whole theory is substantially that of the Indian pantheism, according to which all finite existence is an error and an unreality, so his scheme of redemption logically carried out should have resulted in the absorption of all finite and relative existence into the bosom of the infinite and absolute. The remains of the Christian influence which Valentinus had received during his communion with the Church, appear to have prevented the development of his doctrine to this extreme conse-

[1] Cf. Hippolytus, *Ref. Hær.* vi. 36.

quence, and perhaps in so eclectic a thinker it would be hardly natural to expect a complete logical development of any single idea. Yet the germ of such a consequence may be traced, though it does not ripen into its mature fruit. Redemption, in the highest sense, is reserved for the spiritual element alone; all those powers and operations of the soul which are directed to the relative and the finite are destined to fall entirely away, and nothing remains immortal but the faculty of immediate intuition whose object is the absolute and infinite.[1] In the language of Aristotle, whose teaching this part of the theory closely repeats, the active intellect, the Divine element in man, is alone immortal; the passive intellect, to which belongs memory and self-consciousness, is perishable and will be cast aside.[2] Such a destiny as this, an indestructibility of the intellect rather than an immortality of the soul, cannot be called a personal immortality at all; and Valentinus, in accepting the theory, is at least so far more consistent than his master that he expressly denies to the highest order of mankind the one attribute on which personality depends, and which holds a foremost place in Aristotle's teaching, that of free will. His view of the nature and destiny of mankind has been not inaptly likened to the supralapsarian theory of predestination.[3] Some men are born into the world as spiritual, the children of God, and these are incapable of falling away, and inevitably destined to salvation; others, equally without their own choice, have a material nature, and these by a like necessity are destined to destruction.[4] A kind of choice is permitted only to the intermediate race, the psychical men, who are capable of inclining to good or

[1] Cf. Neander, *Church Hist.* II. p. 84 (Bohn).
[2] *De Anima* i. 4, iii. 5. Cf. Neander, *l. c.*; Zeller, *Phil. der Griech.* II. 2. pp. 441, 465.
[3] Harvey's *Irenæus* I. p. cxli.
[4] Irenæus, i. 6, 2.

evil, but these have no admission into the Pleroma; the very fact of their freedom, we might almost say of their personality, makes them incapable of redemption in the highest sense of the term. A doctrine like this is not explicitly pantheistic, but it escapes from pantheism only by being inconsistent with itself. The moral results of this teaching, in the disciples at least, if not in the masters, were, if Irenæus may be accepted as a witness, pernicious in the extreme. The spiritual man, according to their teaching, was incapable of corruption by any course of life whatever. As gold, they said, when lying buried in mud, does not lose the nature of gold, but remains distinct from the mud, so the spiritual man, in whatever course of action he may be engaged, retains his spiritual nature and is incapable of deterioration. 'Hence,' says Irenæus, 'the most perfect among these commit without fear all forbidden acts. They are indifferent about eating meats offered to idols, maintaining that they are not contaminated thereby; they are the first to attend at every Gentile feast in honour of idols, and some of them do not abstain from the sanguinary and abominable exhibitions of combats of wild beasts and gladiators. Some surrender themselves insatiably to carnal pleasures, saying that they give to the flesh the things of the flesh, and to the spirit the things of the spirit.'[1] No doubt this description, which in the original is carried into further details, was applicable only to the worst portion of the sect; but the character of the theory is unhappily such that it may be applied in practice with equal facility to the most rigid asceticism or the most abandoned profligacy.

Valentinus was for a time the most popular of the Gnostic teachers, and became, through his numerous disciples, the founder of the largest number of subordi-

[1] Irenæus, i. 6. 2, 3.

LECT. XII. VALENTINUS AND THE VALENTINIANS.

nate schools. Secundus, Ptolemæus, Marcus, Colarbasus, Heracleon, Theodotus, and Alexander were distinguished as leaders of Valentinian schools;[1] and Bardesanes, whom we have already noticed as one of the Syrian Gnostics, was for a time a disciple of Valentinus, though he afterwards left him and wrote against some of his opinions.[2] The most celebrated of the Valentinians were Ptolemæus, Marcus, and Heracleon. Ptolemæus, as we have before noticed, was the Gnostic whose writings principally gave occasion to the refutation by St. Irenæus. There is still extant, preserved by Epiphanius,[3] a letter of his addressed to a lady named Flora, whom he desired to bring over to his belief. In this letter he discusses the question of the origin of the world and of the Law of Moses, and combats the opinions of those who attributed them to the Supreme God, as well as the opposite extreme of those who maintained that they proceeded from an evil being. Ptolemæus maintains an intermediate position, asserting that the law is partly of Divine, partly of human origin; some of its precepts resting merely on the personal authority of Moses or of the elders who were associated with him (a conclusion which reminds us of what we have heard of late concerning 'the dark patches of human passion and error which form a partial crust upon' Holy Scripture),[4] while others are of a higher inspiration. The Divine portion however of the law he ascribes, according to the general theory of the Gnostic school, not to the Supreme God, but to an intermediate being, the Creator of the world, whose goodness falls far short of absolute perfection. In this way Ptolemæus accounts for the imperfections which he professes to find even in the Divine

[1] Matter, II. p. 101.
[2] Eusebius, *H. E.* iv. 30.
[3] *Hær.* xxxiii. 3–7.
[4] Wilson in *Essays and Reviews*, p. 177.

portion of Scripture, while at the same time, by denying that the Supreme God is the Maker of the world, he ingeniously evades any argument that may be drawn from the analogy of revelation to the constitution and course of nature. Marcus, another disciple of Valentinus, and the founder of the subordinate sect of Marcosians, seems to have been the conjuror and wonder-worker of the school, bearing somewhat the same relation to the πνευματικοὶ or spiritual men of the Valentinians' doctrine that the modern 'spiritualist,' the necromancer who juggles with rapping spirits and dancing tables, bears to the contemplative mystic. Marcus figures in the writings of Irenæus as a clever charlatan, deluding weak minds, especially women, by his tricks of magic, and employing the influence thus gained for profligate purposes.[1] He taught a system of theosophy agreeing in the main with that of Valentinus, but with a difference in illustration and imagery. His favourite vehicle of illustration (or obscuration) was the alphabet with the numerical powers of its several letters, and his speculations in this respect bear considerable affinity to those of the Jewish Kabbala, which, as a native of Palestine, he may possibly have known.[2] His methods of finding mystical meanings in each letter of which a word is composed, and again in the letters composing the name of that letter (e.g. the five letters in the word *Delta*), and so on, are given in detail by Irenæus.[3] His followers are accused of forging apocryphal Scriptures in support of their doctrines, and an anecdote cited by Irenæus from an apocryphal Gospel employed by them is still found in the extant work called the Arabic Gospel of the Infancy, which, though itself of

[1] Irenæus, i. 13.
[2] See Harvey's *Irenæus* I. p. 159. For the probable Palestinian origin of Marcus, see Matter, *Hist. du Gnost.* II. p. 107; Neander, *Church Hist.* II. p. 104.
[3] Irenæus, i. 14 *seq.*

later origin, may have been partly taken from this source.[1] Heracleon,[2] another disciple of Valentinus, has acquired a reputation as the earliest-known commentator on a canonical Gospel.[3] He wrote an exposition of the Gospel of St. John, portions of which he endeavoured, by means of allegorical interpretations, to wrest to the support of Gnostic theories. Fragments of this commentary are cited in the work of Origen on the same Gospel.[4] Yet though wild and fanciful when carried away by his Gnostic theosophy (as may be seen in his exposition of the discourse of our Lord with the woman of Samaria, which he regards as a figurative representation of the relation of the πνευματικοὶ to the Valentinian Σωτήρ), Heracleon seems in other places to have exercised a sound judgment, and to have produced an exposition more simple and natural than that of his censor, Origen.[5] His philosophical theory is said to have been nearly the same as that of his master Valentinus.[6]

The fragments of this commentary of Heracleon, and the epistle of Ptolemæus to Flora, are the most considerable literary remains of the Valentinian school which have come down to modern times. In addition to these there are extant a considerable extract from a work by an anonymous member of the sect, cited by Epiphanius,[7]

[1] Cf. Tischendorf, *Evang. Apoc. Proleg.* § viii.

[2] Hippolytus (vi. 35) mentions Heracleon (with Ptolemæus) as belonging to the Italian school of the Valentinians. Matter (II. p. 113), without naming any authority, speaks of him as teaching at Alexandria.

[3] Ueberweg, *Gesch. der Phil.* II. p. 35.

[4] He also appears to have written a commentary on St. Luke, if we may judge from the citation of Clem. Alex. *Strom.* iv. 9, p. 595 (Potter). All the fragments of Heracleon are collected in the appendix to Massuet's *Irenæus* (p. 1291, *seq.* Migne).

[5] Neander, *Ch. Hist.* II. pp. 95, 97.

[6] Pseudo-Tertullian, *De Præscr.* c. 49 'Extitit præterea Heracleon alter hæreticus, qui cum Valentino paria sentit.'

[7] *Hær.* xxxi. 5, 6. That this fragment is not, as Blondel supposed, the work of Valentinus himself, but of an anonymous disciple, see Massuet, *Diss. Præv.* i. § 10.

and a few fragments of the writings of Valentinus himself, preserved by Clement of Alexandria and Origen; to which must now be added the citations from a work, possibly of Valentinus himself, made by Hippolytus.[1] It was at one time supposed that there was still in existence an entire work of Valentinus in a Coptic translation. Tertullian, in his treatise against the Valentinians (c. 2), speaks of the *Valentinian Sophia* in a manner which has led some critics to imagine that Valentinus wrote a work with this title; and a Coptic MS in the British Museum entitled Πίστις Σοφία was at one time supposed to be the work in question.[2] Against this supposition however it may be urged that there is no satisfactory evidence that Valentinus ever wrote such a work, the interpretation of Tertullian being very questionable;[3] and secondly, that the aforesaid MS, which has recently been published with a Latin translation, contains internal evidence to show that it does not belong to the Valentinian school. A recent examination of this work by Köstlin seems to establish conclusively that the doctrine which it teaches is widely different from that of Valentinus;[4] and it is at least more probable that it belongs to a late modification of the Ophite heresy, and was written not earlier than the middle of the third century.[5]

The system of Valentinus, like that of Basilides, is in principle pantheistic, which is indeed the tendency and

[1] Clem. Alex. *Strom.* ii. 8, 20, p. 448, 488; iii. 7, 13, p. 538, 603; vi. 6, p. 767; Pseudo-Origen, *Dial. de Recta Fide* sect. iv (I. p. 840, De la Rue). These fragments are collected in the Appendix to Massuet's edition of Irenæus. The extracts in Hippolytus, vi. 29-37, are supposed by Bunsen (*Hippol.* I. p. 65) to be from the *Sophia* of Valentinus.

[2] This conjecture was originally made by Woide. Cf. Matter, *Hist. du Gnosticisme* II. p. 39. The work was published by Petermann, with a Latin translation by Schwartze. Berlin, 1850, 1853.

[3] Cf. Massuet, *Diss. Præv. in Iren.* i. § 9.

[4] See Köstlin, *Das Gnostische System des Buches* Πίστις Σοφία, in *Theol. Jahrb.* Tüb. 1854, p. 185.

[5] Köstlin, pp. 189, 194.

the danger of every system of philosophy which aspires to solve the mystery of the origin of derived existence from one absolute principle. To this pantheistic conception both the Platonism and the Judaism of the author's Alexandrian studies are made subordinate, as well as some minor details which may possibly have been directly taken from other sources. Thus the doctrine of emanations, though common to the Persian and the Indian philosophy, appears in Valentinus in a form which, though Indian in its pantheistic principle and method, yet more resembles the dualistic Persian scheme in some of its subordinate particulars. The Jewish Kabbala, in which this portion of the Persian philosophy was adapted to a monotheistic, or rather to a pantheistic assumption, offers in this respect the nearest resemblance to Valentinianism; and, were we quite certain of its chronological priority, we should have no hesitation in naming this as the channel through which the Persian *Amshaspands* and *Izeds* became the source of the Valentinian *Æons*.[1] As it is, we cannot help regarding the resemblance between the two systems as one of the data for forming an opinion on this controverted chronological question; and the use made of the Hebrew language by some of the disciples of Valentinus, if not by the master himself,[2] seems to point

---

[1] Massuet (*Diss. Præv. in Iren.* i. § 21) denies on chronological grounds the influence of the Jewish Kabbala on the Valentinian system; but he perhaps goes too far, when he denies that there is any trace in the early Fathers of the Kabbalistic trifling with the letters of the alphabet. The theories of Marcus recorded by Irenæus, i. c. 14–17, though not expressly referred to the Kabbalists, are Kabbalistic in character; and it is on the whole perhaps more probable that a secret Kabbalistic teaching existed at this time, and was partly known to some of the Gnostics, than that Gnostic doctrines were copied by Jews in the ninth or thirteenth century.

[2] On the employment of Hebrew terms by the Marcosians, as well as on some points of affinity between the Kabbala and the Valentinian Æons, see above, Lecture III, p. 41 *seq.* On the Aramaic names of the Æons in Epiphanius, which perhaps were not due to Valentinus himself, see a note in Lecture XI, p. 176.

to the existence of Kabbalistic doctrines in a traditional form, if not in written documents, through which the Palestinian or Pantheistic form of Jewish theosophy may have combined with the Alexandrian or Platonic form in the production of the Valentinian hybrid.

LECTURE XIII.

ASIATIC GNOSTICISM—MARCION.

THE third great geographical division of Gnosticism, that of Asia Minor, so classified from the country of its most distinguished representative, Marcion of Pontus, differs in many important points from the other systems; yet, as regards its historical appearance, it is introduced to us in the first instance, apparently as a mere offshoot from the Gnosis of Syria. We are told that the predecessor of Marcion was one Cerdon, a Syrian,[1] who came to Rome during the pontificate of Hyginus (A.D. 139–142), and taught that the God who was proclaimed by the Law and the Prophets was not the Father of our Lord Jesus Christ, for that the one was known and the other unknown, and that the one was just and the other good. To him, it is added, succeeded Marcion of Pontus, who expanded his doctrine.[2]

Yet, notwithstanding this coincidence in doctrine as well as in the exaggerated asceticism of his practical teaching, we should form a very imperfect notion of Marcion and his system if we considered him merely as a disciple of the Syrian Gnosis represented by Saturninus. Though the theology of Marcion ultimately coincided in some respects with that of the earlier Gnostics, he approached the question from the opposite side, and with a

---

[1] For the Syrian origin of Cerdon, see Epiphan. *Hær.* xli. 1.
[2] Irenæus, i. 27.

widely different character and training of mind. The earlier Gnostics were for the most part philosophers who approached Christianity from the side of heathen speculation, and endeavoured, by means of fusion and perverted interpretation, to form an eclectic system out of these separate elements. Marcion on the other hand was originally a Christian, contemplating all other religious teaching from the Christian stand-point as understood by himself, and refusing all alliance with or toleration of every mode of thought which was not in accordance with this pattern. The earlier Gnostics were, or attempted to be, positive thinkers, attaining by their own power of spiritual intuition to a knowledge of Divine things, and having thereby a gauge and criterion to which all other religious teaching, that of the Gospel included, must be adapted. Marcion assumed the position of a negative thinker, rejecting without compromise all that would not be reconciled to his supposed Christian standard, but making no attempt to discover a higher philosophical truth under the apparently conflicting representations. Their method was mystical and ontological; his was rationalistic and critical. They professed to teach a special wisdom, accessible only to a chosen few; he professed to teach a plain Christianity, within the reach of all Christian men; and though his criticisms ultimately carried him to the threshold of the Gnostic shrine, he did not attempt to penetrate into its inner mysteries.

Marcion was a native of Sinope in Pontus, and is said to have been the son of the bishop of that Church and to have been expelled from the Christian community by his own father.[1] The moral offence assigned as the cause of

---

[1] Epiphan. *Hær.* xlii. 1. He seems to have at one time been a sailor. Tertullian, *Adv. Marc.* i. 18, calls him 'nauclerus;' Rhodon (in Euseb. *H. E.* v. 13) ὁ ναύτης. Massuet (*Diss. in Iren.* i. § 135) thinks that this may be merely a play on the name of his country, *Pontus*.

this expulsion is alien to the character of the man and of his teaching, and rests upon very doubtful authority;[1] and it is not improbable that the excommunication may have really been due to his errors of doctrine, and not to any profligacy of conduct. From Sinope he betook himself to Rome, where he seems to have become acquainted with Cerdon and to have adopted some of his Syrian theories; but he must have done so chiefly because he forced them to adapt themselves to a system which he had already elaborated on different grounds. An anecdote, in itself highly probable, narrated by Epiphanius[2] seems to show that he came to Rome with his own theory already formed, and probably hoping to find a more favourable reception for it in the Gentile capital than it had met with in the more judaizing churches of Asia. It is said that when the presbyters of the Roman church refused to receive him into communion, he asked them what was the meaning of our Lord's injunction against putting new wine into old bottles—evidently alluding to the antagonism which he supposed to exist between the Old Testament and the New.[3] Finding that they did not adopt this view and persevered in refusing to admit him to communion, he determined to found a separate church of his own, and joined himself for that purpose with the Gnostic Cerdon.

The character of Marcion's own teaching may be

---

[1] Pseudo-Tertull. *De Præscr.* c. 51 'propter stuprum cujusdam virginis ab ecclesiæ communicatione abjectus:' cf. Epiphan. *Hær.* xlii. 1. But the real Tertullian says nothing of this charge; on the contrary, he contrasts the offence of Apelles with the continence of Marcion; *De. Præscr.* c. 30.

[2] *Hær.* xlii. 2.

[3] Tertullian's account (*Adv. Marc.* iv. 4; *De Præscr.* c. 30) seems to imply that Marcion was for a time admitted into communion, and gave a sum of money to the Church, which was afterwards rejected when he was excommunicated. This account may be reconciled with that of Epiphanius, if we suppose it to refer to his first arrival at Rome, before the news of his excommunication at Sinope was known.

described as a combination of rationalism proper with what is now commonly known as the 'higher criticism.' The first element was manifested in his rejection of the entire Old Testament, as well as all the evidences of natural religion derived from the constitution of the world, because in both alike he discovered phenomena which he considered to be different from what ought to be expected from a Being of perfect wisdom and goodness. The second was manifested in his rejection of a large portion of the New Testament, as a corruption of what he assumed to be the pure doctrines of Christianity. Among the Christian Scriptures, Marcion accepted only ten of the Epistles of St. Paul,[1] whom he regarded as the only preacher of the true revelation of Christ, together with a pretended original Gospel, which he asserted to be that used by St. Paul himself (so he interpreted the expression 'according to my Gospel'[2]) and which was in reality a mutilated copy of the Gospel according to St. Luke.[3] The other books of the New Testament he discarded, as the works of judaizing teachers who corrupted the primitive truth.[4] Marcion's gospel seems to have contained very few additions to the canonical text of St. Luke, but on the other hand very considerable portions of that text were omitted in his recension as not compatible with his theory of the Person of Christ and the character of Christianity. All that relates to the birth and

---

[1] These were arranged by Marcion in the following order: Galatians, 1, 2 Corinthians, Romans, 1, 2 Thessalonians, Ephesians, Colossians, Philemon, Philippians. Even these were received in a mutilated and corrupted form. The Pastoral Epistles were rejected. See Epiphan. *Hær.* xlii. 9.

[2] Rom. ii. 16, xvi. 25 (2 Tim. ii. 8). Cf. Origen. *in Evang. Ioann.* t. v. sect. 4; Pseudo-Orig. *Dial. de Recta Fide*, sect. 1 (p. 807, De la Rue).

[3] Cf. Neander, *Church Hist.* II. p. 149.

[4] Cf. Tertullian, *Adv. Marc.* iv. 2, 3. This part of Marcion's teaching was revived in the eighteenth century by Morgan, the 'Moral Philosopher,' and again in the present century by the Tübingen critics.

infancy of our Lord, together with the genealogy, was omitted.[1] All appeals to the writers of the Old Testament as bearing witness to Christ, and passages that did not tally with the ascetic teaching of the critic, such as the contrast between our Lord's way of life and that of John the Baptist, and the mention of those who shall *sit down* (ἀνακλιθήσονται) in the kingdom of God,[2] were remorselessly excluded, as corruptions detected by the critical insight of the reformer. Other passages were retained in an amended form. The words, 'It is easier for heaven and earth to pass than one tittle of the law to fail' (Luke xvi. 17), became 'It is easier for heaven and earth and for the law and the prophets to fail, than one tittle of the words of the Lord.' 'When ye shall see Abraham and Isaac and Jacob and all the prophets in the kingdom of God' (Luke xiii. 28), was transformed into, 'When ye shall see the righteous in the kingdom of God.'[3] The perverse criticism of the Tübingen school, whose mode of dealing with Holy Scriptures bears no small resemblance to Marcion's own, has endeavoured of late years to defend the paradox, in part suggested by Semler and others, that Marcion's recension was the original, the canonical text the interpolated Gospel;[4] though there is not a scrap of

---

[1] Cf. Irenæus, i. 27. 2. Marcion's Gospel seems to have commenced with the words Ἐν ἔτει πεντεκαιδεκάτῳ τῆς ἡγεμονίας Τιβερίου Καίσαρος [Pseudo-Orig. *Dial. de Recta Fide*, p. 823 (De la Rue), adds ἡγεμονεύοντος Ποντίου Πιλάτου τῆς Ἰουδαίας] ὁ Θεὸς κατῆλθεν εἰς Καπερναοὺμ πόλιν τῆς Γαλιλαίας καὶ ἦν διδάσκων ἐν τοῖς σάββασι, compiled from Luke iii. 1, iv. 31, the early part of c. iv, except a few verses transposed, being omitted on account of the references to the O. T. Cf. Tertullian, *Adv. Marc.* iv. 7; Epiphan. *Hær.* xlii. 11; Iren. i. 27, iii. 10; Origen, *in Ioann.* xx. (IV. p. 165 De la Rue); Theodoret, *H. F.* i. 24; Pseudo-Origen, *Dial.* pp. 823, 869. See Thilo, *Codex Apocr. N. T.* p. 403. For some details of Marcion's alterations in St. Luke and St. Paul's Epistles, see Lardner, *Hist. of Heretics* c. x. §§ 35-53.

[2] Luke vii. 21-35, xiii. 29.

[3] Cf. Bleek, *Einleitung in das N. T.* pp. 124, 125.

[4] Semler imagined that St. Luke's and Marcion's Gospel were both later recensions of an original text. He was followed by Schmidt, who suggested that Marcion's was the original gospel. Ritschl (*Das Evang. Mar-*

historical evidence to show that the mutilated recension was ever heard of before Marcion's time, and though there is positive evidence to show that Marcion must have possessed and made use of passages of St. Luke's original Gospel which were omitted in his mutilated edition.[1]

The circumstance that Marcion approached the question from a critical, not from a historical point of view, and chiefly from a persuasion of the contrariety between the revelations of the Old and New Testament, will serve to account for some of the peculiarities of his system as compared with those of the other Gnostics. The metaphysical element is kept entirely in the background, and large portions of it disappear altogether.

Marcion's theory recognises no emanations of Æons as connecting links between the Supreme God and the world, for from his point of view the Supreme God was not even indirectly the Author of the world. There is no attempt at a description of the spiritual world, no hypothesis to depict the development of absolute into relative existence; for the object of Marcion was simply to avail himself of the surface of the Gnostic theories for the solution of a critical difficulty: he had no taste for plunging into the depths of ontological speculation. Matter is indeed admitted into his system as an eternal self-existent principle,[2] but no consequences are deduced from this assumption with reference to the constitution of the world: for the mind of the Author was almost wholly occupied with

---

cions u. das Kanon. Evang. des Lucas) and Baur (*Kanon. Evang.* p. 397-427) maintain that Marcion's gospel was interpolated to form the received text of St. Luke. Schwegler (*Das nachapost. Zeitalter* I. p. 260-284) maintains the negative portion of the same view, viz. that Marcion did not mutilate St. Luke. Ritschl subsequently retracted, and Baur modified his view. Cf. Bleek, *l. c.* p. 129.

[1] For a full examination of the question, see Bleek, *Einleitung in das N. T.* pp. 129-138

[2] Tertull. *Adv. Marc.* i. 15 'Et materia enim Deus, secundum formam divinitatis, innata scilicet et infecta et æterna.'

the supposed contrasts between the two Testaments and their respective authors; he paid little or no attention to theories of cosmogony. And hence, though in reality he recognised three original principles, Matter, the Demiurge, and the Supreme God, he makes no positive use of the first, and his system is frequently described as if it were a pure dualism recognising the two last only.[1]

Marcion's heretical opinions seem to have begun in a minute and captious criticism of the Old Testament, which he insisted on interpreting everywhere in the most literal manner, and consequently imagined to contain numerous self-contradictions and unworthy representations of God. He wrote a work entitled 'Ἀντιθέσεις, professing to point out contradictions between the Old Testament and the New, as well as to show that parts even of the latter were interpolated and corrupt.[2] The following may be given as specimens of his mode of dealing with the Jewish Scriptures. The God whom these Scriptures reveal, he says, cannot have been a God of wisdom and goodness and power; for after having created man in his own image he permitted him to fall, being either ignorant that he would fall, or unwilling or unable to prevent him from falling.[3] He is represented as calling to Adam in the garden, 'Adam, where art thou?' showing that he was ignorant where Adam was.[4] He commanded the Israelites at the exodus to spoil the Egyptians.[5] He forbade the

---

[1] Thus one of the earliest antagonists, Rhodon (in Euseb. *H. E.* v. 13) speaks of Marcion as holding two principles, as does the Pseudo-Tertullian, *De Præscr.* c. 51. Hippolytus, vii. 31, attributes two principles to Marcion, but in x. 19, he enumerates three. Later expositors add a fourth, an evil being or Satan ; Theodoret, *Hær. Fab.* i. 24. This last was probably a later modification of the theory ; see Dilthey, in Herzog, vol. IX. p. 98.

[2] Tertull. *Adv. Marc.* i. 19 'Antitheses Marcionis, id est, contrariæ oppositiones, quæ conantur discordiam Evangelii cum lege committere.' *Ibid.* iv. 4 'Evangelium Lucæ per Antitheses suas arguit ut interpolatum a protectoribusJudaismi.'

[3] Tert. *Adv. Marc.* ii. 5.

[4] *Ibid.* ii. 25.

[5] *Ibid.* ii. 20.

making of graven images, and yet commanded Moses to raise up the brazen serpent in the wilderness, and cherubim to be placed over the mercy seat.[1] He chooses Saul to be king over Israel, and is afterwards said to have repented of his choice.[2] He threatens to destroy the children of Israel, and is turned away from his purpose by the intercession of Moses.[3] On these and other accounts, Marcion censures the Old Testament representation of God, as being that of an imperfect being; but instead of adopting the hypothesis of the modern rationalists, and denying the fidelity of the representation and consequently the inspiration of the book, he finds an apparent solution of his doubts in the Gnostic hypothesis of a distinction between the Supreme God and the Demiurge. The Old Testament, he argued, represents God as imperfect, because the God of the Old Testament, the Creator of the world, the Author of the elder revelation, is in truth, not the Supreme God, but an imperfect being. He did not however, with the majority of the Gnostics, regard the Demiurge as a derived and dependent being, whose imperfection is due to his remoteness from the highest cause; nor yet, according to the Persian doctrine, did he assume an eternal principle of pure malignity. His second principle is independent of, and co-eternal with, the first; opposed to it however, not as evil to good, but as imperfection to perfection, or, as Marcion expressed it, as a just to a good being.

The choice of the term *just*, which Marcion seems to have borrowed from Cerdon, seems at first sight a strange one to express the character of so imperfect a being as Marcion professed to see in the God of Israel. But in truth Marcion's interpretation of *Justice* was very similar to that in which Aristotle speaks of it as improperly used

[1] Tertull. *Adv. Marc.* ii. 22.   [2] *Ibid.* ii. 24.
[3] *Ibid.* ii. 26.

in opposition to *equity*.[1] He conceived of it as the severe, rigid enforcement of every particular of a law which in itself possessed all the infirmities of the legislator by whom it was enacted. His conception of the law of Moses was as if its whole spirit and purpose was summed up in the single precept, 'an eye for an eye and a tooth for a tooth.'[2] He exaggerated and distorted the teaching of his professed master, St. Paul, concerning the law as weak through the flesh,[3] and as causing offence to abound,[4] and as giving the knowledge of sin;[5] but omitted altogether the other side of the picture, which represents the law as holy and just and good,[6] as being our schoolmaster to bring us to Christ,[7] as causing offence to abound only that grace might much more abound;[8] and on the other hand, in the spirit of some of the Deists of Bishop Butler's day, to whom his method of criticism bears no small resemblance, he regarded the character of the true God as one of pure benevolence,[9] overlooking, or rather purposely, as a part of his system, setting aside, all those aspects of nature as well as of revelation, which represent Him as a Moral Governor.

Though it is a slight digression from our main topic, it may not be unprofitable to turn aside for a moment to notice the manner in which Tertullian meets the cavils of Marcion against the Old Testament. Some he simply dismisses as misrepresentations of the fact; the brazen serpent, for instance, and the cherubim were not erected to be worshipped, and therefore were not opposed to the second commandment. Other features of the Divine government he vindicates by showing them to be per-

[1] *Eth. Nic.* v. 14.
[2] Tertull. *Adv. Marc.* ii. 18.
[3] Rom. viii. 3.
[4] Rom. v. 20.
[5] Rom. iii. 20.
[6] Rom. vii. 12.
[7] Gal. iii. 24.
[8] Rom. v. 20.
[9] Butler, *Analogy*, part i. c. 2. Cf. Tertullian, *Adv. Marc.* i. 6; Baur, *Die Chr. Gnosis* p. 251.

fectly compatible with the goodness of their Author, even as judged by his antagonist's own standard. The fall of Adam was not caused by God's appointment, but by man's abuse of his free will; and the goodness of God is shown in His having given to man this excellent gift of freedom, which exalts him above all the rest of the animal creation, and was necessary in fact, to constitute his likeness to his Maker.[1] Even those institutions of the law which Marcion produces as proofs of the harshness and severity of God will, on examination, be found to tend to the benefit of man. The 'lex talionis' was a law adapted to the Jewish people, and instituted for the purpose of repressing violence and injustice. The prohibition of certain kinds of food was designed to inculcate self-restraint, and thereby to preserve men from the evils of excess. The sacrifices and other burdensome observances of the ceremonial law, independently of their typical and prophetical meaning, answered the immediate purpose of preventing the Jews from being seduced into idolatry by the splendid rites of their heathen neighbours.[2] The gold and silver of Egypt he regards as a payment justly due to the Israelites for their many years of labour and service in that country.[3]

But beyond these, there is another consideration to which Tertullian appeals, and one which is too often kept out of sight in dealing with similar difficulties—man's ignorance of God, and the necessity of speaking of divine things in a manner adapted to human capacities.

You have,' he says, 'a God, certain and undoubted, as may be seen even from this, that you see Him to be one whom you know not, save in so far as He is pleased to reveal Himself.' ... 'Isaiah exclaims, "Who hath directed the Spirit of the Lord, or being His counsellor hath

[1] Tertull. *Adv. Marc.* ii. 5, 6.
[2] Bp. Kaye *Tertullian*, pp. 462, 463. Cf. Tertull. *Adv. Marc.* ii. 18.
[3] Tertull. *Adv. Marc.* ii. 20.

taught Him? With whom took He counsel, and who instructed Him, and taught Him in the path of judgment, and taught Him knowledge, and showed to Him the way of understanding?" (Isaiah xl. 13, 14). And St. Paul agrees with him, saying, "O the depth of the riches both of the wisdom and knowledge of God! how unsearchable are His judgments, and His ways past finding out" (Rom. xi. 33)—ways of understanding and knowledge which no one has shown Him, except, it may be, these critics of Deity who say, God ought not to do this and ought to do that, as if any one can know the things of God but the Spirit of God (1 Cor. ii. 11). . . . God is then most great when He seems to man to be little; and then most good when He seems to man to be not good.'[1] In a later passage, in answer to the objection against attributing to God human feelings and passions, he says, 'We have learnt our God from the prophets and from Christ, not from Epicurus and the philosophers. We who believe that God dwelt on the earth, and humbled Himself to adopt a human nature for man's salvation, are far from believing that to have a care for anything is unworthy of God. . . . Fools, to prejudge of Divine things by human; as if, because the passions of man belong to his corrupt condition, they must be assumed to be of the same character in God. Distinguish between the two substances, and interpret differently as the difference of substance requires, though you use terms which seem to be the same. . . . This must be regarded as the image of God in man, that he has the same affections and senses as God, but not such as God has; for their conditions and ends differ as God differs from man. Our very gentleness, patience, mercy, and goodness, the source of all, are not perfect in us as they are in God, who is alone perfect. . .

[1] Tertull. *Adv. Marc.* ii. 2.

He has our affections, but after His own manner, as it becomes Him to have them; and through Him man has the same affections, but in his own manner also.'[1]

As Marcion attempted to separate the God of the Old Testament from the God of the New, so he likewise attempted to distinguish between two Redeemers, separating the Messiah of the prophets from the true Christ.[2] The Jewish Messiah, he said, still harping on his literal interpretation, is foretold as a warrior who shall destroy the enemies of Israel, and bring back his people to their own land, and finally give them rest in Abraham's bosom;[3] Christ did none of these things. He suffered on the cross, whereas the law declares every one accursed that hangeth on a tree.[4] He was sent by the good God for the deliverance of the whole human race, whereas the Messiah of the Jews is destined by the Creator to restore the dispersed Israelites only.[5] On account of these supposed discrepances Marcion maintained that the Hebrew prophecies were still unfulfilled, and pointed to a second Christ, the son of the Demiurge, who was hereafter to appear as the temporal and spiritual deliverer of the Jewish people.

With regard to the Christ of the New Testament, the doctrine of Marcion was Docetic in the extreme, beyond that of any previous Gnostic teacher. Matter was the instrument of the Demiurge, which he employed in the formation of the world; and such was the hostility which he supposed between his two deities, that Christ, the representative of the Supreme God, could have nothing to do with a material body, or with any part of that human nature which the Demiurge had made. Other Gnostics, who denied the reality of Christ's humanity, had allowed

[1] Tertull. *Adv. Marc.* ii. 16.
[2] *Ibid.* iv. 6.
[3] *Ibid.* iii. 12, 24.
[4] *Ibid.* iii. 18.
[5] *Ibid.* iii. 21.

to Him at least a human soul and a seeming birth into the world.¹ Marcion denied both; his Christ appears suddenly on the world, sent down from that higher region which is the dwelling of the Supreme God,² with the appearance, but none of the reality of mature humanity, not even in appearance born of any human mother (so he interpreted the words, '*Who is my mother?*,' Matt. xii. 48),³ nor passing through any stages of infancy and growth. His gospel is said to have commenced with the words, ' In the fifteenth year of the reign of Tiberius Cæsar, God came down to Capernaum, a city of Galilee, and taught on the sabbath days '—a verse, with the interpolation of the word *God*, compounded of Luke iii. 1, and iv. 31, the intermediate portions of the Gospel being omitted or transposed.⁴ A seeming death his Christ was permitted to suffer, for death is a diminution of the kingdom of the Demiurge; but of birth, which increases that kingdom, not even the appearance was to be tolerated.⁵ The seeming death of Christ Marcion represented as being caused by the malice of the Demiurge, who beheld the power of a new and unknown God manifested on earth,⁶ despising his law and drawing away his subjects, and therefore roused the anger of the Jews against Christ, to persecute and put him to death.⁷ Yet the contest is continued in another world. Christ descends into hell to proclaim the kingdom of the true God to the spirits of

---

¹ Cf. the psychical Christ and the birth ὡς διὰ σωλῆνος of Valentinus.

² On Marcion's higher world, cf. Justin M. in *Apol.* i. c. 27 ἄλλον δέ τινα, ὡς ὄντα μείζονα, τὰ μείζονα παρὰ τοῦτον ὁμολογεῖν πεποιηκέναι: Tertull. *Adv. Marc.* i. 15 'Esse et illi conditionem suam et suum mundum.' On the suddenness of Christ's coming into the world, cf. Tertull. *Adv. Marc.* iv. 11, 'Subito Christus, subito et Ioannes; sic sunt omnia apud Marcionem.'

³ Tertullian, *De Carne Christi* c. 7.

⁴ Tertull. *Adv. Marc.* iv. 7. See above, p. 207.

⁵ Cf. Dilthey in Herzog IX. p. 33. A similar view seems to have been previously held by Saturninus: cf. Irenæus, i. 24. 1 ' Salvatorem innatum demonstravit.'

⁷ Tertull. *Adv. Marc.* iv. 20.

those who were disobedient to the law of the Demiurge and condemned by him as transgressors. Cain, Esau, Korah, Dathan and Abiram, the men of Sodom, the Egyptians, all who in the Old Testament appear as the enemies of the God of Israel, join themselves to Christ in Hades, and are received into his kingdom, while Abel and Enoch, and Noah, and the patriarchs and prophets of the chosen people, remained in the service of their own God, and were left in Hades.[1]

But while Marcion thus emphatically denied any real assumption by Christ of human nature, he seems on the other hand to have left His relation to the Supreme God vague and undetermined.[2] There is no hint in his teaching of any theory of emanation from the Supreme God, which forms an essential feature in the other Gnostic systems, both Docetic and Ebionite. He speaks of God as having revealed Himself in human form,[3] as the Demiurge or his angels appeared in seemingly human bodies to the patriarchs;[4] but in what manner he distinguished between the persons of the Father and the Son, or whether indeed he made any distinction at all, cannot be certainly decided from our present sources of information. It is not improbable however, as Neander conjectures, that he intended to represent, as his language seems to imply, that the Supreme God himself appeared, without any Mediator, in the kingdom of the Demiurge on earth,[5] and thus that he virtually, if not explicitly, adopted the Patripassian doctrine, which was distinctly a very short time after-

---

[1] Irenæus, i. 27; Theodoret, *Hær. Fab.* i. 24; Epiphan. *Hær.* xlii. 4. The Armenian Bishop Esnig adds a strange story of a second descent of Christ into hell, where he confronts the Demiurge, and charges him with the murder of himself, and thus justifies himself for carrying away his enemy's nominal subjects. Cf. Baur, *Die Chr. Gnosis* p. 273; Dilthey in Herzog IX. p. 34.

[2] Cf. Dilthey in Herzog, p. 33.
[3] Irenæus, i. 29.
[4] Tertull. *Adv. Marc.* iii. 9.
[5] *Church History* II. p. 143.

wards taught by Praxeas and Noetus.[1] Though Tertullian did not prominently dwell upon this point in his work against Marcion, as he did in his controversy with his contemporary and personal antagonist Praxeas, yet there are not wanting incidental expressions to show that this doctrine, or something very nearly approaching to it, was the interpretation which he put upon Marcion's language.[2] It was a natural consequence of Marcion's views concerning the Demiurge and his kingdom that he should deny the resurrection of the body.[3] It was also natural that, on the same grounds, he should inculcate the duty of the most rigid asceticism during this life. In the same spirit in which he had denied the birth of Christ, he condemned marriage as increasing the kingdom of the Demiurge. No married person was permitted to receive the baptism by which proselytes were admitted into his sect, and which he regarded as a renunciation of the Demiurge and his works.[4] This baptism he permitted to be repeated a second and a third time in the case of those who fell into sin after its first administration.[5] He also prohibited the use of animal food, except fish, which he regarded as a more holy food than flesh,[6] and enjoined a rigid fast on the sabbath day as a mark of hostility to Judaism.[7] In

---

[1] Marcion came to Rome after the death of Hyginus (Epiphan. *Hær.* xlii. 1). He flourished under Anicetus (Irenæus, iii. 4). It is probable, though Tertullian asserts the contrary, that he died before the pontificate of Eleutherus, A.D. 176. Cf. Massuet, *Diss. Præv. in Iren.* i. § 137. Praxeas came to Rome in the pontificate of Victor (A.D. 192–201) or perhaps of Eleutherus (A.D. 176–192). Cf. Neander, *Antignosticus* p. 510 (Bohn). Tertullian's birth may probably be placed A.D. 160.

[2] *Adv. Marc.* ii. 28 'Tuus [Deus] semetipsum voluit interfici.' Cf. i. 11.

[Tuus Deus] 'et descendit et prædicavit, et passus resurrexit.'

[3] Irenæus i. 27. 3 'Salutem autem solum animarum esse futuram earum quæ ejus doctrinam didicissent; corpus autem, videlicet quoniam a terra sit sumptum, impossibile esse participare salutem.'

[4] Tertull. *Adv. Marc.* i. 29 'Non tingitur apud illum caro, nisi virgo, nisi vidua, nisi cælebs, nisi divortio baptisma mercata.'

[5] Epiphan. *Hær.* xlii. 3.

[6] Tertull. *Adv. Marc.* i. 14.

[7] Epiphan. *Hær.* xlii. 3.

these practices we see the consistent disciple of the Syrian Gnosticism, which had descended to Marcion through Cerdon from Saturninus.

The principal speculative distinction between the system of Marcion and that of his Syrian predecessors, besides that which we have noticed already, the absence of any theory of emanations in connection with the doctrine of creation or redemption, consisted in the non-recognition of any principle of pure evil. He assumed only three principles: the Supreme God, the Demiurge, and the eternal matter, the two latter being imperfect, but not essentially evil.[1] Some of the later Marcionites seem to have added an evil spirit as a fourth principle, but this must be regarded as an innovation on the teaching of the master, who does not appear to have recognised any other evil being than the Demiurge, whose economy, originally of a mixed character, combining good and evil together, might in certain relations assume the character of positive evil, namely, when placed in direct antagonism to the redeeming work of the higher God. This feature of Marcion's system may be traced to the character of his mind, averse from abstract speculation, and dealing with philosophical hypothesis to no further extent than was actually required by the phenomena to be explained. The actual appearance of the world presented phenomena of a mixed character, partly good and partly evil, and an author of a similar nature seemed to him sufficient to explain these without the need of analysing this assumption into any simpler and purer elements.

Marcion is the least Gnostic of all the Gnostics. Though not in point of time the latest holder of Gnostic

---

[1] Theodoret, *Hær. Fab.* i. 24. Cf. Dilthey in Herzog, IX. 28. Epiphanius, *Hær.* xlii. 3, mentions the Devil as a third principle added by Marcion to the two recognised by Cerdon, the Supreme God and the Demiurge.

[2] Cf. Baur, *Die Chr. Gnosis* p. 281.

doctrines, he is the latest original thinker of this class, and his teaching represents the point of transition at which Christian speculation passes over from philosophy to pure theology. Cosmological and ontological problems, attempts to connect Christianity with the objects and method of heathen speculation, had, for a time at least, worn themselves out. The traces of them in Marcion himself are feeble and incidental, and in the next phase of religious thought they pass out of sight to make way for speculation more directly arising out of the Christian revelation, as manifested in the Monarchian controversy.

LECTURE XIV.

JUDAIZING REACTION—THE CLEMENTINES—THE ELKESAITES.

IF we compare the doctrines of the earliest Gnostic proper (omitting Simon and Menander, whose teaching is anti-Christian rather than heretical) whose name is known to us, with those of the latest master of any Gnostic school of reputation, we shall see that the Christian element in Gnosticism had in the course of rather more than half a century come round to a point almost opposite to its original position. Cerinthus, the precursor of Ebionism, regarded Christianity as the completion of Judaism, and maintained the continued obligation of the Jewish law. Marcion regarded Christianity as irreconcilably antagonistic to Judaism, and manifested his hostility to the Jewish law in every possible way both of teaching and practice. Cerinthus regarded Jesus as a man born after the manner of other men; Marcion, in the other extreme, regarded Him as having descended suddenly from heaven, and refused to ascribe to Him even the appearance of a birth from any human parent. Cerinthus considered the Divine mission of Jesus as having commenced at His baptism; Marcion omitted all mention of the baptism in his mutilated Gospel. Cerinthus separated the person of Christ from that of Jesus, regarding them as two wholly distinct beings, the one purely spiritual, the other purely human; Marcion not only rejected the humanity of our

Lord altogether, but seems hardly, if at all, to have recognised any distinction between the Divine Person of the Father and that of the Son. It was natural that the extravagant hostility of Marcion to the Jewish religion should call forth a reaction equally extravagant in the opposite direction; and accordingly, the next step which we are called upon to notice in the transmutation of Gnosticism is a return (with some important variations in detail however) to the judaizing standpoint of Cerinthus and the Ebionites. The work in which this reaction is represented is the so-called Clementine Homilies, a production, it is hardly necessary to observe, not of the Apostolic Father, Clement of Rome, whose name it bears, but of a later writer making use of his name. It can hardly be called a forgery, for it may be doubted whether the author had any intention of passing it off as a genuine production of Clement. It was necessary to the plot of his romance to carry the scene back to Apostolic times, to bring on the field St. Peter, the Apostle of the Circumcision, and his earliest antagonist, Simon Magus, the precursor and representative of the anti-Jewish Gnosticism; and Clement, who, according to one tradition preserved by Tertullian,[1] was ordained Bishop of Rome by St. Peter himself, was so far a person whom it was natural to select as the companion of the Apostle in his journeys and the reporter of his acts and teaching; though at the same time there is some incongruity in choosing a man who is generally identified with one of the fellow-labourers of St. Paul, to be the vehicle of a judaizing reaction against the teaching which Marcion professed to derive from St. Paul's own writings.[2]

---

[1] *De Præscr.* c. 32. So the *Clem. Hom. Epist. Clem.* c. 2.

[2] If Clement is the same who is mentioned in Phil. iv. 3, he is more likely to have been the companion of St. Paul than of St. Peter.

The collection called *The Clementines*, to adopt the name now commonly given to the whole series of cognate works,[1] comprises three separate writings of similar character, and emanating from one school, namely; (1) *The Homilies*, professing to be an account written by Clement, at the desire of St. Peter, to St. James the Bishop of Jerusalem, narrating his introduction to and travels with the Apostle, together with the disputations between St. Peter and his companions on the one side, and Simon Magus and his disciples on the other. (2) *The Recognitions* ('Αναγνώσεις), so called from the discovery by Clement of his parents and brothers, which forms an interesting episode in all these works, though giving its title to one only. (3) *The Epitome*, an abbreviated recension of the Homilies,[2] with some slight additions from other sources. The *Recognitions* are now extant only in a Latin translation by Rufinus; the two other works have come down to us in the original Greek, the concluding portion of the *Homilies*, which were for a long time imperfect, having been recently recovered from a MS in the Vatican Library. The contents of all the works are cognate to each other, and in parts substantially identical, but the Gnostic element predominates in the *Homilies*,[3] which were probably (though this point has been much disputed) the earliest of the three writings in their present form.[4] For our present purpose it will be sufficient to confine our attention to this work, the date of which may probably be placed about

---

[1] On the proper use of this title, see Uhlhorn in Herzog, vol. II. p. 744.

[2] By Dressel, who published it at Göttingen in 1853. The new portion embraces the latter part of *Hom.* xix from the middle of § 14, and the whole of *Hom.* xx.

[3] Cf. Uhlhorn in Herzog, II.

p. 754.

[4] For an account of this dispute, see Uhlhorn, *l. c.* p. 750 *seq.* Of recent writers, Schliemann, Schwegler, and Uhlhorn (as well as Dorner, *Person of Christ* I. p. 446) give the priority to the *Homilies*; Hilgenfeld, Köstlin, and Ritschl, to the *Recognitions*.

A.D. 160 or a little later, though some portions of it may be a very few years earlier.[1] To the *Homilies* is prefixed a brief introduction containing (1) a supposed letter from St. Peter to St. James the Bishop of Jerusalem, recommending to him the record of his own teaching which he is about to send, and desiring that it may be preserved as a secret doctrine, to be communicated only to those who should be found worthy to receive it—a caution which of itself betrays the apprehension of the writer that his system is different from that received by the Catholic Church.[2] (2) A supposed speech of St. James to his assembled presbytery, containing the measures which he proposes for the safe custody and transmission of the secret doctrine. (3) A letter purporting to be written by Clement to St. James, giving an account of his own appointment by St. Peter just before his martyrdom, as his successor in the episcopate of Rome, with the directions given to him, and to the presbyters, deacons, catechists, and people, by the Apostle for their conduct in their several offices; and finally introducing the narrative which he had drawn up by St. Peter's command, to be transmitted to St. James. Then follow the Homilies themselves, twenty in number, the contents of which may be briefly summed up as follows. Clement, a Roman citizen, anxious for a knowledge of truth, and having vainly sought for it in the schools of philosophy, at last hears of Jesus and His teaching and miracles in Judea, and determines to visit that country to inquire into what he had heard. Having sailed to Alexandria, and being detained there by adverse winds, he becomes acquainted with St. Barnabas, whom he follows to Cæsarea, and is

---

[1] Cf. Uhlhorn in Herzog, II. p. 756. The earliest part of the work (*Hom.* xvi-xix) combats Marcion, and therefore can hardly be earlier than A.D. 150.

[2] Cf. Dorner, *Person of Christ* I. p. 212.

introduced by him to St. Peter, who first instructs him in the nature of the true Prophet as the expounder of Divine truth, and then invites him to be present at a disputation to be held on the following day between himself and Simon the magician. On the next day Clement becomes acquainted with some of the companions of St. Peter, amongst others with two brothers, named Nicetas and Aquila, who had formerly been disciples of Simon Magus, but had now left him and followed St. Peter. He is now further instructed in the character and office of the true Prophet, who alone is the teacher of the truth, and whose teaching must be implicitly followed. He is also told that God is both good and just, and that the justice may be reconciled with the apparent inequalities of man's fortunes in this life if we believe that there is a future state in which all men will be rewarded or punished according to their deeds. He is further told that Simon the Samaritan denies the justice of God (an evident allusion to the doctrine of Marcion), and this circumstance gives occasion to introduce the doctrine of $\sigma u\zeta u\gamma l a\iota$, or pairs of opposites, which run through the constitution of all things. Justice must exist, for injustice exists, and the existence of the one implies that of the other; and if justice exists anywhere, it must be in God, the source of all things. God, who is one, has made all things in pairs, a better and a worse, represented as male and female, e.g. heaven and earth, day and night, sun and moon, life and death. In other parts of creation the masculine or better element is first and the feminine second; in man alone the order is reversed, and the inferior takes precedence of the superior. Thus this life, which is temporal, precedes the next life, which is eternal, and among the generations of men the worse comes before the better, Cain before Abel, Ishmael before Isaac, Esau before Jacob, Aaron before Moses, and now Simon Magus before Peter, who is come to undo his work. After this Clement is recommended to Aquila and Nicetas, who narrate to him the previous history of Simon Magus, following for the most part the usual traditions concerning the impostor, with some additional particulars.

The dispute being then postponed for another day, Peter proceeds to inform Clement of the subject of the intended controversy. The Scripture, he says, contains falsehood mingled with truth; the introduction of falsehood having been permitted by God in order to try men's faith. Simon, he continues (here there is an evident allusion to Marcion), means to adduce these false passages which give unworthy representations of God, that he may lead men away from the faith. Such, for example, are those places in Scripture which speak of God as showing his power with others, as being ignorant, as repenting, as being jealous, as hardening men's hearts, as pleased with sacrifices, as dwelling in a tabernacle, and the like. Such also are those which speak evil of just men, as, for instance, the disobedience of Adam, the drunkenness of Noah, the polygamy of Jacob, the homicide of Moses. All these will be more fully explained hereafter. On the third day the disputation between Peter and Simon commences, and lasts for three days. Before its commencement Peter gives some further information to his companions concerning the opinions of Simon, still with evident allusion to the teaching of Marcion. He charges him with maintaining that the Creator of the world is not the Supreme God, but that there is another superior and unknown God; and he then proceeds to dwell on the unity of God as the foundation of all true religion, and on the dignity of Adam, the first true prophet, and on the spirit of false prophecy, represented by Eve, which teaches a plurality of Gods.¹ After this the disputation commences. Peter maintains the existence of one God, who created the world and all that it contains for the benefit of man. Simon on the contrary maintains Marcion's doctrine of two Gods, and enlarges on the imperfections of the God revealed in the Old Testament, to which Peter replies by means of his previous distinction between the true and the false Scriptures.² At the end of the third day Simon withdraws and escapes by night to Tyre, while Peter remains at Cæsarea to confirm the Church in that city, appointing Zacchæus (the publican of St. Luke's Gospel) as its Bishop.

In the meanwhile he sends Clement with Aquila and Nicetas to Tyre to inquire into the proceedings of Simon.³ After their arrival at Tyre they find that Simon, after exhibiting many sorceries, has departed to Sidon, leaving however behind him three of his followers, Appion or Apion, a grammarian of Alexandria (meant for Apion the antagonist of Josephus, whose hatred to the Jews makes him a fit companion for Simon, the representative of Marcion), Annubion, an astrologer, and Athenodorus of Athens, an Epicurean philosopher.⁴ Clement holds a disputation with Apion concerning the fables of the heathen mythology, Clement condemning their immoral character, and Apion defending them as allegorical representations of natural phenomena.⁵ This dispute occupies the time till the arrival of Peter at Tyre. After this Peter, with his companions, follows Simon from place to place, counteracting the effect of his sorceries and instructing the people.⁶ At Tripolis he stays three months, and delivers several discourses to the people, giving them among other

¹ *Hom.* iii. 1-29.
² *Hom.* iii. 30-57.
³ *Hom.* iii. 58-73.
⁴ *Hom.* iv. 6.
⁵ *Hom.* iv. 11—vi. 25.
⁶ *Hom.* vi. 26—vii. 12.

things some very curious information on the subject of demonology and witchcraft.¹ At this place Clement is baptized, and then departs with Peter for Antioch, in search of Simon. In the course of this journey he relates to Peter his own history and discovers his mother, who had fled from Rome in his infancy. Afterwards, at Laodicea, he recognises his two elder brothers in Nicetas and Aquila, and finally recovers his father, who had also left him at a later age.² These several recognitions are the circumstances which give the title to the second Clementine work, in which they are also contained. The journey to Antioch is interrupted by the arrival of Simon at Laodicea, where a second disputation takes place between him and Peter, and is carried on for four days.³ This disputation, which is probably the original groundwork of the book,⁴ turns in the first place, like that in the third homily, which is probably a later revision, on the question of the unity of God and the representations of Him in the Old Testament. Simon endeavours to prove that the Scripture acknowledges a plurality of Gods; while Peter, disposing of apparently adverse testimonies by his former distinction between the true and the false portions of Scripture, maintains the perfect unity of God, and denies that the name can be given to any other being. In this discussion it should be remarked that Peter is made to deny that Christ Himself ever asserted His own Divinity,⁵ and to declare that the Son, as being begotten, must be of a different nature from the unbegotten God.⁶ Subsequently Simon is represented as urging the Marcionite distinction between two Gods, the one good, the other merely just,⁷ while Peter maintains that the Supreme

¹ *Hom.* viii–xi.
² *Hom.* xii–xiv.
³ *Hom.* xvi–xix.
⁴ Uhlhorn in Herzog II. p. 755.
⁵ *Hom.* xvi. 15.
⁶ *Hom.* xvi. 16.
⁷ *Hom.* xvii. 4, 5.

God, in whose image man was made, has himself a form and members like those of man, though not made of flesh; he also expounds the relation of the Divine Being to space, emanating from Him as from a centre in six directions, up and down, right and left, backwards and forwards, which he calls the mystery of the Hebdomad, figured by the six days of creation with the rest of God on the seventh; and finally he maintains the superiority of his own knowledge as having seen and conversed with Christ, over those who pretended to know Divine things by dreams and visions.[1] The controversy concludes with two discussions, neither of them leading to any very definite conclusions, on the supremacy of God and on the origin of evil.[2] After the departure of Simon, Peter again discourses with his own disciples on the free will of man, on the nature of evil, and on the Devil as the prince of this world; in which discourse he advances the strange doctrine that the Devil is a being appointed by God for the punishment of wicked men; that he himself, though of evil nature, does no evil, but accomplishes God's will; and that his final condemnation is not a punishment but a translation to the kingdom of darkness, which is congenial to his nature.[3] Then follows a strange story, how Simon, hearing that he was to be arrested by order of the emperor, bewitched Faustus the father of Clement, and changed his face into a likeness of himself, hoping that Faustus might be arrested in his stead. Peter however turns Simon's device against himself by sending Faustus to Antioch, and bidding him in the character of Simon

[1] *Hom.* xvii. 6–19. This passage has probably reference to the Docetism of Marcion, which reduced Christ to a mere vision; but there is also a covert attack on Marcion's assumed authority, St. Paul, whose knowledge of Christ through visions and revelations (2 Cor. xii. 1) is contrasted with St. Peter's intercourse with Him during his earthly life. Cf. Baur, *Die Chr. Gnosis* p. 384.

[2] *Hom.* xviii, xix.

[3] *Hom.* xx. 1–9.

retract all the calumnies which he had uttered against Peter, and thus prepare the people for a favourable reception of the Apostle and his companions. After ten days a message arrives from Faustus, announcing that his task is performed, and the work concludes with the departure of Peter for Antioch.[1]

From the constant antagonism to Simon Magus and the praises of Peter which appear in the work, it might at first sight be supposed to be a protest of an orthodox Christian against Gnosticism in the person of its first representative. In truth however it is only the protest of one Gnostic school against another—the Ebionite against the Marcionite. The Gnostic tendency of the work, though not prominently put forward, appears in it almost from the commencement. The purpose of God's dealings with men is declared to be to instruct them in the truth of things as they are;[2] and it is for this purpose that revelations have been given through the instrumentality of the true prophets. The true prophet knows all things, past, present, and to come, and even the thoughts of all men; he is without sin and the only authorised guide to truth.[3] This knowledge he has by the innate and perpetual dwelling in him of the Divine Spirit;[4] indeed the true prophet is the Spirit himself, who from the beginning has passed through the ages of the world in various forms, labouring in this world and destined to eternal rest in the world to come.[5] Eight different persons are named in whom the Spirit has successively manifested himself, namely, Adam, Enoch, Noah, Abraham, Isaac, Jacob, Moses (who are called the sure pillars of the world[6]), and finally Jesus.[7] The doctrine taught by

[1] *Hom.* xx. 11–23.
[2] *Hom.* ii. 15 (cf. ii. 5). See Uhlhorn in Herzog II. p. 746.
[3] *Hom.* ii. 6, 10, iii. 11.
[4] *Hom.* iii. 12.
[5] *Hom.* iii. 20.
[6] *Hom.* xviii. 14.
[7] *Hom.* xvii. 4, xviii. 13. Cf. Schliemann, *Die Clementinen* p. 194.

all these is one and the same; indeed the teachers themselves are but reappearances of one and the same teacher, Adam the first son of God, manifested in various forms at subsequent times, as the revelation given by him became corrupt and needed renovation.[1] Thus Christianity and Judaism are one and the same religion in all respects; only that this identity must be understood of the true Judaism as revealed by the true prophet, not of the corrupted form which appears in the false passages of Scripture proceeding from evil inspiration.[2] The true Judaism consists in acknowledgment of one God and obedience to His commands; the commands however being apparently limited to the moral law only. Sacrifices are especially condemned;[3] circumcision is passed over without notice;[4] and the ordinances urgently enjoined as those of true Judaism are the Christian sacrament of baptism, together with abstinence from meats offered to idols and from things strangled.[5] Abstinence from all animal food is highly recommended, though not absolutely commanded.[6] But the most striking feature in this Clementine identification of Christianity with Judaism is the distinct denial of the Divinity of our Lord (a denial which the author regards as indispensable to monotheism[7]), and the addition of His name to the catalogue of Jewish prophets as the successor of Adam and Moses.[8] Whether the author,

---

[1] *Hom.* iii. 20. Cf. Baur, *Die Chr. Gnosis* pp. 343, 362; Schliemann, *Die Clementinen* p. 195.

[2] *Hom.* xi. 16, iv. 13. Cf. Baur, *Die Chr. Gnosis* p. 365.

[3] *Hom.* iii. 45, 56, ix. 7, 14. Cf. Schliemann, p. 222.

[4] Cf. Schliemann, p. 225. The mention of Peter in the διαμαρτυρία as αἱρούμενος ἐμπερίτομος is hardly an exception to this statement. Peter is the Apostle of the circumcision, and the representative of the true Judaism of the author; but his position does not therefore represent the rite as binding on Christians.

[5] *Hom.* vii. 8. Cf. Schliemann, pp. 223–225.

[6] *Hom.* iii. 45, viii. 15. Cf. Schliemann, p. 223.

[7] *Hom.* xvi. 15.

[8] *Hom.* xviii. 14. Cf. Schliemann, p. 194; Uhlhörn in Herzog II. p. 746, 747.

like Cerinthus and the Ebionites, denied the supernatural birth of our Saviour, is a matter of dispute; the only passages which bear upon the question being capable of interpretation in two ways;[1] but the direct antagonism to Marcion which is everywhere manifest in the work makes it at least probable that, as Marcion went to the extreme of denying to the Saviour all human parentage, his opponent, in the opposite extreme, did not distinguish His birth from that of other men.[2]

Hostility to Marcionism is indeed the leading feature of the work. It is Marcion who for the most part is represented under the character of Simon Magus, though there is also here and there a covert attack upon St. Paul, whose Epistles were the only Apostolic writings which Marcion accepted as authoritative.[3] And yet, though the doctrines of Marcion, and in a secondary relation other Gnostic systems, are attacked in this work, the teaching of the work itself exhibits Gnosticism in another phase. Not merely in the negative feature of the Cerinthian and Ebionite humanitarianism does this appear, but also in the positive tenets of the system; in the representation of religion as a philosophy teaching the true nature of things; in the acknowledgment of Christ merely as a teacher of this knowledge; in the speculations on the nature and origin of matter and of evil, which, though

---

[1] The two passages which bear on this question are iii. 17, and iii. 20. For the different interpretations, see Schliemann, p. 200.

[2] This interpretation, which is rejected by Schliemann, by Neander (*Ch. Hist.* I. p. 493, Bohn), by Baur in his later view (*Die Chr. Gnosis* p. 760, and by Dorner (*Person of Christ* I. p. 441), but supported by Credner (in Schliemann, p. 201) is perhaps now confirmed by the testimony of Hippolytus, ix. 14, who says that Elchesai, whose teaching much resembles that of the Clementines, taught that Christ was born like other men, but had appeared often in different bodies. This is in fact the Hindoo doctrine of Avatars, which allows a natural origin for the human medium of the incarnation.

[3] See *Hom.* xvii. 6-19, and Baur, *Die Chr. Gnosis* p. 384.

holding a subordinate place, still appear as part of the religious system;[1] in the law of antagonism between good and evil, which was established from the beginning in the constitution of things, and which appears, though in an inverted order in man, notwithstanding his free will;[2] in the denial of Adam's transgression, and the consequent contemplation of the first sin, not as a voluntary act of rebellion against God, but as the consequence of the same law by which evil exists in the universe;[3] in the mystical character assigned to Adam as the ideal man, and to Adam and Eve as the ideal representatives of two opposite systems of prophecy, the masculine and feminine principles, to which truth and error are respectively referred.[4] In all these points we may discern the method and the spirit of the elder Gnostic systems, though pursued with enfeebled vigour and less exclusive interest. In this respect both in Marcion and in the antagonistic Clementine doctrine the Gnostic spirit may be regarded as in its decline, and as bearing symptoms of transition to another phase of religious speculation. The Christian faith was gradually emancipating itself from its uncongenial connection with the problems of heathen philosophy, and the inquiries pursued in connection with it were assuming a more purely theological character. The doctrine of the Person of Christ, and of His personal relation to the Father, was being disentangled from speculations of ontology and cosmogony, and becoming the principal and central point of religious thought. And as the diluted Gnosticism of Marcion gives evidence in this respect of a transition to the Patripassian theories of Praxeas and Noetus, so the

---

[1] *Hom.* xix. 12, 13, xx. 2. Cf. Schliemann, pp. 154, 521.

[2] *Hom.* ii. 15, 16. Cf. Baur, *Die Chr. Gnosis* p. 398.

[3] *Hom.* ii. 16, 52, iii. 21.

[4] *Hom.* iii. 22 *seq.* Cf. Schliemann, p. 177. This theory resembles the Pythagorean συστοιχία, in which *male* and *female* are placed as opposite principles of good and evil.

LECT. XIV. *THE CLEMENTINES, THE ELKESAITES.* 233

diluted Gnosticism of the Clementines gives evidence of a similar transition to the opposite form of Monarchianism, the Humanitarian heresy of Theodotus and Artemon.

As regards the external history of the pseudo-Clementine writings, the mention (which here occurs for the first time in ecclesiastical literature)[1] of St. Peter as having been Bishop of Rome, and the prominence given to Clement as the Apostle's supposed successor, seem to point out the author, at least of that portion of the work, as a member of the Roman Church, which even then was beginning to assert its supremacy, though in a modified form and with a subordination to the mother church of Jerusalem, whose Bishop, St. James, appears as the superior of St. Peter, and is addressed as 'Lord and Bishop of the Holy Church,' and 'Bishop of Bishops.'[2] But though the origin of the book is probably Roman,[3] the doctrines which it contains must be assigned to an Eastern origin, and the conflicting theories on this question may perhaps be reconciled with each other, if we suppose that at Rome, which at this time was the great centre to which various religious speculations, orthodox and heterodox, naturally converged, some philosophically educated Christian, distracted by the various doctrines around him, and especially by the spread of Marcionism, had adopted the idea of seeking for a primitive Christianity in the Jewish birthplace of the faith, and had fancied

[1] Cf. Gieseler, *E. H.* I. pp. 208, 264 (Eng. Tr.).

[2] The letter of St. Peter commences Πέτρος Ἰακώβῳ τῷ κυρίῳ καὶ ἐπισκόπῳ τῆς ἁγίας ἐκκλησίας. The letter of Clement commences Κλήμης Ἰακώβῳ τῷ κυρίῳ καὶ ἐπισκόπων ἐπισκόπῳ. Cf. Schliemann, pp. 86, 213; Gieseler, *E. H.* I. p. 207 (Eng. Tr.).

[3] The Roman origin of the book is maintained by Baur, Schliemann, Hilgenfeld, and Ritschl, as well as by Gieseler, *E. H.* I. p. 206. Uhlhorn (in Herzog, II. p. 755) questions this, and assigns the work to Eastern Syria. Gieseler's view that the author is Roman, the doctrine Eastern, meets Uhlhorn's objections, while recognising what is weighty in his arguments.

himself to have discovered it among the speculations of judaizing heresy.[1] The sect to whose doctrines the Clementine writings bear most affinity, is that mentioned by authors of the next century,[2] under the name of Elkesaites, who are said to have been so called from one Elxai or Elchesai, their founder, who is probably a later personification of a Hebrew appellative signifying *concealed power*.[3] According to the statement of Epiphanius, this sect had its origin in the region bordering on the Dead Sea, and its disciples were originally called Ossenes (probably only a local pronunciation of Essenes), but were afterwards, in the reign of Trajan, joined by Elxai, who pretended to be a prophet and compiled a book for which he claimed Divine inspiration.[4] Of this Elxai, Epiphanius adds, 'He was by birth a Jew and held Jewish doctrines, yet did not live according to the law.... He taught men to swear by salt, and water, and earth, and bread, and heaven, and æther, and wind. Sometimes he speaks of seven other witnesses, namely,

---

[1] Cf. Gieseler, *E. H.* I. p. 206.

[2] The earliest writer who mentions them is Hippolytus, ix. 13, followed by Origen in Euseb. *H. E.* vi. 30. A fuller account is given by Epiphanius, *Hær.* xix, xxx. 3, 17, 18, liii; in the last place under the name *Sampsæi*, which he interpret ἡλιακοί (שִׁמְשִׁי). Cf. Gieseler, *E. H.* I. p. 100, 101, for these and th *Ossenes*.

[3] חֵיל כָּסִי, δύναμις κεκαλυμμένη, Epiphan. *Hær.* xix. 2, who however does not himself accept the derivation. Gieseler, *E. H.* I. p. 100, aptly compares this with the δύναμις ἄσαρκος of Clem. *Hom.* xvii 16, and supposes that the titles of two books called חֵיל כָּסִי and יָהּ כָּסִי, the latter treating of the concealed Deity, and the former of his concealed power, may have given rise to the names of the two supposed brothers Elxai and Iexeus. Other less probable derivations are mentioned by Gieseler, *l. c.*

[4] Hippolytus (ix. 13) says that this book was brought to Rome by one Alcibiades of Apamea in Syria, who described it as a work inspired by an angel (whose dimensions are given with exact measurements), and brought from the Seræ of Parthia by Elchesai, who gave it to Sobiai. The latter name is probably derived from שָׁבַע, *swearing*, the book being kept secret under an oath. Cf. Ritschl *Altkath. Kirche* p. 208. Origen (in Euseb. *H. E.* vi. 30) also mentions the book, which, he says, they regarded as having fallen from heaven.

heaven, and water, and spirits, and holy angels of prayer, and oil, and salt, and earth. He is an enemy to virginity, condemns continency, and compels men to marry.'[1] A little later he adds, 'He anathematizes sacrifices and offerings, and denies that they were appointed by God, or offered under the law or by the fathers. ... He condemns the eating of flesh as practised by the Jews, and the altar, and fire, as offensive to God, but water he approves as acceptable.'[2] Epiphanius then adds that Elxai also joined himself to the Ebionites, and that he was adopted as a teacher by four sects, the Ebionites, two divisions of the Nazarenes, and the Ossenes.[3] In a subsequent chapter Epiphanius tells us that the Ebionites, who at first held Jesus to be the son of Joseph, afterwards diverged into various opinions, and that, as he supposes, it was after Elxai had joined them that they adopted fanciful opinions concerning Christ, some maintaining that He was the same as Adam, the first man.[4] Though there is some chronological difficulty in these statements as they are here given,[5] we may at least infer from them with historical probability that the Ebionites and the Elkesaites were cognate sects derived from the influence of a spurious Christianity on the Jewish Essenes; the latter, though professing Judaism, being less strict observers of the letter of the Jewish law than the former. On the authority of Origen we are further told that the

---

[1] Epiphan. *Hær.* xix. 1. Cf. Hippolytus, ix. 15.

[2] Epiphan. xix. 3.

[3] *Ibid.* xix. 5.

[4] *Ibid.* xxx. 3. Cf. Hippol. ix. 14 τὸν Χριστὸν δὲ λέγει ἄνθρωπον κοινῶς πᾶσι γεγονέναι· τοῦτον δὲ οὐ νῦν πρώτως ἐκ παρθένου γεγεννῆσθαι, ἀλλὰ καὶ πρότερον καὶ αὖθις πολλάκις γεννηθέντα αἱ γεννώμενον πεφηνέναι καὶ φύεσθαι, ἴσοντα γενέσεις καὶ μετενσωματούμενον.

[5] If Elxai, as both Hippolytus (ix. 13) and Epiphanius (*Hær.* xix. 1) say, belongs to the reign of Trajan, he can hardly have joined the sect of the Ebionites, which (though some of their doctrines had been previously asserted by Cerinthus and Carpocrates) do not appear under this name till after the founding of Ælia by Hadrian.

Elkesaites rejected portions of the Scriptures, and the whole of the teaching of St. Paul;[1] and Epiphanius in like manner says of the Ebionites of his day (after their teaching had been modified by that of the Elkesaites) that they repudiated St. Paul,[2] and that among the prophets of the Old Testament they accepted Abraham, Isaac, Jacob, Moses, and Aaron, and Joshua, but repudiated all who came afterwards, as David and Solomon, Isaiah, Jeremiah, Daniel, and Ezekiel, as well as Elijah and Elisha, asserting that they were not prophets of the truth, but only of intelligence.[3] Hippolytus further says that the Elkesaites used frequent baptisms employing them not only for the purification of such of their followers as had committed deadly sins, but also as a cure for bodily diseases.[4] Epiphanius professses to give an account of the Ebionites and Elkesaites (whom he calls Sampsæans)[5] as they existed in his own day, some two centuries later than the probable origin of the Clementines. But while the changes which may have taken place during that interval will probably account for a portion at least of the variations in his description, the points of resemblance which remain, between the doctrines and practices of these heretics and those advocated in the Clementines, can hardly be accounted for without supposing a common origin. The δύναμις κεκαλυμμένη, which Epiphanius gives as the interpretation of the name *Elxai*, reminds us of the invisible δύναμις ἄσαρκος ascribed by

---

[1] Euseb. *H. E.* vi. 38 ἀθετεῖ τινα ἀπὸ πάσης γραφῆς . . . τὸν ἀπόστολον τέλεον ἀθετεῖ.

[2] *Hær.* xxx. 16.

[3] *Ibid.* xxx. 18. By προφῆται συνέσεως καὶ οὐκ ἀληθείας seems to be meant prophets only by human sagacity, not by divine inspiration.

[4] Hippol. ix. 15, 16.

[5] Epiph. *Hær.* liii. 1 Σαμψαῖοί τινες . . . τῶν δὴ καὶ 'Ελκεσαίων καλουμένων αἵρεσίς τις. Epiphanius interprets this name by ἡλιακοί (Hebr. שֶׁמֶשׁ, 'the sun') probably because they turned, when praying, to the rising sun. Cf. Gieseler, *Eccl. Hist.* I. p. 103.

the Clementines to God and angels,[1] and warrants the suspicion that the name, originally applied to the book which claimed a divine origin, and which was even said to have fallen from heaven, was subsequently understood as designating a supposed founder of the sect. The Jewish origin of this supposed Elxai and his departure from the strict letter of the law, answer to the distinction drawn in the Clementines between true and false Judaism, the latter including most, if not all, of the ceremonial observances.[2] The mention of salt among the things held sacred by Elxai recalls the passage in the Clementines where St. Peter is said to have administered the Eucharist with bread and salt.[3] The compelling men to marry is but an exaggeration of the advice which St. Peter is represented as giving to the Roman Church.[4] The rejection of sacrifices is a common feature in both doctrines: St. Peter in the Clementines, like Elxai in Epiphanius, expressly denying their divine appointment.[5] Abstinence from flesh is recommended if not commanded by both,[6] while the condemnation of fire and approbation of water corresponds in a remarkable manner to the words which the author of the Clementines puts into the mouth of St. Peter: 'Fly to the water, for this alone can quench the fury of the fire.'[7] Finally the two remarkable parallels, the identification of Christ with Adam, and the rejection of the later prophets, with the especial honour paid to the early patriarchs,[8] are sufficient to give extreme probability to the conjecture that in the Clementine writings we

---

[1] *Hom.* xvii. 16.
[2] Cf. Gieseler, *Eccl. Hist.* I. p. 100.
[3] *Hom.* xiv. 1.
[4] *Epist. Clem.* c. 7.
[5] *Hom.* iii. 45, 56.
[6] *Hom.* viii. 15. Cf. Schliemann, p. 223.
[7] *Hom.* xi. 26. By the fire is meant the power of the demons (*Hom.* ix. 11, 19). Cf. Schliemann, p. 229.
[8] *Hom.* iii. 20, xvii. 9, 10, xviii. 14, iii. 22–24, 38. Cf. Schliemann p. 193.

possess a work chiefly exhibiting the early teaching of the Elkesaite sect.

The work which we have been examining in this lecture is the last important monument of Gnostic teaching. From this time Gnosticism, while it continued for a season to transmit the doctrines of its early speculators, cannot be regarded as originating any new development. The literary interest after this period is transferred to the Christian antagonists of Gnosticism, of whom it is my intention to attempt a brief notice before concluding this course of lectures.

LECTURE XV.

CHRISTIAN OPPONENTS OF GNOSTICISM, IRENÆUS, TERTULLIAN.

THE teaching of Marcion and the judaizing reaction of his opponent, the author of the Clementines, bring us to the beginning of the latter half of the second century. After this date no Gnostic teacher of any eminence arose, and Gnosticism may be considered as having entered on the period of its decline, though some of its sects continued to linger on till the sixth century. The chief literary interest of the latter part of the second and the beginning of the third century turns upon the writings of those Fathers of the Christian Church who came forward as the antagonists of Gnosticism. The principal of these are Irenæus, Clement of Alexandria, and Tertullian, to whom must now be added Hippolytus, Bishop of Portus, the greater part of whose work on the 'Refutation of all Heresies,'[1] having been long lost, was recovered and published in the year 1851 under the title, generally acknowledged to be incorrect, of the 'Philosophumena of Origen.'[2]

The earliest of these Fathers, Irenæus Bishop of Lyons, is the author of a work usually quoted as the 'Five Books

---

[1] See books iv–x. Book i had been previously known and printed among Origen's works, though acknowledged by the best critics not to be his. See De la Rue's *Origen*, I. p. 872.

[2] Origenis *Philosophumena, sive Omnium Hæresium Refutatio*; e Codice Parisino nunc primum edidit Emmanuel Miller. Oxon. 1851.

against Heresies,' but of which the proper title is, 'Five Books of the Refutation and Overthrow of Knowledge falsely so called' (Ἐλέγχου καὶ ἀνατροπῆς τῆς ψευδωνύμου γνώσεως βιβλία πέντε).[1] Of this work the greater part of the original text is lost, but the whole survives in a barbarous Latin translation, probably executed not more than ten or fifteen years after the original. The work itself may with good reason be placed somewhere between A.D. 182 and 188,[2] and the translation, having been used by Tertullian, can hardly have been composed later than the end of the same century.[3]

Of the five books of which the work of Irenæus is composed, the first is mainly devoted to a historical account of various Gnostic heresies, chiefly of the Ptolemæan branch of the Valentinians, with whose system the author had become acquainted both by a study of the writings in which it was contained and by personal intercourse with some members of the sect.[4] An account of the doctrines of these heretics is given in the first nine chapters of the work. After this, by way of contrast to the heretical teaching, there follows a declaration of the faith of the Catholic Church throughout the world, which is remarkable, both as the earliest distinct statement of that faith formally drawn up in a series of propositions,[5] and also for its complete conformity in substance, and nearly in language, with the creeds afterwards formally adopted by the Church, especially with the Eastern type,

---

[1] Eusebius, *H. E.* v. 7. (Cf. Harvey's *Irenæus* I. p. clxiii; Massuet, *Diss.* ii. § 46). This title is also acknowledged by Irenæus himself in the Preface to bk. ii.

[2] It was composed after Theodotion's translation of the O. T. A.D. 181, which is mentioned by Irenæus, iii. 21. and before the death of Pope Eleutherus, A.D. 189, who closes the list of Roman bishops given iii. 3. Cf. Harvey, I. p. clviii.

[3] Tertullian uses it in his treatise against the Valentinians, written probably early in the third century. On this, see Massuet, *Diss.* ii. § 53.

[4] Irenæus, i. 1. 2.

[5] Cf. Heurtley, *Harmonia Symbolica* p. 5 *seq.*

as represented by the Nicene Creed.[1] 'The Church,' he says, 'throughout the world, spread out as she is to the ends of the earth, carefully preserves the faith that she received from the Apostles and from their disciples, believing in one God, the Father Almighty, who made heaven and earth, the seas and all that in them is; and in one Christ Jesus, the Son of God, who was incarnate for our salvation; and in the Holy Ghost, who by the prophets proclaimed the dispensations and the advents of our dear Lord Christ Jesus, and His birth of a Virgin, and His suffering, and His resurrection from the dead, and His ascension in the flesh into heaven, and His coming from heaven in the glory of the Father to sum up all things, and to raise up all flesh of the whole human race; that to Christ Jesus, our Lord and God and Saviour and King, according to the good pleasure of the invisible Father, every knee should bow, of things in heaven and things on earth and things under the earth and that every tongue should confess Him, and that He should have righteous judgment upon all.'[2] 'The Church,' he continues, 'scattered as she is over the whole world, having received this message and this faith, diligently guards it, as though she inhabited but one house; and her faith is conformable to these doctrines, as though she had but one soul and one heart; and she preaches these things harmoniously, and teaches and hands them on, as though she had but one mouth. For, dissimilar as the languages of the world may be, still the power of the tradition is one and the same; and neither have the churches established in Germany believed otherwise or transmitted any other doctrine, nor those of Spain, nor

---

[1] Heurtley, *Harmonia Symbolica* p. 6.

[2] Irenæus, i. 10. 1. See Harvey, *History and Theology of the Three Creeds* vol. I. pp. 43, 44.

R

those among the Celts, nor in the East, nor in Egypt, nor in Libya, nor those established in the middle of the world. But as the sun, the creature of God, is one and the same in all the world, such also is the preaching of the truth in its universal phase, enlightening all men who wish to approach the knowledge of the truth. He that among the Bishops of the Church is mightiest in the word speaks no other doctrine than this, for none is above his Master; neither shall he that is weak in the word be found to minish aught of the tradition; for, the faith being one and the same, he that hath much to say concerning it hath nothing over, and he that hath little hath no lack.'[1] After this emphatic declaration of the unity of the Catholic faith, Irenæus proceeds to contrast it with the diversity of opinions put forth by various teachers of heresy, even within the school of Valentinus;[2] the contrast being subsequently heightened by a further account of the different opinions of the earlier Gnostic sects from Simon Magus downwards.[3] This list includes Simon Magus and Menander (c. xxiii), Saturninus and Basilides (c. xxiv), Carpocrates (c. xxv), Cerinthus, the Ebionites and the Nicolaitans (c. xxvi), Cerdon and Marcion (c. xxvii), Tatian and the Encratites (c. xxviii), and finally various branches of the Ophites (cc. xxix–xxxi).[4] This part of the work is chiefly historical, and the materials which it supplies have been made use of in the preceding lectures.

The second book of Irenæus is chiefly devoted to a philosophical refutation of the tenets of the Valentinians (other Gnostics being incidentally noticed), interspersed with criticisms on their false interpretations of Scripture.

[1] Irenæus, i. 10. 2. Cf. Harvey, *l. c.* p. 45.
[2] cc. 11–21.
[3] cc. 23–31.
[4] The Barbelists of c. xxix are identified by Theodoret, *H. F.* i. 13, with the Naassenes, of whom a fuller account is given by Hippolytus, v. 6–11.

The philosophical arguments are mainly directed to the following points: 1. To maintain the unity of God, and the absurdity of the Gnostic separation between the Supreme God and the Creator of the world (cc. i–vi). 2. To overthrow the Platonic hypothesis of a correspondence between the intelligible and the visible world, on which so many of the Valentinian theories rested (cc. vii, viii). 3. To point out the absurdities and inconsistencies in the details of the Valentinian theory, and in the arguments by which it is supported (cc. xii–xix). After this follows a refutation of the false interpretation of Scripture which these Gnostics adduced in support of their theories (cc. xx–xxiii); a criticism of the mystical signification attached, particularly by the Marcosians, to numbers, letters, and syllables (cc. xxiv–xxvi); and some judicious remarks on the plain, natural, and universally intelligible mode of interpreting Scripture, as distinguished from the secret and fanciful meanings which the Gnostics adopted, and which any man can invent according to his own imagination (c. xxvii). Then follow some wise remarks on the limitation of man's knowledge, on the duty of leaving many mysteries unsolved, the knowledge of which belongs to God alone, and of believing in revealed truths concerning Divine things, though we cannot comprehend the manner in which they are as they are revealed to be (c. xxviii). Then follows a refutation of some of the remaining details of the Gnostic doctrines, as regards the future destiny of the soul and the body (c. xxix), and their own claims to a superior spiritual nature (c. xxx). To this succeeds an application of the preceding argument to other sects besides the Valentinians (c. xxxi); a denunciation of the licentious doctrines and practices of some of these heretics (c. xxxii); a refutation of the theory of transmigration, and a vindication of the consciousness of the soul in its separate state after death (cc. xxxiii, xxxiv); and finally, a refutation of those who maintained that the prophets were inspired by different gods (c. xxxv).

The third book is chiefly occupied with a refutation from Scripture of the heretical opinions of the Gnostics; first, concerning the unity of God; and secondly, concerning the person of Christ. After asserting the superior authority of the Apostles, as inspired by the Holy Ghost, over these pretended teachers of a higher knowledge (c. i), Irenæus proceeds to show that the Gnostic tradition was not known to the Church in the West or in the East, neither to the Roman Church which was founded by St. Peter and St. Paul, whose Bishops he enumerates down to his own time, nor to the Asiatic Churches, as represented by his own teacher Polycarp, the disciple of St. John. These agree in one primitive faith, while, on the contrary, the doctrines of these several sects were never heard of before the time of the heresiarchs whose names they bear (cc. ii–iv). He then proceeds to show that the Scriptures, both of the Old and the New Testament, agree in teaching that there is but one God, the Father of our Lord Jesus Christ, and the Maker of all things, and do not give the name of God or Lord to any other (cc. v–xii); in the course of which argument he takes occasion to assert the canonicity and the inspiration of the four received Gospels, and of these alone, to the exclusion of the false Gospels used by the heretics, and points out the characteristics of each as typified by the four living creatures of the Apocalypse (c. xi). He then proceeds to refute those who attempted to establish an antagonism between the teaching of St. Paul and that of the other Apostles, whether on the side of the Marcionites who accepted St. Paul alone, or of the Ebionites who rejected him; and he cites St. Paul's own testimony that one and the same God wrought in Peter to the Apostleship of the Circumcision, and in himself toward the Gentiles[1] (cc. xiii–xv). Proceeding then to the Gnostic heresies concerning the distinction of the Æon Christ from the man Jesus, he shows that the Apostolic writings unanimously acknowledge but one Christ Jesus, and that the Being who descended upon our Lord at His baptism was not the Æon Christ, but the Holy Ghost (cc. xvi–xviii). He then proves, on the same authority, the pre-existence and the real incarnation and suffering of Christ, and that He is very God, the eternal Son of the Father, and very Man, born of the Virgin Mary for our salvation (cc. xix–xxii). In the course of this argument he vindicates the prophecy of Isaiah (vii. 14) from the misinterpretation of the Ebionites and the later Jews, and shows that the Septuagint translation, ἡ παρθένος, is the true rendering, and not ἡ νεᾶνις, which is substituted in the later versions of Aquila and Theodotion (c. xxi). He then refutes the arguments of Tatian against the salvation of Adam (c. xxiii), and concludes with a recapitulation of his previous positions, and a re-assertion of the unity and providence of God (cc. xxiv, xxv).

The early part of the fourth book is employed chiefly in showing, from the testimony of our Lord Himself, that He acknowledged but one God and Father, and that this God and Father is the same who was proclaimed of old by Moses and the prophets, speaking the words of Christ. With this argument is united a refutation of the Gnostic perversions of our Lord's words to support their own theories (cc. i–vii). Irenæus then refutes the false teaching of Marcion, who endeavoured to exclude Abraham and his posterity from salvation through Christ, and shows that

[1] Gal. ii. 8.

there is one Author and one End of both the Covenants, and that the Old Testament Scriptures foretold Christ, thus showing that they were inspired by one and the same God from whom Christ came (cc. viii–xi). He then shows that Christ confirmed the moral precepts of the law while condemning the traditions of the elders which were contrary to the law, and that those ceremonial and typical observances which are no longer in force were necessary for the discipline and correction of the Jewish people until Christ should come (cc. xii–xvi). He then goes on to maintain that oblations still continue in the Church, though the name of them is changed; that the prophecy of Malachi (i. 10, 11) that the Jewish sacrifices should cease, and yet that a pure offering should be offered in every place to the Lord, is fulfilled in the Eucharist, in which the Church offers to God the first-fruits of His creatures, not as needed by God, but as giving thanks to God and as sanctifying the creatures (cc. xvii, xviii). From this argument the author returns to the question of the unity of that God, of whose spiritual things these earthly things are the type; who, though invisible and unspeakable as regards His nature and magnitude (qualis et quantus est), is manifested, as regards His love, through His works, and is revealed through Christ His Word (cc. xix, xx). The author then goes on to say that Abraham's faith was identical with ours, and that Christ came for the sake of the patriarchs of old as well as of the men of later times; that the patriarchs and prophets foretold Christ, and thus prepared the way for the preaching of the Apostles; and that the true exposition of the Scriptures is that given by the Church (cc. xxi–xxvi). The book concludes with a vindication of the Old Testament Scriptures against the cavil which had been raised against them by the Gnostics, chiefly by the school of Marcion, as regards the sins of the patriarchs, which, he says (citing the teaching of a presbyter who had been instructed by the disciples of the Apostles[1]), were recorded for our warning and instruction; as regards the judgment of God against sinners, on which point the Old Testament is not contrary to the New; and as regards the hardening of Pharaoh's heart and the spoiling of the Egyptians, which he defends by arguments similar to those afterwards advanced by Tertullian in his treatise against Marcion (cc. xxvii–xxx).

The fifth book is chiefly devoted to a refutation of the Gnostic opinions concerning the Resurrection of the Body. In opposition to the Valentinians on the one side, and to the Ebionites on the other, he maintains the true Humanity and the true Divinity of Christ, and shows how both are necessary to the truth of our Lord Himself, and to the redemption of mankind. In opposition to those who deny that the flesh is capable of salvation, he appeals to our redemption by the blood of Christ and to our partaking of His body and blood in the Eucharist, by which our bodies are nourished and preserved to everlasting life (cc. i, ii). He asserts that God, who was able to create man's body, is equally able to raise it from the dead; and that the body, which was worthy of God's care in the one case, is not less so in the other; His strength, as St. Paul said of his own infirmity,[2] being made perfect in weakness (c. iii). He urges that the heretics themselves who deny that God raises up the body may be refuted on their own principles, for they make God either less powerful or less gracious than their own pretended Demiurge, who made the body (c. iv). He appeals to the power of God over-

---

[1] Who this presbyter was, can only be conjectured; Polycarp, Papias, Clement, Justin, have been suggested. Harvey thinks that Pothinus, the predecessor of Irenæus in the see of Lyons, is intended.

[2] 2 Cor. xii. 9.

coming the infirmity of the flesh, as shown in the longevity of the patriarchs before the Flood, in the translation of Enoch and Elijah, and in the preservation of Jonah in the belly of the whale, and of Ananias, Azarias, and Misael in the fiery furnace (c. v). He shows that to the perfection of man the body is needed as well as the soul and the spirit, and cites the prayer of St. Paul for the Thessalonians,[1] that their whole spirit and soul and body might be preserved blameless unto the coming of our Lord Jesus Christ, and his declaration to the Corinthians[2] that their bodies are the temple of the Holy Ghost and the members of Christ (c. vi). He urges the resurrection of Christ with His body, the language of St. Paul on the resurrection of the body,[3] and the spiritual gifts vouchsafed to man while in the body; and refutes the heretical perversion of St. Paul's words,[4] 'Flesh and blood cannot inherit the kingdom of God,' by showing that it refers to carnal-minded men, not to the body as incapable of resurrection, and that the works of the flesh are contrasted by the Apostle with the works of the Spirit (cc. vii–xii). He then appeals to the miracles of our Lord in raising up the daughter of Jairus, the widow's son, and Lazarus, as a type of our resurrection hereafter in the same bodies, and cites various passages in proof of the same truth from the Epistles of St. Paul (c. xiii). He then proceeds to show that the flesh and blood of Christ were of the same nature with those of other men, and cites St. Paul in proof of this; and thus shows again that it is impossible with any consistency to adopt the Gnostic interpretation of their favourite text, 'Flesh and blood cannot inherit the kingdom of God' (c. xiv). He then proceeds to show how the

[1] 1 Thess. v. 23.
[2] 1 Cor. iii. 16, vi. 15.
[3] 1 Cor. xv.
[4] 1 Cor. xv. 50.

same truth is indicated in the Old Testament, and thence again argues for the identity of the God of the Old Testament with the God of the New, and for the efficacy of the redemption effected by Christ's birth from a woman, as co-extensive with the evil sustained by Adam's fall through a woman (cc. xv–xix). He then repeats the argument in the third book, contrasting the novelty and variety of the heretical theories with the primitive character and unity of the teaching of the Church, and exhorts to obedience to the teaching of the Church, and to Christ, the Head of all things in heaven and in earth,[1] the promised Seed of the woman, who bruised the head of the serpent by overcoming the temptations addressed to His human nature, and thus again showed the unity of God in the Law and in the Gospel (cc. xx–xxii). Irenæus then proceeds to speak of the works of the Devil as a liar from the beginning, in hostility to Christ, and of the future coming of Antichrist in the power of the Devil, as foretold by the prophet Daniel, by St. Paul, and by St. John in the Apocalypse (cc. xxiii–xxvi). He then proceeds to speak of the future coming of Christ to judge the world, and to separate the sheep from the goats, and of the eternity of reward on one side and of punishment on the other, and of the great apostacy which shall precede Christ's coming (cc. xxvii, xxviii). This gives occasion to speak of the number of the name of Antichrist, and the various attempts which had been made or might be made to explain it; on which he judiciously remarks that some of these explanations are plausible, but that, had it been intended that the prediction should be understood at the present time, it would have been explained by the Apostle himself who beheld the vision, not very long ago, but as late as towards the end of the reign of Domitian (cc. xxix,

[1] Ephes. i. 10.

xxx). The author then returns to the original question of the resurrection of the body, and adduces the fact of Christ's burial and resurrection as an argument against the Gnostic assumption of an immediate ascent to the Pleroma of the soul separated from the body (c. xxxi). He then says that it is just that those who have suffered in the body should also be recompensed in the body (c. xxxii), and then proceeds to describe the future kingdom of Christ as it is foretold in Scripture. He argues in behalf of a literal millennial reign of Christ on earth with His risen saints, and quotes, among genuine texts of Scripture, a strange apocryphal saying attributed to our Lord on the testimony of Papias. After the millennium will come the general resurrection and the judgment, and the new heaven and earth where men shall dwell with God (cc. xxxiii–xxxvi). With this description the work ends.

As the writings of Irenæus are directed principally against the Valentinian branch of the Gnostics, so those of Tertullian are directed chiefly, though not exclusively, against the school of Marcion. It is scarcely possible to imagine a greater contrast of character than between the gentle and modest though zealous Irenæus,[1] and the rough, fiery, one-sided Tertullian; and this difference appears in their respective modes of dealing with their subject, except where, as in Tertullian's treatise against the Valentinians, he does little more than copy his predecessor. Three works of Tertullian may be selected as his principal contributions to the controversy against Gnosticism—the 'Præscriptio adversus Hæreticos,' the tract against the Valentinians, and the five books against Marcion.[2] Of these the two last are generally allowed to

---

[1] ὁ μὲν Εἰρηναῖος φερώνυμός τις ὢν τῇ προσηγορίᾳ αὐτῷ τε τῷ τρόπῳ εἰρηνοποιός, Euseb. H. E. v. 24.

[2] Three minor works may be

have been written after their author became a Montanist;[1] the first is of doubtful date, but may with considerable probability be assigned to a period before his secession from the Church.[2]

The 'Præscriptio adversus Hæreticos' is accepted as a genuine work of Tertullian down to the middle of the forty-fifth chapter; the latter part of the work, which is chiefly historical, is a subsequent addition by another hand.[3] The term *Præscriptio* is used in its legal sense of an *exception* or *demurrer*; and the title is characteristic of the temper of the man. Tertullian proposes to put the heretics *eo nomine* out of court, as teaching a new doctrine contrary to the traditions of the Church, and therefore not entitled to a hearing. He says that we must not be surprised that heresies are permitted to exist for the trial of men's faith, but that our duty is to avoid them as we would some deadly sickness; that they are foretold, and at the same time condemned beforehand in Scripture; that they are the offspring of a perverse will and idle curiosity, doctrines of demons, borrowed from heathen philosophy, with which Christians ought to have nothing to do (cc. i–vii). He meets the objection that men are bidden to seek and they shall find,[4] by the reply that this precept is addressed to those who are not yet Christians, but that those who have received the faith must not seek any other; that they who are always seeking will never find anything to believe; that the Church has a rule of faith

---

added, treating of special points taught by some of the Gnostics. The *Scorpiace*, written to enforce the duty of martyrdom in preference to idolatry; the treatise *De Carne Christi*, written against those who denied the reality of Christ's body; and the *De Resurrectione Carnis*, which contains arguments similar to those of Irenæus against those who denied the resurrection of the body. For an account of them, see Bp. Kaye, *Tertullian* pp. 141, 251, 256.

[1] See Bp. Kaye, *Tertullian* pp. 52, 55.
[2] See Neander, *Antignosticus* p. 425 *seq.* (Eng. Tr.).
[3] *Ibid.* p. 426.
[4] Matt. vii. 7.

to be accepted without further seeking (cc. viii–xiv). This rule of faith he exhibits in the form of a creed, in substance agreeing with that professed by Irenæus, but in language more nearly approaching to the Roman type, which received its ultimate form in the Apostles' Creed [1] (c. xiii). After these preliminary remarks Tertullian proceeds to lay down his main proposition, namely, that heretics should not be admitted by orthodox believers to any disputation concerning the Scriptures, which they interpret differently from the Church. This *præscriptio* he maintains on the following grounds:—1. Because perverse disputings, especially with heretics, are forbidden by St. Paul [2] (c. xvi). 2. Because the heretics reject or corrupt Scripture, and therefore no advantage can be gained by disputing with them (cc. xvii, xviii). 3. Because the faith was committed by Christ to the Apostles and their successors, and no other teachers should be sought than those who were instructed in all truth by Christ and the Holy Ghost, and who taught no secret doctrine beyond that which has been handed down by the Church (cc. xix–xxvi). 4. Because the truth of the teaching of the Church is proved by its unity and antiquity, and the error of heresies by their diversity and novelty (cc. xxvii–xxxi). 5. Because, if there be any older heresies going back to the Apostolic age, they have no succession of bishops to preserve their continuity as a Church (c. xxxii). 6. Because the earliest heresies were condemned by the Apostles themselves (cc. xxxiii, xxxiv). He then shows that none of the above *præscriptio* applies to the Catholic Church (cc. xxxv, xxxvi), and further urges against the heretics that,

---

[1] Cf. Heurtley, *Harmonica Symbolica* p. 14. Another citation of a creed more nearly approaching to the exact form is given by Tertullian, *De Virg. Velandis*, c. 1.

[2] He refers to 1 Tim. vi. 4, and Titus iii. 10.

not being Christians, they have no share in the Christian Scriptures; that they have perverted and mutilated the Scriptures; that their teaching is from the Devil, introducing profane imitations of Christian rites; that in their religious services they observe no distinction of orders and degrees, and show no reverence to their own rulers; and finally, that they are guilty of magical practices (cc. xxxvii–xliii). Lastly, he denounces future judgment against the heretics and those who unite with them (c. xliv).

It will be observed that Tertullian, like Irenæus, appeals to the unity and primitive character of the Church's teaching as handed down from the Apostles through their successors the Bishops, and contrasts it with the variety and novelty of the Gnostic theories. Yet, though appealing to the same authority, the two Fathers do so in a different spirit, according to the diversity of their own characters. Irenæus, while insisting on the Church's rule of faith, expresses the conviction that this rule may be obtained by the sound independent exposition of Holy Writ, as well as by tradition.[1] To him it was something certain in itself, and the two sources of knowledge proceeded independently, side by side. Tertullian went further. He made the traditions of the Church a standard of Scripture exposition, and denied the competence of heretics to expound the Scriptures at all, so far as they did not agree with the Apostolic Church. He occupies, as Neander has shown, a middle position between Irenæus and that later development of which Vincentius Lirinensis is the type.[2] It should be observed however, that in thus appealing to Catholic tradition rather than to Scripture for the defence of the faith

[1] Cf. Irenæus, ii. 27. 1, 2 ; 28. 1. See Beaven's *Irenæus*, p. 138. [2] See Neander, *Antignosticus* p. 441.

against heretics, Tertullian gives no countenance to any assertion of the authority of a tradition differing from or even opposed to Scripture. The question turns on the origin of the rule of faith, not on the nature of its contents. It may be perfectly true, as Tertullian intimates, that the rule of faith was not originally deduced from Scripture; nay, it is certain that there must have been an oral teaching employed by the Apostles and their disciples before the canonical books were written, and still more before they were known and received in all the churches; and such teaching might be handed down by the Church independently of Scripture, though agreeing with it. The controversy of modern times on the respective authority of Scripture and tradition turns on the question, not whether there existed an independent and pure tradition in Tertullian's day, but whether that tradition has been preserved uncorrupted down to the present time. It should be observed also that though Tertullian thus appeals to the tradition of the Church in dealing with opponents who, like Marcion, corrupted or rejected the canonical Scriptures, he constantly himself appeals to the Scriptures in his controversies with those who, like Praxeas, agreed with the Church in accepting them.[1] The treatise against the Valentinians is chiefly taken from the first book of Irenæus,[2] and is valuable as proving the early existence of the Latin translation of that work which was manifestly used by Tertullian.[3] The five books against Marcion are the longest and most important of Tertullian's anti-Gnostic writings. I have already called your attention to some portions of this work in the lecture on the heresy against which it is directed, and a short survey of

---

[1] See Bp. Kaye, *Tertullian* pp. 282, 283.
[2] *Ibid.* p. 482.
[3] Massuet, *Diss. Præv. in Iren.* ii. § 53.

its general plan and contents will be sufficient to complete the former incidental notices.[1] The first book is devoted to a refutation, on general grounds, of Marcion's distinction between the Supreme God and the Creator of the world. This distinction Tertullian, like the author of the 'Clementines,' regards as in fact an assertion of the existence of two Gods, and the greater part of this book is employed in showing the absurdity of such an assertion. The definition of God, he urges, involves the idea of Supreme Power, Eternal Duration, and Self-existence. The unity of the Deity is the necessary consequence from this definition, since the supposition of two Supreme Beings involves a contradiction in terms (cc. iii, iv). Two Deities in every respect equal are in fact only one Deity; nor, if you introduce two, can any satisfactory reason be assigned why you may not, with Valentinus, introduce thirty (c. v). On the other hand, if one of the Deities is inferior to the other, the superior alone is God; the other is not properly entitled to the name at all (cc. vi, vii). Continuing this latter supposition, Tertullian further argues that it is absurd to suppose that during the whole time between the Creation and the coming of Christ, the superior Deity should have remained unknown, while the inferior received the worship of mankind and manifested his power and godhead in the works of creation (cc. ix–xii). In answer to the objection that the world is too imperfect to be the work of the Supreme Being, he replies that Christ Himself has allowed the things of this world to be employed in His own sacraments, that the Marcionites themselves are compelled to use them for sustenance and enjoyment, and that

[1] Cf. Kaye's *Tertullian*, p. 452 seq., from which the following analysis is chiefly abridged. For other expositions of this part of Tertullian's teaching, see Neander, *Antignosticus* p. 488 seq. (Eng. Tr.); Baur, *Die Chr. Gnosis* p. 471 seq.

during the whole time that has elapsed since the coming of Christ, the work of this supposed hostile power has been permitted still to exist, and has not been superseded by a new creation (cc. xiii–xv). Against the supposition that Christ came to deliver men from the power of the Demiurge, and to reveal a new God, he urges the long time during which the supposed deliverance was delayed, and that this very revelation, supposed to be made by Christ, continued itself to be unknown till it was discovered by Marcion (cc. xvi–xix). He then proceeds to examine Marcion's argument for the antagonism between the Law and the Gospel derived from the teaching of St. Paul, and urges that St. Paul's teaching really proves the very opposite conclusion to that which Marcion would draw from it. The whole necessity of St. Paul's argument arises from the fact that the Law and the Gospel proceed from the same Author, and the Apostle has to show why observances which God enjoined at one time were not equally required at another (cc. xx, xxi). He then appeals, as in the *præscriptio*, to the authority of the Church (c. xxii), and finally contends that Marcion's theory does not even prove what it is intended to establish—the benevolence of the Supreme God, for that on Marcion's own showing He permitted all the evils which have taken place under the rule of the Demiurge, if He did not directly produce them; He saves the soul only, not the body; His goodness is not such as to abhor and punish evil, and therefore it is not able to check sinners in their evil courses; and does away with the necessity of baptism for the remission of sins (cc. xxii–xxviii). This leads some concluding remarks on the Marcionite practice of refusing baptism to married persons, which he censures as incompatible with the doctrine of the goodness of God (c. xxix).

In his second book Tertullian proceeds to show that the appearances of evil in the world are not inconsistent with the perfect goodness of its Author. He dwells on man's ignorance and inability to judge of the Divine dispensations (c. i). He appeals to the proofs of the Divine goodness exhibited in the material world, in the creation of man, and in the law given to Adam; the superiority of man to the other animals being shown by the very fact that a law was given to him which he was capable of obeying or disobeying (cc. iii, iv). He maintains that the freedom of man's will was part of his likeness to his Maker, and that if he abused that freedom and fell, his fall does not detract from the goodness of God (cc. v–x). Having thus shown that God is not the author of evil, Tertullian proceeds to maintain that the punishment of sin is not inconsistent with the goodness of God, but belongs to His justice which is part of His goodness, and that God may fitly be moved with anger against sin and compassion towards suffering, though these passions are not in Him such as they are in man (cc. xi–xvii). Tertullian then proceeds to answer the objections of Marcion against particular portions of the Old Testament, such as the *Lex Talionis*, the sacrifices and ceremonies of the Mosaic Law, the spoiling of the Egyptians, the apparent violation of the Sabbath, the lifting up of the brazen serpent, the repentance ascribed to God, &c. (cc. xviii–xxix).

The third book is directed to the refutation of Marcion's opinion that Christ was not sent by the Creator of the world, but by the Supreme God to counteract the work of the Creator. He says that Marcion's supposed Supreme God gave no intimation of the Christ He was hereafter to send, and that the miracles which Christ performed would not have sufficed to prove His Divine mission without the corroborative evidence of prophecy. He concludes therefore, that Christ must have been sent by the Creator of the world who predicted His coming through the prophets of the Old Testament (cc. ii, iii). After some cautions on the interpretation of prophecy, he then proceeds to show that both the Jews and the Marcionites erred through not distinguishing between the two advents of Christ—the one in humiliation, the other in glory; and dwells at some length on the absurdities of the Marcionite doctrine that the body of Christ was a mere phantom (cc. v–xi). The remainder of the book consists principally of references to various passages in the Old Testament which prove that Jesus was the Messiah foretold by the prophets (cc. xii–xxiv).[1]

The fourth book is designed as a refutation of Marcion's 'Antitheses,' a work which professed, by exhibiting supposed points of opposition between the Old and New Testaments, to show that they could not have proceeded from the same author. Tertullian allows the different character and purpose of the two dispensations, but maintains that this very difference was foretold by the prophets, and is therefore an argument for, not against, the unity of authorship (c. i). He then protests against Marcion's mode of comparing the Law and the Gospel by means of a garbled revision of St. Luke's Gospel alone, and by exalting the authority of St. Paul in opposition to the other Apostles. He maintains that all the Apostles and all the Evangelists must be alike received, and that St. Paul's teaching is not opposed to that of the other

[1] Much of this portion of the book is repeated almost in the same words in the tract *Adversus Judæos*, whence Neander (*Antignosticus* p. 530) conjectures that that tract as originally written went no further than the beginning of the ninth chapter, and that the remainder was afterwards supplied by a later hand from the treatise against Marcion. Cf. Bp. Kaye, *Tertullian* p. xix.

Apostles (cc. ii–v). He then enters on an examination of the special passages in the Gospels, and shows from them that the things said and done by Christ correspond with those foretold of the Messiah by the Hebrew prophets, answering also the various charges of contradiction between the two Testaments which had been alleged by Marcion (cc. vi–xliii).

In the fifth book Tertullian pursues, with reference to St. Paul's Epistles, the same argument which in the previous book he had applied to the Gospels. Marcion professed an exceptional respect for St. Paul, as the only preacher of true Christianity; and the object of Tertullian is to prove that the writings of this Apostle, far from being at variance, are in perfect unison with the teaching of the Old Testament (c. i). He proceeds to examine in succession the ten Epistles whose authority was acknowledged by Marcion: first, the Galatians (cc. ii–iv); then the two Epistles to the Corinthians (cc. v–xii); then that to the Romans, which he states to have been grievously mutilated by the Marcionites (cc. xiii, xiv); then the two to the Thessalonians (cc. xv, xvi); then the Ephesians, Colossians, and Philippians (cc. xvii–xx); and ends with a remark on the Epistle to Philemon, which he says had alone, on account of its brevity, escaped corruption at the hands of Marcion. The Epistles to Timothy and Titus are omitted because Marcion refused to acknowledge them, affecting, as Tertullian says, to falsify the number of the Epistles, as well as their contents (c. xxi).

Of the two theologians whose writings we have hitherto examined, Irenæus represents for the most part the calmness and moderation of the judge; Tertullian, the vehemence and to some extent the one-sidedness of the advocate. Both, though occasionally dealing with philosophical arguments, are, in the general tone of their minds, theologians rather than philosophers, and, while zealous in defending the revealed truth, hardly appreciate the philosophical positions occupied by their adversaries who corrupted it. In our next lecture we shall endeavour to show how this point of view was taken up and controverted by the writer who is especially the Christian philosopher of this period, Clement of Alexandria.

LECTURE XVI.

CLEMENT OF ALEXANDRIA—HIPPOLYTUS.

ALEXANDRIA, the great centre of intellectual and practical activity under the Roman empire, the confluence where the thought of Egypt, Asia, Palestine, and Greece came together, possessed a Christian catechetical school for the instruction of converts in the faith, which is said to have existed from the time of St. Mark.[1] About the middle of the second century it assumed a different character, and from a school for catechumens became a seminary for training the clergy and for completing the instruction of the most highly educated converts.[2] The mastership was held by a succession of eminent men, among whom the first that can be named with certainty was Pantænus, a convert from the Stoic philosophy.[3] Pantænus was succeeded by his disciple Clement, usually called, from the place of his residence, Clement of Alexandria, though he was probably a native of Athens.[4] Clement was originally a heathen, and it is uncertain at what period of his life he was converted to Christianity;[5] but from the comparatively favourable estimate which, in common with his

---

[1] Hieron. *De Viris Illustr.* 36. Cf. Robertson, *History of the Christian Church* vol. I. p. 87.

[2] Robertson, *l. c.*

[3] Euseb. *H. E.* v. 10.

[4] Epiphan. *Hær.* xxxii. 6. Cf. Bp. Kaye, *Clem. Alex.* p. 8.

[5] Neander (*Ch. Hist.* II. p. 453) speaks of him as converted to Christianity at a mature age, though he supposes his conversion to be earlier than his intercourse with Pantænus. The latter supposition is doubted by Davidson, Art. 'Clement,' in Smith's *Dict. of Biography*.

predecessor Justin Martyr,[1] he forms of the Greek philosophy, differing in this respect from the majority of the Christians of his day, it is probable that, like Justin, he had studied philosophy, and learned to estimate its value, before his acquaintance with the higher truths of Christianity.[2] While Irenæus looks upon philosophy chiefly as the source of the errors of Gnosticism, while Tertullian regards it as a corruption proceeding from Satan and altogether devoid of truth,[3] Clement sees in it a gift of God, imperfect indeed and corrupted by human devices, but designed by God for the training of the Gentile world, as an education preparing the Gentiles for the coming of Christ, as the law was to the Jews.[4]

The three principal extant works of Clement—the 'Cohortatio ad Græcos,' the 'Pædagogus,' and the 'Stromateis' or 'Miscellanies'—may be regarded as forming a connected series, since his starting point is the idea that the Divine Teacher of mankind, the Logos, first conducts the rude heathen sunk in sin and idolatry to the faith; then still further reforms their lives by moral precepts; and finally elevates those who have undergone this moral purification to that profounder knowledge of Divine things which he calls *Gnosis*. Thus the Logos appears first as exhorting sinners to repentance, and converting the heathen to the faith ($προτρεπτικός$); then as forming the life and conduct of the converted by his discipline ($παιδαγωγός$); and, finally, as a teacher of the true knowledge to those who are purified.[5] The work with which we are princi-

---

[1] In his *Apologies*, not in the (probably spurious) *Cohortatio*. Cf. Neander, *Ch. Hist.* II. p. 418.

[2] Cf. Euseb. *Præp. Evang.* ii. 2; Neander, *Ch. Hist.* II. 454.

[3] Neander, *Ch. Hist.* II. p. 236.

[4] *Strom.* i. 5, p. 331; vi. 8, p. 771. Cf. Bp. Kaye, *Clem. Alex.* pp. 116, 191. Clement however followed the Alexandrian tradition handed down from Aristobulus, which maintained that the Greek philosophy was in great part stolen from the Jewish Scripture, though he allows that some parts may have been directly given by God: see *Strom.* i. 17, p. 366. Cf. Kaye, p. 122.

[5] *Strom.* iv. 1, 2.

pally concerned is the Στρωμάτεις, a title which perhaps may be fairly rendered 'Miscellanies,' the word στρωματεὺς in its literal signification meaning a patchwork quilt of various colours. The title is not inappropriate to the character of the work, which is, as he himself describes it,[1] a miscellaneous collection passing from one subject to another, to suit the tastes of discursive readers; the main design however being to bring together a chaotic assemblage of truth and error out of the Greek philosophers and the systems of the Gnostic sects, in connection and contrast with portions of the true Gnosis. Availing himself of the distinction, to which I have adverted in a former lecture as recognised in the writings of St. Paul, between the knowledge with which the followers of Christ are enriched by Him,[2] and the knowledge falsely so called[3] which the Christian teacher is bidden to avoid, Clement endeavours to wrest from his adversaries the title on which they prided themselves, and to turn whatever attractions it possessed to the service of the Church by claiming the title of Gnostic as properly belonging to the perfect Christian, and sketching a portrait of the true Gnostic as contrasted with the false. What he has actually produced however is 'not so much a portraiture of the perfect Christian as a representation of different portions of the Gnostic character thrown upon the canvas without order or connection.'[4] His design seems to have been to form an ideal sketch of Christian excellence in its highest conceivable perfection; to describe the model Christian as he ought to be, after the manner of the perfectly good man of Aristotle's Ethics or the imaginary wise man of the Stoic philosophy, Christian graces and Divine illumination being substituted for the sovereign reason of the heathen

[1] Cf. Neander, *l. c.* p. 455.
[2] 1 Cor. i. 5.
[3] 1 Tim. vi. 20.
[4] Bp. Kaye, *Clem. Alex.* p. 260.

philosophers. Like Aristotle, Clement placed the highest state of the Gnostic soul in contemplation.[1] Like the Stoics, he regarded the perfection of the human character as consisting in apathy or exemption from passion.[2] To both he added a Christian consummation, the contemplation being an intercourse with God to be completely realised in a future life; the apathy being a perfect subjection to the law of God, extinguishing all struggle between the flesh and the spirit. Clement's anxiety to place Christianity in such a light as might conciliate the favour of the learned heathen caused him to assimilate the model of Christian as much as possible to that of philosophical perfection;[3] and like the heathen philosophies he has constructed an imaginary man framed on an *à priori* hypothesis, rather than a type actually realisable in human nature. The antagonism of Clement to the false Gnosticism—that is to say, to the Gnosticism commonly so called—principally relates to two points in their teaching. 1. Their denial of the free will of man, and consequent perversion of the moral relation of man to God. 2. Their condemnation of the material creation, and consequent hostility to marriage as a means whereby material existence is multiplied.[4]

I have before observed that the Gnostic philosophy in general entirely lost sight of the proper conception of sin as a voluntary transgression by man of the law of God, and merged it in the general notion of evil inherent in the constitution of the universe, to be traced, not to the fall of man, but to the creation of the world and the original nature of things. Moral evil in human actions

---

[1] *Strom.* vii. 10, p. 865 (Potter). Cf. ii. 17, p. 469; v. 14, p. 732. See Bp. Kaye, *Clem. Alex.* p. 254.

[2] *Strom.* ii. p. 484; iv. p. 581; vi. 9, 14, p. 775, 776, 797; vii. 14, p. 883, 886. Cf. Kaye, p. 251.

[3] Kaye, p. 261.

[4] Baur, *Die Christ. Gnosis,* p. 489.

being thus identified with natural evil in the system of
the world, it was perfectly consistent to regard the characters of men, and consequently their moral relations
to God, as determined by the cosmical conditions under
which each man came into existence, not as in any way
connected with his own choice or free will. The Gnostics,
at least the better portion of them, recognised indeed the
distinction between good and evil men; nay, they prided
themselves especially on the superiority of the Gnostic or
spiritual man over the inferior degrees of men, psychical
or material; but the pre-eminence was wholly a natural
gift, bestowed upon some men and denied to others by
inevitable necessity, without any choice on their part.[1]
Against this doctrine of natural necessity, as held by
Basilides and Valentinus, Clement asserts in the strongest
terms the responsibility and free will of man. 'The
followers of Basilides,' he says, 'suppose that faith is a
natural gift assigned to the elect, which discovers knowledge without demonstration by intellectual apprehension.
The disciples of Valentinus, on the other hand, ascribe
faith to us simple persons; but for themselves, who, by
the superior excellence of their formation, are naturally
destined to be saved, they claim knowledge, which they
say is yet more removed from faith than is the spiritual
from the psychical. The followers of Basilides moreover
maintain that faith and election together are appropriated
to each person according to his grade,[2] and that, in consequence of the supermundane election, the mundane faith
of every nature is determined, and that correspondent to
the hope of each[3] is also his gift of faith. Faith then
is no longer a voluntary right action, if it is a natural

---

[1] See above, Lecture XII on the Valentinians.

[2] Καθ' ἕκαστον διάστημα, 'nach jeder Stufe der Geisterwelt,' Baur, *Die Chr. Gnosis* p. 489.

[3] κατάλληλον τῇ ἐλπίδι, i.e. apparently according to the destiny or expectation allotted to each person.

privilege; nor can he who does not believe be rightly punished for that which is not his own fault; as also he who believes is not the cause of his own belief. Nay, the whole peculiarity and distinctive character of belief and unbelief, if we consider rightly, will not be amenable to praise or blame, being predetermined by a natural necessity ordained by Almighty power; and in us, if we are mere lifeless machines, pulled by our desires as with strings, volition or compulsion and the impulse which precedes these are mere superfluities.' 'I cannot,' he continues, 'conceive a living being whose active principle is moved necessarily by an external cause. How, upon this supposition, can he who believes not repent and receive remission of sins? Baptism is thus no longer reasonable, nor the blessed seal (of confirmation[1]), nor the Son, nor the Father; but their God becomes nothing more than a natural distribution of things, not having that which is the basis of salvation, voluntary faith.'[2] In a later passage he combats the doctrine of natural destination to immortality, together with the Valentinian distinction between the Supreme God and the Demiurge, the one being the author of the spiritual, the other of the psychical portion of mankind; and shows how this theory limits the saving work of Christ and perverts the true nature of the redemption.[3] And again in another passage he maintains that if men arrive at the knowledge of God by nature, as Basilides maintains, faith is not a reasonable assent of a free soul, but a beauty conferred by immediate creation; and that for such persons, being, as Valentinus says, saved by nature, the commandments are superfluous, and even the redemption by Christ not needed.[4] In

---

[1] οὐδὲ μακαρία σφραγίς. This term sometimes means baptism, sometimes confirmation. Here the context seems to indicate the latter.

[2] *Strom.* ii. 3, p. 433 *seq.*
[3] *Ibid.* iv. 13, p. 603.
[4] *Ibid.* v. 1, p. 645.

another place Clement maintains that the merit of the martyr depends upon the fact that he suffers voluntarily, for the sake of the faith, torments which he might have avoided by apostasy; and combats a strange theory of Basilides, that these sufferings are incurred on account of sins committed in a former life—a theory which Clement censures as subversive of the justice of God, and dishonouring to the faith of the martyr.[1] In another place he combats the pantheistic tendency of the Gnostic theory, and points out its monstrous consequences in those remarkable words, 'God has no natural relation to us, as the founders of the heresies assert, whether He formed us out of nothing or out of matter, since the former has no existence, and the latter is in every respect different from God; unless some one should venture to assert that we are part of God, and of the same essence with Him; and I understand not how he who knows God can bear to hear such an assertion, when he contemplates our life and the evils in which we are involved. Were this the case God would in part sin, if the parts of the whole go to complete the whole; but if they do not go towards its completion, they are not parts. But God, being by His nature rich in pity, in His goodness watches over us, who are neither part of Him nor His children by nature. . . . The riches of God's mercy are manifested in this: that He calls to the adoption of sons those who belong not to Him in essence or nature, but simply in being the work of His will.'[2]

On the second feature of the Gnostic heresies to which Clement opposes himself, their contempt and dislike of the material creation, and especially of the human body, he expresses himself in general terms in a beautiful

[1] *Strom.* iv. 12, p. 599.
[2] *Ibid.* ii. 16, p. 467, translated by

Bp. Kaye, *Clem. Alex.* p. 142. Cf. Baur, *Die Chr. Gnosis* p. 492.

passage towards the end of the fourth book. 'Those,' he says, 'who censure the creation and speak evil of the body, speak without reason, for they do not consider that the structure of man is erect, and fitted for the contemplation of heaven, and that the organs of sensation contribute to the acquisition of knowledge, and that the members are formed for that which is good, not for pleasure. Hence the body becomes the habitation of the soul, which is most precious to God, and is thought worthy of the Holy Spirit by the sanctification of the soul and body, being perfected by the perfection of the Saviour.' . . . . 'We admit,' he continues, 'that the soul is the better part of man, the body the worse; but neither is the soul good by nature, nor the body bad by nature, nor is that which is not good necessarily bad; there are things between the two, and of these some preferred, some rejected.[1] As man was to be placed among sensible objects, he was necessarily composed of different, but not opposite parts, a soul and a body. . . . Basilides speaks of the *election* as strangers to the world, being naturally above the world. But this is not so, for all things are of one God; and no one can by nature be a stranger to the world, there being but one essence and one God; but the elect live as strangers, knowing that all things are to be possessed, and then laid aside. They use the three good things of which the Peripatetics speak;[2] but they use the body as men who are taking a long journey use the inns on the road—minding the things of the world as of the place in which they sojourn, but leaving their habitations and possessions and the use of them without regret; readily following Him who withdraws them from life, never looking behind,

---

[1] καὶ προηγμένα καὶ ἀποπροηγμένα. Cf. Cicero, *De Fin.* iii. 4. 15, 'proegmenis et apoproegmenis . . . quamquam hæc quidem præposita recte et rejecta dicere licebit.'

[2] *i. e.* goods of the soul, goods of the body, and goods external. Cf. Aristotle, *Eth. Nic.* i. 8.

giving thanks for the time of their sojourning, but blessing their departure, and longing for their mansion in heaven. . . . The heretical notion that the soul is sent down from heaven into these lower regions is erroneous. God ameliorates all things; and the soul, choosing the best course of life from God and righteousness, receives heaven in exchange for earth.'[1]

The Gnostic hostility to matter and the material body assumed in some of these schools, though not in all, a practical direction in relation to marriage; and to this question Clement gives a special examination, often giving, in the latter part of the second book, his own views on the subject of marriage, which, he says, is ordained by God and counselled in Scripture, though not to be entered into rashly, nor by every one, but with due regard to time and person and age and circumstances; and after mentioning the opinions of some of the ancient philosophers on this subject, Clement proceeds in the third book to examine the views of the different schools of Gnosticism. The Valentinians, he says, approve of marriage; the followers of Basilides, though preferring celibacy, allow marriage in certain cases, while some of this sect have perverted the teaching of their founders to licentious conclusions; the disciples of Carpocrates and Epiphanes profess communism after the manner of brutes, and practise open and shameless licentiousness; the followers of Marcion condemn marriage out of hostility to the Creator and unwillingness to add to His kingdom.[2] Clement then proceeds to divide the heretics into two classes—those who taught the indifference of human actions, and those who inculcate an overstrained continence through impiety and enmity to the Creator,

---

[1] *Strom.* ii. 26, p. 638. See Bp. Kaye, *Clem. Alex.* p. 172. Cf. Baur, *Die Chr. Gnosis* p. 493 *seq.*

[2] *Ibid.* iii. 1–3, p. 508 *seq.*

and argues at considerable length against both, on grounds drawn partly from natural reason and partly from Scripture. 'We are at liberty,' he says, 'to marry or to abstain from marriage; a life of celibacy is not of itself better than a married life. They who, in order to avoid the distraction of a married life, have remained single, have frequently become misanthropic, and have failed in charity; while others, who have married, have given themselves up to pleasure, and have become like unto beasts.'[1] His concluding advice on the subject is in the same moderate tone. 'They,' he says, ' who inculcate continence out of enmity to the Creator, act impiously, when they might choose celibacy agreeably to the second rule of piety; giving thanks for the grace imparted to them, but not abhorring the creature or despising those who marry, for the world is the work of a Creator, as well as celibacy itself; but let both (the married and single) give thanks for the state in which they are placed, if they know for what purpose they are placed in it.'[2]

Clement's direct refutation of particular portions of the Gnostic teaching, as exhibited in the above extracts, is mainly directed to moral and practical questions. The general principles of the Gnostic theories he does not attack directly, but refutes them indirectly by his counter-sketch of the true Gnostic, or perfect Christian. The true Gnostic is he 'who unites in himself all Christian perfections, intellectual and practical, who combines knowledge, faith, and love, and therefore is one in his judgment, truly spiritual, formed into a perfect man, after the image of the Lord by the Artificer Himself, worthy to be called brother by the Lord, at once a friend and son of God.'[3] He is distinguished from the common believer in

[1] *Strom.* iii. 9, p. 541. Cf. Kaye, p. 153.
[2] *Ibid.* iii. 18, p. 560. Cf. Kaye, p. 156.
[3] *Ibid.* iii. 10, p. 542. Cf. Kaye, p. 242.

that he acts from love, not from fear of punishment or hope of reward.[1] He has faith in common with all believers, but his faith is made perfect by knowledge. His knowledge however, on the other hand, is founded upon faith; he must proceed from faith and grow up in faith, in order that through the grace of God he may receive knowledge concerning Him as far as it is possible.[2] 'Faith is a compendious knowledge of things which are of urgent necessity; knowledge, a firm and valid demonstration of things received through faith, built upon faith through the instruction of the Lord, and conducting us on to an infallible apprehension. The first saving change is from heathenism to faith; the second from faith to knowledge, which, being perfected in love, renders that which knows the friend of that which is known.[3] The believer merely tastes the Scriptures; the Gnostic, proceeding further, is an accurate judge (γνώμων) of the truth, as in matters of ordinary life the artificer is superior to the common man, and can express something better than the common notions.'[4]

Yet, however highly Clement may rate the knowledge which he attributes to his true Gnostic, several features are worthy of notice by which it is distinguished from that knowledge claimed for themselves by the Gnostic heretics. First, it is not a special gift of nature, but a habit painfully acquired by preparation and discipline. Secondly, it is not a mere apprehension of speculative theories, but a practical principle, embracing action and love. Thirdly, it is founded on faith; the matter and substance of its doctrine is that which is revealed through Christ; its pre-eminence consists in the manner and certainty of its

---

[1] *Strom.* iv. 18, 22, pp. 614, 625. Cf. Kaye, p. 244.
[2] *Ibid.* vii. 10, p. 864. Cf. Kaye, p. 245.
[3] *Ibid.* vii. 10, p. 865. Cf. Kaye, pp. 245–6.
[4] *Ibid.* vii. 16, p. 891. Cf. Kaye, p. 246.

apprehension, not in any new and distinct teaching. Fourthly, it is a knowledge imparted as far as is possible,[1] possessed in this life according to man's capacity to receive it; and the limits of that capacity Clement has pointed out in several remarkable passages. In one place he says, 'The Divine nature cannot be described as it really is. The prophets have spoken to us, fettered as we are by the flesh, according to our ability to receive their saying, the Lord accommodating Himself to human weakness for our salvation.'[2] In another he says, 'It is manifest that no one during the time of this life can have a clear apprehension of God. The pure in heart shall see God when they shall have arrived at the last perfection.'[3] In another, describing the purification of the true Gnostic by the elevation of the soul above the objects of sense, he says, 'If, then, rejecting whatever belongs to bodies and to things called incorporeal, we cast ourselves into the greatness of Christ, and go forward with holiness into immensity, we shall approach to the notion of the Almighty, knowing not what He is, but what He is not.'[4] And in a fourth passage he expressly declares, 'The first principle of all things cannot be named; and if we give it a name not properly (οὐ κυρίως), calling it either One, or the Good, or Intellect, or the Very Existent, or Father, or God, or Maker, or Lord, we speak not as declaring its name, but by reason of our deficiency we employ good names, in order that the reason may be able to rest upon these, not wandering around others. For these names are not severally indicative of God, but all collectively exhibit the power of the Almighty; for the names of things are given to them either from the properties belonging to

---

[1] *Strom.* vii. 10, p. 864, χάριτι τοῦ Θεοῦ τὴν περὶ αὐτοῦ κομίσασθαι, ὡς οἷόν τέ ἐστιν, γνῶσιν. Cf. Kaye, p. 245.
[2] *Ibid.* ii. 16, p. 467. Cf. Kaye, p. 141.
[3] *Ibid.* v. 1, p. 647.
[4] *Ibid.* v. 11, p. 689. Cf. Kaye, p. 184.

them, or from their relation to each other; but none of these can be received concerning God.'[1]

It may be interesting to compare these admissions of the philosophical Clement with the cognate language of the other Catholic opponent of the Gnosticism of the period. Irenæus says of the Gnostic attempts to explain the origin of the universe, and to solve problems which the Scriptures have left unexplained, 'If we cannot discover explanations of all those things which are sought for in the Scriptures, let us not therefore seek after any other God besides Him who is truly God; for this is the greatest impiety. We ought to leave such things to God who made us, being fully assured that the Scriptures are perfect, being spoken by the Word of God and His Spirit; but we in proportion as we are inferior to, and the latest creation of the Word of God and His Spirit, in that proportion are destitute of the knowledge of His mysteries. And there is no cause to wonder if we are thus circumstanced with regard to spiritual and heavenly things, and those which require to be made known by revelation, since even of those things that are before our feet (I mean the things in this created world, which are handled and seen by us and are present to us) there are many which have escaped our knowledge; and these, too, we commit to God.'[2] . . . 'If any one,' he continues, 'should ask, "What was God doing before He made the world?" we reply that the answer to this question rests with God. That this world was made perfect by God, and had a beginning in time, the Scriptures tell us; but no Scripture reveals what God was doing before this. The answer therefore rests with God, and it is not [fitting] that we should wish to discover foolish and rash and blasphemous

---

[1] *Strom.* v. 12. Cf. Uberweg, *Gesch. der Philosophie*, II. p. 61.

[2] Irenæus, ii. 28. 2.

inventions, and, by imagining that we have discovered the origin of matter, to set aside God Himself who made all things.'[1] A little later he applies the same rule to curious inquiries concerning the mysteries of the Divine nature: 'If any one should say to us, "How was the Son begotten of the Father?" we reply that that production, or generation, or nomination, or revelation, or by whatever name we may call that unspeakable generation, no one knows, not Valentinus, nor Marcion, nor Saturninus, nor Basilides, nor Angels, nor Archangels, nor Principalities, nor Powers, but only the Father who begat, and the Son who is begotten.'[2] And in more general terms he concludes: 'Although the spirit of the Saviour that is in Him searcheth all things, even the deep things of God, yet, as to us, there are diversities of gifts, diversities of ministrations, and diversities of operations, and we on the earth, as Paul says, know in part and prophesy in part. . . . But when we seek things which are above us, and which we are not able to attain, [it is absurd] that we should aspire to such a height of presumption as to lay open God and things which are not yet discovered, as if by one man's talk about emanations we had found out God, the Maker of all things.'[3] I have quoted in a previous lecture the strong language in which Tertullian, in his work against Marcion, dwells on the unsearchableness of God and the ignorance of man; and the *consensus* of the three writers is the more remarkable when we consider the difference in their natural dispositions and in their modes of conducting their respective controversies. These writers represent the first direct collision between a metaphysical philosophy of the Absolute with its inevitable tendency

---

[1] Irenæus, ii. 28. 3. [*decet* supplied from Grabe's conjecture].
[2] *Ibid.* § 6.
[3] Irenæus, ii. 28. 7. [*absurdum* supplied from Massuet's conjecture].

to Pantheism, and the Christian revelation with its firm hold on the belief in a personal God; and the method which these Fathers' inaugurated has been pursued by their ablest successors in the Catholic Church in subsequent generations.

The fourth Christian writer against heresies to whom I have referred, Hippolytus, pursues a different method from the other three. The value of his work is chiefly historical, in which respect it contains much new and interesting information. But he does not attempt a philosophical or theological refutation of the various heresies which he notices. His principal object is to show that their doctrines are borrowed from heathen sources: and he seems to think that the refutation of these doctrines is sufficiently accomplished when he has traced them back to this unchristian origin, and shown that theories which the heretics put forth as of Divine inspiration are really stolen from the inventions of heathen men.[1] His theological controversy with the heretics is limited to an exposition, by way of contrast, of the true doctrine concerning God the Creator of all things; concerning the Logos by whom the world was made, and who became man; and concerning the free will and future destiny of men. The last portion is not completed in the work as it has come down to us, which ends abruptly in the middle of a sentence.

[1] Hippolytus, *Ref. Hær.* ix. 31.

INDEX.

ABE

ABEL, evil spirit of the Cainites, p. 101
Abraham, said to have written Book of Creation, 38
Abrasax or Abraxas, 153
Absolute Existence, problem of, 11, 16
Achamoth, 169, 184 & *ff.*
Adam identified with Christ, 237
Adam Kadmon of the Zohar, 37; in theory of Simon Magus, 87
Adamites, 122
Æons, 178; how used in N.T. 61 & *ff.*; by Valentinus and Simon Magus, 62; in Valentinian theory, 168, 171; same as Roots of Simon Magus, 86; same as Diathesis of Ptolemæus, 173
Ahriman, Zoroastrian evil spirit, 26
Akiba, Rabbi, traditional author of Book of Creation, 38
Alcibiades of Apamea, 234
Alexander the Valentinian, 197
Alexander and Hymenæus in N.T., 57
Alexandria, school of, 261
Amshaspands, the six, of the Zoroastrian system, 26
Anaxagoras, 4, 21; borrowed from by Basilides, 149
Angels of Valentinus, 181
Announcement, the Great, of Simon Magus, 88 & *ff.*
Annubion, 226
Antichrist, Irenæus on the name of, 249
Antitactæ, 123
Antithesis of Marcion, 209 & *ff.*
Apocalypse, see John, Revelation of Saint

BAS

Appion, 226
Archelaus, bp. of Caschar, 159
Archon, first of Basilides, 152, 155; second do. 154, 155
Aristotle on the 'Existence of Evil,' 22; use of word 'wisdom,' 1
Asceticism of Saturninus, 134
Athenodorus, 226
Aquila, 225, 226, 227
Augustine and Valentinianism, 183

BALAAM and the Nicolaitans, 73
Baptism, for the dead, 116; a Gnostic initiatory rite, 41; Marcion's rite, 217
Barbelists, 242
Barcabbas, 164
Barcoph, 164
Bardesanes, 139, 197; his teaching, 139, 140; his hymns, 141
Baruch, Gnostic book of, 102
Basilides, 144; date of, 145; teaching of, destroys free-will, 14; relation to the Kabbala, 42; seed of the world, 148; threefold sonship, 150; account of Creation, 151; Ogdoad and first Archon, 152; Hebdomad, 152, 154; theory of Redemption, 154; second Archon, 154, 155; illumination of the universe, 156; accepts history of the Gospels, 157; not Docetic, *ib.*; not dualistic, *ib.*; his theory externally allegorical, 159; internally pantheistic, *ib.*; emanations, 160; relation to Plato, 161; relation to the Pythagoreans,

162; Caulacau, *ib.*; no idea of Providence or free-will, 165; source of his teaching, 146; first principle, a non-existent deity, *ib.*; a non-existent world, 148; borrows from St. John, 150

Baur, classification of Gnostic sects by, 46; quotes Irenæus unfairly against St. John, 177

Beghards, or Brethren of the Free Spirit, 122

Bisexual principle of Simon Magus, 89; of the Naassenes, 97

Buddhist doctrine of Annihilation, 30

Bunsen, view of Simon Magus, 83, 91

Burton, estimate of Simon Magus, 91

CAIN and the Cainites, 100, 101
Caius, presbyter of Rome, gives an account of Cerinthus, 114

Carpocrates, 117 & *ff.*; on Person of Christ, 117; licentiousness of his teaching, 120; relation to Cerinthus, 119; his son Epiphanes, 121

Carpocratians adopt title Gnostic, 7, 117; their teaching on the Resurrection, 59; their treatment of the Gospel, 121

Caulacau, 163

Celbes, 102

Cerdon, 203

Cerinthus, 112 & *ff.*; his relation to St. John, 14, 74, 75; to St. Paul, 53; to Philo, 75, 114; to Carpocrates, 119; his teaching, 74; refuted by Gospel of St. John, 116; germs of his teaching opposed in Ep. to Col. 53; his Christology, 115; said to have forged the Apocalypse, 114; the precursor of the Nazarenes and Ebionites, 123

Christ, Person and work of, recognised by Gnosticism, 5; errors in relation to Person of, 110

Christian elememt in Gnosticism, 220

Christology of Cerinthus, 115; of Clem. Hom. 237; of Sethites, 102

Cipher, supposed derivation of, 37

Clement of Alexandria, his date, 8; contrasts true and false Gnosticism, 8, 9; his charges against Basilides and Valentinus, 14, 160; his tradition about Ep. to the Hebrews, 61; places Apocalypse before Gospel of St. John, 71; identifies Nicolas the Deacon as founder of the Nicolaitans, 72; his account of Epiphanes and his book 'On Justice,' 121; the Antitactæ, 123; Tatian, 137, &c.; Basilides, 145, &c.; preserves fragments of writings of Valentinus, 200; his position, 261; a philosopher, 262; his writings, 262 & *ff.*

Clement of Rome, said to have been ordained by St. Peter, 221; his letter to St. James in the Clem. Hom. 223

Clementine Homilies, 221; their external history, 233; their Christology, 237

Colarbasus, 197

Colossians, Ep. to, alludes to Gnosticism, 53

Conception, *see* Ennoia

Confirmation, 266

Constitutions, Apostolical, 93

Corinth., Epp. to, contain first allusions to Gnosticism in N.T., 48

Creed of Tertullian, 252

DARKNESS, Persian evil principle, 87

Decad of Valentinus, 174, 175

Democritus, 21

Demiurge, lower in Gnostic systems than in Philo, 19; of Ophites, 99; of Valentinus, 186, 190; of Marcion, 209, 210, 214 & *ff.*

'Depth' of Valentinus, 169, 173

Devil of Valentinus, 190

Diathesis, Æons so called by Ptolemæus, 173

Dionysius, Bp. of Alexandria, his account of Cerinthus, 114

Docetism, 58, 111; germs of, derived from India, 32; in teaching of Simon Magus, 85; in teaching of Marcion, 214; the earliest form of Gnosticism, 127; referred to in Ep. to Ephes. 55; in Ep. to Heb. 60; opposed by St. John, 76

Dodecad of Valentinus, 175, 176

Dogma and Christianity, 78

Dorner, estimate of Simon Magus, 91

Dositheus and Simon Magus, 85

Draco, the constellation, 99

Dualism, characteristic of the Syrian Gnosis, 142

EBI

EBION the heretic, a myth, 124
  Ebionism, 58, 111
Ebionites, 123, 124, 236; precursors of, at Corinth, 50
Ebionite Gospel, 126
Egyptian Gnosis, 144
Eleatics, 3, 21
Elkesaites, 236
Elxai or Elchesai, 234
Empedocles, 5, 21
Encratites, 136, 142
Ennoia of Simon Magus, 82; of Ophites, 98
En Soph in the Zohar, 36
Ephesians, Epistle to, alludes to Gnosticism, 51 & ff.; on the Incarnation, 55
'Ephesian Letters,' 51 & f.
Ephraim, St., his hymns superseded by those of Bardesanes, 142
Epiphanes, son of Carpocrates, 121.
Epiphanius, account of the Ophites, 98–100; his date of the Apocalypse, 71; account of Cerinthus, 112 & ff.; baptism for the dead, 116; Saturninus, 132 & ff.; Bardesanes, 138 & ff.; the Encratites, 142; Basilides, 144 & ff.; Valentinus and the Valentinians, 166 & ff.; Marcion, 204, 216 & ff.; Elxai, 234 & ff.; Ebionites and Elkesaites, 234 & ff.
Esau, a hero, 100
Essenes, 65, 234
Euphrates, one of the founders of the Peratæ, 102
Eusebius, account of Polycarp and Marcion, 14; date of Apocalypse, 71; of Carpocrates, 118; the Cainites, 120; Jewish Bishops of Jerusalem, 125; Saturninus and Basilides, 129 & ff.; Bardesanes, 138 & ff., 197; account of Irenæus, 239 & f.
Evil, Origin of, 11, 18; no longer sin, 12; in Greek philosophy, 20, 24; in Eastern philosophies, 24

FALL, the, in the Ophite theories, 99
Faustus, story of, in Clem. Hom. 228.
Fire, the primary principle of Simon Magus, 86 & f.
Fire-worship, the meaning of, 87
Flora, letter of Ptolemæus to, 197
Franck, on the Kabbala and Gnosticism, 42

HEL

Free-will destroyed by Gnosticism, 12, &c.

GENTILE Bishops of Jerusalem, 126
Gieseler, classification of Gnostic sects, 45
Glaucias, teacher of Basilides, 146
Gnosis, meaning of term in Plato, 1; in LXX, and N. T. 6, 7; in Clem. Alex. 262; first used in a depreciatory sense, 49; Syrian, 142; Egyptian 144
Gnostes, use of, in LXX, 6
Gnostic, first used, 7, 105, 117; estimate of Christianity, 9; taught a twofold religion, 10; acknowledge Christ as a Redeemer, 18; list of, given by Irenæus, 242; classification of sects by Mosheim, 44; Gieseler, 45; Neander, ib.; Baur, 46; Matter, ib.
Gnosticism, distinctive title of Christian heretics, 3; characteristics of in time of St. Paul, 8, 53; of Clem. Alex. 8, 265, 267, 269; regarded as Antichristian by St. John, 13; and early Fathers, 13; two schools of, 20; sources of, 31, 32; its relation to Materialism, 14; alluded to in N. T., 6, 48 & ff.; prophecies of in N. T. 64; earliest form of, Docetic, 127
God, Personality of, destroyed by Gnostics, 12
God of the Jews, his position in the Gnostic theories, 19
Gospels, effect of the Synoptic, 127 & f.
Greek philosophy, idea of evil, 3; of Redemption, 20

HAM, Sethite account of, 101
  Harmonius, 141
Heathen Mythologies and the Ophites, 104
Hebdomad of Basilides, 152, 154
Hebrews, Gospel of, 126
Hebrews, Epistle to, date and author, 59 & ff.; to whom addressed, 61; allusions to Gnosticism, 60
Hegel, 147, 165; similarity to the Kabbala, 35; to the Ophite theories 107
Helena, see Simon Magus

INDEX.

HER

Heracleon, 197; first commentator on the Gospel of St. John, 199
Heraclitus, 3; and Simon Magus, 87
Hippolytus, account of title Gnostic, 7; Æons first used by Valentinus, 62; Nicolas and the Nicolaitans, 72; Ophites, 73, 95 & *ff*.; Gospel of St. John, 74; Simon Magus, 83; the 'Great Announcement,' 85 & *ff*.; analogy between Simon and Heraclitus, 87; Peratæ, 99; the Ophite Jesus, 110; Cerinthus, 110 & *ff*.; Ebionites, 123; Saturninus, 129; Basilides, 146 & *ff*; Valentinus, 170 & *ff*.; Elchesai, 231; the book of Elchesai, 234; his date, 235; his own writings, 275
Horus of Valentinus, 169, 180
Hydroparastatæ, 137
Hyginus, Bishop of Rome, 203
Hymenæus, 51, 57, 111

IALDABOTH, 98
Incarnation, the, and Gnosticism, 55, 58
Indian Religion, 29; Emanation theory of origin of evil, 24; relation to Gnosticism, 29
Innatum, meaning of, 132
Intellect, male principle of Simon Magus, 88
Ionian philosophy, 3, 20
Irenæus, account of St. John and Cerinthus, 13; description of Simon Magus and his teaching, 40; says Simon used Hebrew words at Baptism, 42; date of Apocalypse, 71; Nicolas and the Nicolaitans, 72; Gospel of St. John, 74; account of Simon Magus, 82 & *ff*.; Ophites, 97 & *ff*.; Cerinthus, 110 & *ff*.; title Gnostic, 118; Carpocrates, 118 & *ff*.; Carpocratians and Gospel, 122; Ebionites, 123; Ebionite Gospel of St. Matthew, 126; Saturninus, 129, says, Basilides is Docetic, 157; Valentinus, 166 & *ff*.; Marcion, 203 & *ff*.; his own writings, 239 & *ff*.; list of Gnostics, 242; the 'Presbyter' of, 247

JAMES, St., speech of in Clem. Hom. 223
Jerome, date of Apocalypse, 71; his date of Basilides, 145

MAN

Jerusalem, Bishops of, 126
Jesus of the Valentinians, 181
John, St. and Cerinthus, 14, 75; the Revelation, 71, & *ff*., 96, 105 & *f*.; date, 71; said to have been forged by Cerinthus, 114; Gospel, 74 & *ff*.; opposed to Gnosticism, 74; refutes Cerinthus, 116; borrowed from by Basilides, 150; by Valentinus, 177; earliest commentary on, 199; Epistles opposed to Docetism, 76
Judas Iscariot in Cainite theory, 101; Gospel of, 101
Jude, St., Epistle of, date, 61 & *ff*.; relation to 2nd Epistle of St. Peter, 69
'Just' and 'Justice' in Marcion, meaning of, 210
Justin the Gnostic, 102
Justin Martyr, his account of Simon Magus, 82 & *ff*.

KABBALA, meaning of the word, 33; the Jewish metaphysics, 33; similarity to Spinoza and Hegel, 35; its teaching, 35 & *ff*.; date and author, 38 and *f*.; relation to Gnosticism, *ib*.; to Persian philosophy, 39; to Simon Magus, 40, 87; to Basilides and Valentinus, 42; to Ophite theory, 97; possibly alluded to by St. Paul, 56, 57
Korah, a Cainite hero, 100

LARDNER doubts existence of Cainites, 100
'Laws of Countries,' Book of the, 141
Leucippus, 21
Light, the Persian good principle, 87
Logos, a designation of Christ, 75; in Philo, 17; Simon Magus identifies with himself, 81 & *f*.; Ophites identify with serpent, 99; in Valentinian theory, 171, 181
Luke, St., Gospel of, mutilated by Marcion, 206 & *f*.

MAN, personality of, destroyed by Gnosticism, 12; spiritual in Kabbala, 37; in Ophite theories, 97; ideal of Valentinus, 172 & *ff*.; three classes of, in Valentinian theory, 191; creation of, *ib*.

INDEX. 281

MAR

Marcion, 203 & ff.; and Polycarp, 14; prohibits marriage, 65; refuted by Bardesanes, 139; higher criticism, 206, &c.; his canon, *ib.*; Antithesis, 209; Demiurge, 209, &c.; two Redeemers, 214; Docetic, *ib.*; Patripassian, 216; his Baptism, 217; meaning of his phrase 'just,' 210; how treated by Tertullian, 211

Marcosians, 198; initiatory rites, 41; refuted by Irenæus, 242

Marcus, 197, 198

Materialism and Gnosticism, 14

Matter's classification of Gnostic sects, 46

Matthew, St., Ebionite Gospel of, 126

Matthias, St., Basilides' account of secret teaching given to, 146

Menander, 90, 93 & *f.*; professes to be a Christ, 130; common points with Saturninus, 129; parent of Syrian and Egyptian Gnosticism, *ib.*

Menandrians soon extinct, 94

Monogenes of Valentinus. *See* Nous.

Mosaic account of Creation and Fall, resemblance of Persian Cosmogony to, 27

Moses de Leon, reputed by some to be the author of Zohar, 39

Mosheim, classification of Gnostic sects, 44; estimate of Simon Magus, 91

NAASSENES, 96 & *f.*; assume title Gnostic, 105; quote St. Paul, *ib.*

Nazarenes, 124

Neander on Gnosticism, 10.; on relation of God to the Demiurge, 135; classification of Gnostic sects, 45; estimate of Simon Magus, 91

Neoplatonism of Plotinus, 147; of Proclus, *ib.*

New Testament, first allusions to Gnosticism, 48.

Nicetas, 225 & ff.

Nicolaitans, germ of heresy discerned by St. Paul, 66; referred to by St. John, 72; by St. Jude, 70

Nicolas, 72

Noah, the Sethite spiritual man, 101

Noetus, 217

Non-existent principle and world of Basilides, 146 & ff., 161

PET

Nous of Valentinus, 170, 175, 177, 181

OGDOAD of Basilides, 152; of Valentinus, 170

Old Testament, Marcion's treatment of, 209 & ff.

Ophites, 95 & ff.; date 104 & ff.; of Jewish origin, 103; first assume title Gnostic, 7; alluded to in Apocalypse, 73; their Trinity, 98; Ennoia, *ib.*; idea of Redemption, 103; relation of their system to pantheism, 107

Origen on the commentary of Heraclion, 199

Ormuzd, the good spirit of Zoroaster, 26

Ossenes, 234

PANTÆNUS, 261
Pantheism and Ophite theory, 107

Paradise of Ophites, 99

Parchor, 164

Parsism and Ophite theory, 104

Passions, human, in theory of Basilides, 158

Patripassianism of Marcion, 216

Paul, St., use of Gnosis, 6 & *f.*; combats Gnosticism, 8, 9, 54; encounter with Simon Magus, 92; quoted by Naassenes, 105; by Valentinians, 182; attacked by Clem. Hom. 228; his Epp. in the Canon of Marcion, 206

Pella, Church at, 125

Peratæ, 96, 102

Peripatetics, 4

Persian religion, dualistic, 24; cosmogony resembles Mosaic narrative, 27; contrast to Indian, 29; influence on the Kabbala, 39; on Simon Magus, 87; on Syrian Gnosticism, 133; its sacred books destroyed by Alexander, 28

Person of Christ, errors in relation to, 110

Personality of God and man destroyed by Gnosticism, 12

Peter, St., use of Gnosis, 6; alludes to the Gnostic usage of St. Paul's Epp. 59; prophecies of Gnosticism, 66 & ff.; relation of 2nd Ep. to Ep. of St. Jude, 69; meeting with

PHI

Simon Magus, 92, 95; Ep. to James in Clem. Hom. 223; said by Clem. Hom. to have administered the Eucharist with bread and salt, 237

Philetus, 51, 57, 111

Philo, embodies germs of Gnosticism, 2; Logos and Divine powers, 17, 18; interpretation of Old Testament, 16

Philosophy, Greek. *See* Greek

Pistis Sophia, 200

Plato, use of Gnosis, 1; problem of the Absolute, 16; of the origin of evil, 21; relation to Philo, 16, &c.; to Basilides, 161

Pleroma, 178, 179; meaning of, in N. T., 51, 55

Plotinus, 147

Polycarp and Marcion, 14; anecdote about Cerinthus, 112

Power, one of the titles claimed by Simon Magus, 80

'Powers,' Divine, of Philo, 17

Præscriptio, meaning of, in Tertullian, 251

Praxeas, 217

Prodicus, 122

Prunikos of Ophites, 98; meaning of, 106

Ptolemæus, 177; letter to Flora, 197

Pythagoreans, 21

REDEEMER, Gnostic, higher than Creator, 19

Redemption, distinctive feature of Gnostic philosophy, 3, 5; Gnostic idea of, 18; in Ophite theory, 103; in theory of Basilides, 154; of Valentinus, 179

Resurrection, the, and Gnosticism, 50, 58 & *ff*.

Revelation. *See* St. John.

Romans, Ep. to, possibly refers to Gnosticism, 51

Rome, Bp. of, subordinate to Bp. of Jerusalem in Clem. Hom. 233

'Roots' of Simon Magus, 86, 178

SALT, held sacred by Elxai, 237; used for Eucharist by St. Peter in Clem. Hom., *ib.*

Samaritan estimate of Simon and Helena, 91

Sampsæans, 236

Satan, depths of, 73

SYR

Saturninus, summary of doctrine given by Irenæus, 131; his Cosmogony, 130; his Christology, 131; relation to Menander, 129; borrows from Persian philosophy, 133; asceticism, 134; prohibits marriage, 65, 134

Schelling, 147

Secundus, 197

Seed of the World in Basilides' system, 148

Sephir Yetzirah, 35; date and author, 38 & *f*.

Sephiroth in the Zohar, 36, 37

Serpent, veneration of, 96; various doctrines of, 99 & *f*.; the Brazen, 99

Seth, Christ of the Sethites, 102

Sethites, 96, 101

Shelley, 4

Sichem, *see* Sychar

Silence, primary power of Simon Magus, 86, 88; of Valentinus, 170, 173

Simon ben Jochai, traditional author of Zohar, 38

Simon Magus, 91 & *ff*.; and Dositheus, 85; relation to the Kabbala, 40, 87; to Heraclitus, 87; a Samaritan, 79 & *ff*.; sources of his teaching, 80 & *ff*., 84; a false Christ, 81, 82, 90; Ennoia, 82; Roots, 86, 87; 'Great Announcement,' 85, 88; primary principle, Fire or Silence, 86, 88; male and female principles, 88; bisexual power, 89; regarded as God by Samaritans, 91; Docetic, 85; his Cosmogony, 54; account of him by Irenæus and Just. Mart. 82 & *ff*.; his doctrine explained by Bunsen, 83; different estimates of, 91; accounts of his death, 92 & *f*.; perhaps alluded to in N.T. 66; account of him in Clem. Hom. 225; uniting with St. Peter, 95; his position among Gnostic heretics, 95; supposed statue to, 91 & *f*.

Simonians and the Resurrection, 59

Sophia Achamoth, 169, 180, 184 & *ff*.; among Ophites, 98; Prunikos, 106; among Sethites, 101

Spinoza and the Kabbala, 35

Stoics, the, 4, 23

Sychar, possibly city where Philip preached, 79

Syrian Gnosis, dualistic, 142

INDEX.

TATIAN, 136
Tertullian, his heretic Ebion, 125; makes Basilides Docetic, 157: his accounts of Valentinus, 166, &c.; of Marcion, 203, &c.; use of tradition, 253; contrast with Irenæus, 250, 260; his use of 'Præscriptio,' 251; his writings, 251 & *ff*.
Tetrads of Valentinus, 171
Theodotus, 197
Theodotion's translation of O.T., 240
Therapeutæ, 31 & *f.*
Thought, female principle of Simon Magus, 89
Timothy, Epp. to, allude to Gnosticism, 56, 64, 66; their date, 56
Titus, Ep. to, combats Gnosticism, 57

UNSPEAKABLE, the, of Valentinus, 170

VALENTINUS, 166; relation to the Kabbala, 42, 201; Æons, 62, 86, 178; Pleroma, 178; two Christs, 181; borrows from St. John, 177; and St. Paul, 181; Ogdoad, 170; Orders of Æons, 171; Tetrads, *ib.*; ideal man, 173; Decad, 174 & *f.*; Dodecad, 176; idea of Redemption, 179, 184 & *ff.*; three classes of men, 191; Christology, 192 & *ff.*; philosophy, 194 & *ff.*; his theory pantheistic, 201; refuted by Irenæus, 167, 242; relation to Augustine, 183; charged by Clem. Alex. with destroying free-will, 14

'WISDOM' of God, 168

ZACCHÆUS said to be Bp. of Cæsarea by Clem. Hom. 227
Zohar, 35, 36; author and date, 38, 39
Zoroaster, date, 25; his system, 26; influenced by Judaism, 28

INDEX

OF

PASSAGES IN THE OLD TESTAMENT AND LXX.

GENESIS

	PAGE
I. 3	137, 148
I. 26	131

NUMBERS

XXV. 1, 2	72
XXXI. 16	72

1 SAMUEL

XXVIII. 3, 9 (LXX.)	6

2 KINGS

XXI. 6 (LXX.)	6

JOB

XXVIII.	168

PSALMS

CXVIII. (CXIX.) 66 (LXX.)	6
XXIII. (XXIV.) 1 (LXX.)	179

PROVERBS

VIII.	168
VIII. 12 (LXX.)	6
IX. 1	184, 169
XXX. 3 (Vat. XXIV. 26), (LXX.)	6

ECCLESIASTES

	PAGE
I. 1–10	168
II. 26 (LXX.)	6
XXIV. 1–18	168

ISAIAH

VII. 14	245
XI. 2 (LXX.)	6
XXVIII. 10	163
XL. 13, 14	212

DANIEL

XII. 3	35

MALACHI

I. 10, 11	246

WISDOM (LXX.)

II. 13	6
VII. 17	6
VII. 22–30	168
VIII. 1–9	168
IX. 9–11	168
X. 10	6
XIV. 22	6

ECCLESIASTICUS (LXX.)

XXXVI. 17	88, 178

INDEX

OF

PASSAGES IN THE NEW TESTAMENT

ALLUDED TO OR EXPLAINED.

St. Matthew

	PAGE
VII. 7	251
XII. 48	215

St. Luke

I. 77	6
III. 1	207, 215
IV. 31	207, 215
VII. 21–35	207
XIII. 28	207
XIII. 29	207
XVI. 17	207

St. John

I. 3	74
I. 9	148
I. 14	74
IV. 5	79
IV. 25	81
VII. 48, 49	124
XIV. 6	178
XIX. 26	102
XIX. 35	77
XX. 31	116
XXI. 1 & *ff.*	110

Acts

VIII. 5, 9, 10	79, 80
VIII. 10	41

Acts—*continued.*

	PAGE
XV. 2	112
XVI. 6	105
XVIII. 23	105
XIX. 19	51
XXI. 28	112
XXIV. 5	124

Romans

II. 16	206
III. 20	121, 211
V. 14	155
V. 20	211
VI. 4	59
VII. 12	211
VIII. 3	211
VIII. 19, 22	155
VIII. 33	155
XI. 33	213
XI. 36	181
XVI. 17–19	51
XVI. 25	206

1 Corinthians

I. 2	51
I. 5	6, 263
II. 6	51
II. 11	213
II. 14, 15	10
III. 16	48

INDEX.

1 CORINTHIANS—continued.

	PAGE
VI. 15	248
VIII. 1	7, 49, 72
VIII. 2	49
XII. 8	6
XIII. 8, 10	50
XV.	50, 248
XV. 22	137
XV. 29	117
XV. 50	248

2 CORINTHIANS

IV. 6	6
X. 5	6
XI. 6	50
XII. 9	247

GALATIANS

I. 4	62
II. 2	112
II. 8	246
III. 24	211

EPHESIANS

I. 10	181, 249
I. 21	156
I. 23	52
II. 2	61
III. 19	51
IV. 13	52
IV. 14	52
VI. 21	53

PHILIPPIANS

III. 18	6
IV. 3	221

COLOSSIANS

I. 16, 17	54
I. 18, 19	55
II. 6–9	8
II. 8	54
II. 9	55, 181
II. 12	59
II. 18	54
II. 20–23	55

COLOSSIANS—continued.

	PAGE
III. 3–5	55
IV. 7	53

1 THESSALONIANS

IV. 9	9
V. 23	248

1 TIMOTHY

I. 4	56
I. 17	178
I. 19, 20	57
IV. 1	70
IV. 1–3	64
VI. 4	252
VI. 20	7, 56, 263

2 TIMOTHY

II. 16–18	57
II. 18	59
III. 1	70
III. 1–7	65, 66

TITUS

I. 14	57
III. 9	57
III. 10	252

HEBREWS

I. 1, 2	60
I. 2	62
II. 14, 16, 17	60, 61
XI. 3	62

2 ST. PETER

I. 5, 6	6
II. 1	69
II. 1, 2	67
II. 10, 12	67
II. 13, 15	67
II. 15	71
II. 18, 19	67
III. 2	70
III. 3	69
III. 16	59
III. 18	6

1 St. John

	PAGE
I. 1–3	76
II. 22	14, 77, 78
IV. 1–3	76
IV. 2	112
IV. 3	78
IV. 15	77
V. 6	77

2 St. John

7	77

St. Jude

	PAGE
4	69
11	71
17, 18	70

Revelation

II. 6	72, 73
II. 14	71
II. 14, 15	72
II. 15	72
II. 24	73, 96, 105
XII. 9	106

ABOUT THE AUTHOR

Henry Longueville Mansel, D.D. (1820 – 1871) was an English philosopher and ecclesiastic writer. He was born at Cosgrove, Northamptonshire (where his father, also Henry Longueville Mansel, fourth son of General John Mansel, was rector). He was educated at Merchant Taylors' School, London and St John's College, Oxford. He took a double first in 1843, and became tutor of his college. He was appointed reader in moral and metaphysical philosophy at Magdalen College in 1855, and Waynflete Professor of Metaphysical Philosophy in 1859. He was a great opponent of university reform and of the Hegelianism which was then beginning to take root in Oxford. In 1867 he succeeded Arthur Penrhyn Stanley as regius professor of ecclesiastical history, and in 1868 he was appointed dean of St Paul's. He died in Cosgrove on the first of July 1871.

The philosophy of Mansel, like that of Sir William Hamilton, was mainly due to Aristotle, Immanuel Kant and Thomas Reid. Like Hamilton, Mansel maintained the purely formal character of logic, the duality of consciousness as testifying to both self and the external world, and the limitation of knowledge to the finite and "conditioned." His doctrines were developed in his edition of Aldrich's *Artis logicae rudimenta* (1849) – his chief contribution to the reviving study of Aristotle – and in his *Prolegomena logica: an Inquiry into the Psychological Character of Logical Processes* (1851), in which the limits of logic as the "science of formal thinking" are rigorously determined.

In his Bampton lectures on *The Limits of Religious Thought* (1858) he applied to Christian theology the metaphysical agnosticism which seemed to result from Kant's criticism, and which had been developed in Hamilton's *Philosophy of the Unconditioned.* While denying all knowledge of the super sensuous, Mansel deviated from Kant in contending that cognition of the ego as it really is belongs among the facts of experience. Consciousness, he held – agreeing thus with the doctrine of "natural realism" which Hamilton developed from Reid – implies knowledge both of self and of the external world. The latter Mansel's psychology reduces to consciousness of our organism as extended; with the former is given consciousness of free will and moral obligation.

These lectures led Mansel to a bitter controversy with the Christian socialist theologian Frederick Maurice.

A summary of Mansel's philosophy is contained in his article *"Metaphysics"* in the 5th edition of the *Encyclopædia Britannica* (1860).

He also wrote:

- *The Philosophy of the Conditioned* (1866) in reply to John Stuart Mill's criticism of Hamilton;
- *Letters, Lectures, and Reviews* (ed. Chandler, 1873),
- *The Gnostic Heresies of the First and Second Centuries* (ed. Joseph Barber Lightfoot, 1875).

He contributed a commentary on the first two gospels to the *Speaker's Commentary* (1881).

www.ingramcontent.com/pod-product-compliance
Lightning Source LLC
Chambersburg PA
CBHW020737160426
43192CB00006B/226